Build Your Own
Smart Home

About the Authors

Robert C. Elsenpeter is an author and award-winning journalist. He is co-author of *Windows XP Professional Network Administration*, *E-Business: A Beginner's Guide*, and *Optical Networking: A Beginner's Guide* (all McGraw-Hill/Osborne).

Toby J. Velte, Ph.D., MCSE+I, CCNA, CCDA, is a technology entrepreneur in Minneapolis, MN. He has helped launch four companies including Velte Publishing, a networking and information systems publishing firm. Dr. Velte is co-author of the best-selling *Cisco: A Beginner's Guide* (2001, McGraw-Hill/Osborne) and eight other technology books. He can be reached at tjv@velte.com.

About the Technical Editor

Glen Carty, CCIE, is a data and telecommunications specialist in Odessa, FL. He has held positions with both IBM Global Network and AT&T and is the author of the book *Broadband Networking*, and a contributing author to *Stephen Bigelow's Troubleshooting, Maintaining, and Repairing Networks* (both McGraw-Hill/Osborne).

Build Your Own Smart Home

Robert C. Elsenpeter
Toby J. Velte

McGraw-Hill/Osborne

New York   Chicago   San Francisco   Lisbon   London   Madrid   Mexico City
Milan   New Delhi   San Juan   Seoul   Singapore   Sydney   Toronto

The McGraw·Hill Companies

McGraw-Hill/Osborne
2100 Powell Street, 10th Floor
Emeryville, California 94608
U.S.A.

To arrange bulk purchase discounts for sales promotions, premiums, or fund-raisers, please contact **McGraw-Hill/Osborne** at the above address. For information on translations or book distributors outside the U.S.A., please see the International Contact Information page immediately following the index of this book.

Build Your Own Smart Home

1234567890 QPD QPD 019876543

ISBN 0-07-223013-4

Publisher
Brandon A. Nordin

Vice President & Associate Publisher
Scott Rogers

Acquisitions Editor
Tim Green

Project Editor
Mark Karmendy

Technical Editor
Glen Carty

Copy Editor
Dennis Weaver

Proofreader
Susie Elkind

Indexer
Claire Splan

Composition
Carie Abrew, Kelly Stanton-Scott

Illustrators
Lyssa Wald, Kathleen Fay Edwards,
Melinda Moore Lytle, Jackie Sieben

Series Design
Jean Butterfield

Cover Series Design
Ted Holladay

This book was composed with Corel VENTURA™ Publisher.

Screen shots reprinted by permission from Home Automation, Inc. (HAI)
Screen shots reprinted by permission from HomeSeer Technologies
Compaq iPaq running WebLink II software courtesy Home Automation, Inc.
Product photos reprinted by permission from Smarthome.com

For Calvin and Rowena Pope

Contents at a Glance

Contents

Multiline Systems 237
Installing a Jack 239
Wiring 239
Security Systems 248
Physical 249
Software 249

Part IV
Smart Home Entertainment and Integration

Chapter 13   Audio/Video Systems **255**
Components 256
Audio Components 256
Video Components 261
Zones 265
Single Source Distributed to Multiple Rooms 266
Multiple Zones, Multiple Sources 266
Purpose-Made Zone Systems 267
Designing Your Distribution System 267
Connecting Whole-House A/V 268
A/V Cabinet 269
Wiring 269
Audio Connection 271
Video Connection 274

Chapter 14   Audio and Video Distribution **281**
Remote Control Options 282
X10 282
Wireless 283
Coax Transmission 284
Hardwired 285
Connecting a Bedroom to A/V System 285
Audio 285
Video 290

Chapter 15   Working and Playing Together: The Smart Home Way **297**
Setting Up the Computer 298
Hardware 298
Software 299
Managing Devices 304
Views 306
Managing Events 308
E-mail 313
Web Access 315
Webcam 320
Setup 320
Setting Up the Software 321

Acknowledgments

A book seems like a singular endeavor; however, it cannot really be started, crafted, and completed without the input of a number of individuals. First, we'd like to acknowledge the efforts of acquisitions editor Tim Green at McGraw-Hill/Osborne, who got the ball rolling on this project. Next, we appreciate the work of technical editor Glen Carty and copyeditor Dennis Weaver. Key to the completion and overall appearance of this book were Mark Karmendy and Jean Butterfield.

We would like to acknowledge the help of a number of individuals at different companies who helped support this project, through their guidance and assistance, through supplying products, or through both:

❏ Matt Dean from Smarthome.com

❏ Jay McLellan, Ernie Sieber, Matthew Davis, and Allison Read from Home Automation, Inc.

❏ Richard Helmke from HomeSeer Technologies

Introduction

You're probably not alone if you've ever had the "Clapper®" jingle stuck in your head. Although "Clap on, Clap off, Clap on, clap off...the Clapper" can become a maddening tune running through your head, the Clapper still has the distinction of being one of the first home automation products. It might not seem inherently "smart," but it provides a home-friendly function with just the clap of the hands.

This book steps beyond the simple functions of the Clapper, introducing you to a number of products that can be used for everything from controlling lighting levels, watering your lawn, closing your drapes, and managing sundry appliances in your home.

We start simply, introducing you to some concepts in the world of Smart Home. This includes some of the terminology, an explanation of various products and projects, as well as some design basics. From there, we look at specific projects. Each chapter introduces a new project that you can refer to as you build your own Smart Home.

The core of *our* Smart Home is the Omni II security system by Home Automation, Inc. This provides not only security functions, but also ties in various X10 devices that can react when an alarm is tripped. While this device is not necessary to complete most of the projects in this book, it does provide an understanding for intermediate and advanced Smart Home projects that would utilize a security system or a home automation system.

Again, it is not necessary to spend thousands of dollars on your home automation system. There are a number of very useful, utilitarian, and downright cool projects that you can implement without spending stacks of cash. As such, each chapter explains these projects (like connecting interior lighting, for example) and will give you ideas on how you can modify the project for your own, individual circumstances.

The thought of making your home a Smart Home might seem daunting. Indeed, when you start cutting into walls and pulling cabling through the void, it might seem like you've lost your senses. However, given an understanding of your needs and wants, adequate planning, and some research into the best solution, Smart Home renovation shouldn't be too frightening. It's even less disturbing if you employ some of the easier (and readily available) options like X10. If you've ever thought about increasing the functionality, security, or wow-factor of your home, we're here to walk you through the process of turning your home into a Smart Home.

Part I

Meet the
Smart Home

Chapter 1

Smart Home Foundations

Prior to 1797, the washing machine was little more than a rock against which laundry was beaten. In that year, the washing board was invented, making the process of cleaning one's laundry astronomically easier. More than a century later—in 1908—cleaning one's clothes took another quantum leap forward with the advent of the electric washing machine. Now, as we're fresh into the 21st century, we cannot imagine scrubbing our laundry against a washing board, let alone stumbling down to the river's edge and beating our clothes against a rock.

Similarly, but at a much accelerated pace thanks to computers, we are able to eliminate life's little inconveniences around the home. Home automation is taking a lot of the tedium out of our lives. Sure, it's simple enough to flip a switch to turn on a light—and it's much easier than climbing a ladder to ignite a gas lamp. However, we're at a place in time where we don't even have to touch a light switch anymore—a computer can automatically do it for us. Some might call that "laziness"; we like to think of it as "progress."

From piping audio and video through the home to automatically watering the lawn, there are scores of places where Smart Homes can make your life easier, or make it downright cool. If you've got the time and inclination, there isn't anything that cannot be automated in your home.

Meet Your Smart Home

Smart Homes can be as simple or as complex as you want. Maybe you're only interested in dimming the lights in your kitchen. Or, maybe you want to do something more comprehensive, more complex, like setting up the whole house to be on a certain schedule and to work with your family's daily routine. Whatever your needs, there's a Smart Home gadget or system to handle it for you.

Let's take a look at an average day in the life of Mr. and Mrs. Joe Smarthome, their kids, and their totally tricked out, automated home.

Waking Up

It's 5:30 a.m. and the Smart Home is waking up before Joe and his family have to. After a long night with the temperature turned down to save money, the Smart Home sends a signal to the thermostat—like the Omnistat RC-80 shown in Figure 1-1—to start warming up the house. By 6 a.m., the house is nice and toasty and now it's time to get up. As the security system is automatically deactivated, the lights in the master bedroom come on at a low level. Over the next couple minutes, they get a little brighter. Simultaneously, soft music is pumped into the room. The lights in the kids' rooms remain out and they don't get the serene wake-up music—they don't have to get up for another half hour.

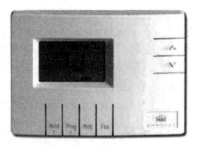

Figure 1-1
An Omnistat RC-80 thermostat by Home Automation, Inc.

The coffee pot started automatically, so by the time Joe makes it downstairs, there's a fresh pot of java ready to go. Outside, he notices that the sprinklers are already spraying, giving the lawn a fresh drink of water. After a few minutes, they shut off by themselves. If it had rained during the night, a sensor in the lawn would have indicated that the lawn had plenty of water, and an automated sprinkling wouldn't have been necessary. As such, the sprinkler would not have come on, saving on water usage.

During the Day

When all the showers have been taken and the dishwasher completed its load of breakfast dishes, the water heater automatically turns off, rather than running constantly. This saves Joe and his family some money, because there is no need to maintain a tank of hot water when no one's home.

Once everyone is out the door and on their way to work or school, the security alarm is set and the Smart Home turns off all the lights the kids forgot about. There are a number of sensors keeping the house safe and secure—they are motion sensors, door and window sensors, and fire detectors, all making sure everything is safe.

A few minutes before everyone hit the door, the thermostat turned off the heat, automatically bringing the temperature down to its "away" level. The dog laps at his water dish periodically throughout the day, the dish automatically refilling itself when it runs low.

During the day, Joe checks his house periodically via his web browser. His Smart Home controls are linked via web software, so he can check the status of various items in his home, even while he's at the office. Noticing that it's overcast out, Joe turns on a light in the kitchen, so Fido doesn't feel shut in.

Welcome Home

At 3:30 p.m., the spa heater automatically turns on, warming the water for Mrs. Smarthome's daily post-work dip. A half an hour later, the water is warm and waiting for her tired muscles, but not so fast!

Potential disaster has threatened the house while everyone was away at work! No, thugs didn't try to break into the home (if they had tried, the security system would have scared them off, notified the police, sent an e-mail to Joe at work, and sent a message to his cellular phone). Instead, the washing machine has overflowed onto the utility room floor. Luckily, when this potential disaster occurred, a sensor detected the spill and immediately shut off the water. The most that Joe will have to do is to mop up a little water and restart the machine. Luckily, water didn't keep shooting out, seeping into other parts of the house, and causing untold and expensive damage.

A Relaxing Evening

After dinner, the family is ready to unwind after a long day at school and work. When everyone can agree on what to watch on television, things go smoothly. Those times are few and far between, however. As such, Joe watches television in the family room—the lights automatically dim to a level he's preset for watching movies. Joe's wife is upstairs reading and listening to the stereo. The stereo, it should be noted, is physically situated next to the television set Joe is watching. However, the audio is piped to various speakers located throughout the house and are controlled remotely, so she can listen to whatever she wants, without having to go into the family room.

In the computer room, Johnny is engrossed in his homework, while Jenny chats on the telephone with her friend. Because they have a digital subscriber line (DSL), Jenny is still able to use the telephone while Johnny is online. The DSL line offers an added benefit to the Smart Home: the computer is always connected to the Internet, so various Smart Home functions can be monitored and managed from anywhere there is a web browser. Occasionally, Joe uses his laptop with its wireless connection to tweak elements of their Smart Home.

When she's done chatting with her friend, Jenny decides to tackle her homework. She's having a little trouble understanding some of the concepts, so she takes her laptop around the house, looking for help. Because her laptop is connected to a wireless LAN, Mrs. Smarthome can help Jenny find the information on the World Wide Web—even from the living room.

Going to Bed

Time for bed. Once everyone is tucked in, the security system is again set and vigilant for any signs of trouble. Joe isn't quite ready to go to sleep yet, so he sits up in bed and reads. He turns on the bedroom light immediately over his side of the bed, just a little bit so he can read, but not enough to keep his wife awake. Meanwhile, music plays softly in the background. It doesn't take long for Joe to be lulled asleep, in spite of his best efforts to get through his book. The Smart Home, however, has been programmed to be aware of Joe's nocturnal reading habits and—at a certain time—turns off the stereo and lights, completely.

The Still of the Night

It's 2 a.m. and everyone's been nestled in for hours. The grandfather clock in the hallway ticks slowly and the dog sleeps at the foot of Johnny's bed. The dog is thirsty and gets up to get himself a drink of water. After sauntering out into the hallway, he passes a number of security system sensors on his way to his dish. However, these sensors, like the one in Figure 1-2, are so-called "pet-immune" and have been adjusted so that Fido doesn't set them off. He gets his drink of water, then goes back to sleep.

Figure I-2
A pet-immune security sensor lets pets wander about without activating the alarm.

At 3:30 a.m., nature calls. Jenny gets out of bed and makes her way to the hall. Rather than flip on the lights and wake up everyone in the house, the Smart

Home detects her presence. Aware of the time and her probable need for a late-night trip out of her room, it activates the lights en route to the bathroom. Don't worry about Jenny getting the corneas blasted out of her head—the lights come on at a very low level. The light is dim enough so she isn't blinded, but she can also see her youngest brother's Thomas the Tank Engine trains scattered throughout the hallway. Once she's returned to her bedroom, the lights automatically turn off.

Smart Home Basics

There is a definite, concrete distinction between what someone needs and what someone wants. Abraham Maslow demonstrated this with his famous "Hierarchy of Needs" in 1943. At the top of his list are such physiological needs as air, food, water, and heat—truly, things we need. As the list progresses, it gets a little more esoteric with things like "self actualization" and "esteem needs." So what does this foray into Philosophy 101 have to do with Smart Homes? Let's be honest: no one needs their home lighting wired to the garage door opener. No one needs to be able to check their house's temperature from a web browser on the other side of the world. Nowhere on Maslow's Hierarchy of Needs are "integrated home security systems" listed. Of course, it could be argued that's just because Maslow didn't live in this day and age.

True, we don't *need* any of the stuff Smart Homes have to offer, but some of us sure do want them. There are a number of benefits inherent to Smart Homes. First—and for many it's an important consideration—a Smart Home can save money. This is achieved through savings in heating, cooling, water, and other utility costs. Additionally, Smart Homes offer more enhanced security measures, reduce a number of rote tasks, and offer an increase in entertainment.

So what, exactly, can you do to smarten up your home? There are a number of home automation projects that can do anything from control your stereo to cascade lights on and off as you walk through the house at night. You can make your Smart Home as simple or as complex as you'd like. Sure, look around for information about sample Smart Home projects, and you're likely to hear about what Bill Gates did to his house and what a handful of other enthusiasts have managed to, pushing the envelope on both home automation and cost. You don't have to do quite that much—but you can.

For example, if you just want to be able to dim the lights in your bedroom without having to get out of bed, that is a simple enough project, and it won't cost more than US$100. If you don't mind getting out of bed to dim your lights, the project will only cost about US$30.

The following explore various Smart Home projects and show where, in this book, we will talk about these projects in more depth.

Home LAN

The core of the Smart Home is its computer network. Of course, the term "computer network" connotes a huge, NASA-style arrangement of dozens of computers connected by miles of wiring to mysterious boxes with flashing lights. The fact of the matter is you don't have to turn your house into the bridge of the starship Enterprise to develop a functional Smart Home. If you're like 51 percent of Americans, you already have a home computer (according to the US Census Bureau). You might even have two or more computers at various locations throughout the house (the home office, your son's room, the kitchen, and so forth). In order for you to make your home local area network (LAN), all you need to do is hook those two computers together. A LAN is also helpful to share your computers' resources—the ability to share an Internet connection, share hard drives, and access files and folders located on each computer. If you only have one computer—and don't see a burning need to buy another one—you can still make your Smart Home work just fine.

In order to fully integrate our Smart Home, we're going to use X10 modules (more on X10 and what it's all about in Chapter 2). These modules are used to connect various appliances, lights, and other goodies with your computer or home LAN. Can't wait to get started on your home LAN? Flip ahead to Chapter 4.

Wiring

Possibly the most frightening aspect of Smart Home modification comes when the notion of wiring is brought up. We won't lie to you: snaking wire through your house is a chore. However, you don't have to put new wiring in your home for each and every project. The fact is that new wiring will be necessary for only very specialized projects. For example, if you decide you want whole-house audio or video, it's a good idea to install some coaxial cable and speaker wire between your home entertainment center and the satellite rooms you wish to connect—it is also helpful to have installed some Cat 5 cabling when connecting your computers into a home LAN.

The inclusion of new wiring improves some projects, simply because there is no signal loss and the wiring provides a better connection. We'll take some of the sting out of home rewiring in Chapter 2 and explain better when and where you might need to undertake a wiring project.

Security

What would a Smart Home be without a security system? Though most security systems are designed as stand-alone units—whether they are monitored or not—many can be controlled as part of a Smart Home set up, like Home Automation, Inc.'s OmniLT device, shown in Figure 1-3. For example, if you're at work, you can use your web browser to check on your home security system. If one of the sensors is tripped, not only can you set your security system to contact the monitoring station, but it can also turn on your TV, stereo, the exterior lighting, and anything else you want to do to scare off would-be intruders (or at least aggravate your neighbors).

Figure 1-3
The OmniLT
Controller by Home
Automation, Inc.

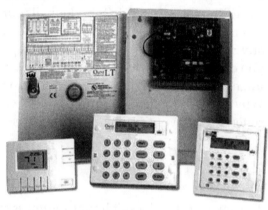

There are also measures you can take to make your home look lived in, even if you're out of town or working late. Setting up some lights on a preset schedule is a preventive measure you can take for the cost of just a few dollars.

Security and the Smart Home is a big topic (after all, once you install all that Smart Home gear, you don't want some thug breaking in and making off with it), and we cover it in Chapter 5.

Lighting

Consider the new, 10,000-square-foot Smart Home on the fringes of Las Vegas. In addition to a number of other home automation accessories, it includes a number of kicked up lighting tools. The home uses a wired Lutron HomeWorks Interactive System and a Lutron wireless HomeServe system, working in tandem, to control more than 300 lights throughout the house which serve a number of amenities, including

- ❑ A club room with wet bar
- ❑ Hidden home theater

❏ Game room

❏ Wine cellar

❏ Fitness room

❏ Spa

❏ Offices

❏ Tower retreat

❏ Basketball court

The wireless portions of the home (including the club room, master bedroom, and hallways) are set up for wireless control, using radio-frequency signals.

You might not need your basketball court and wine cellar to be managed with smart lighting, but isn't it cool to know that you can? One of the cornerstones of any Smart Home project is its lighting capabilities. There are a number of ways you can set up specific lighting needs within the Smart Home. For instance, you might prefer your living room lighting to be at a certain level in the evenings. Why should you have to trudge all the way to a dimmer switch? Let the computer do it for you, automatically. We'll cover more lighting projects and issues in Chapter 9.

Exterior Needs

The Smart Home doesn't limit usefulness to the interior of the house. It isn't all security systems and computers. There are definite needs outside that can be managed by the Smart Home. For example, automatic lighting can be set up to add an additional layer of safety and security. If you want to watch your dog in the backyard, a video camera can be set up to observe Fido chasing rabbits.

In addition, the exterior of your Smart Home can also be managed in such a way that everyday tasks are also tended to. A Smart Home can automatically water the lawn at a specified time each day—there are even robotic lawn mowers that can make your Saturdays a little less sweaty and a little more pleasant. We'll cover the sorts of things that you can do outside your Smart Home in Chapter 8.

Garage

A garage is in the same quasi–Smart Home category as the home's exterior. While not conventionally thought of as part of the house, a garage can still be made into a smart place.

Have you ever gotten up in the morning and stepped out into the garage only to find that the door has been open all night? Maybe you were lucky and no hooligans made off with your golf clubs and reciprocating saw, but a Smart Home can help ameliorate that mistake and make sure you don't go to bed with the garage wide open. Even better—and we'll show you this in Chapter 8—the simple act of opening the garage door can be the signal to turn on other devices in your home. For instance, when you open the garage door, the entryway lights can automatically activate, and some nice music can come on, welcoming you home.

Home Entertainment

We live in a day and age where there's a TV and stereo in every room of the house. But, if you don't want to buy a TV, VCR, DVD player, video game console, stereo, and satellite dish receiver for each and every room yet still want that availability, the Smart Home can help you. By distributing the signal from your home entertainment system throughout the house, you can watch TV in the bedroom while your wife listens to music in the living room while your kids save the galaxy from the alien mutant menace in the family room. We'll show you how to do it in Chapters 13 and 14.

Utilities

All this Smart Home stuff sure is glamorous, isn't it? Security systems, computer networks, distributed audio and video signals...could anything else in the Smart Home be as sensational? Well, maybe not the utilities system, but it's still pretty useful stuff. As we'll show you in Chapter 11, connecting your Smart Home to a heating, ventilating, and air conditioning (HVAC) system can both save you money and make your home a more pleasant place to live. Just about any home utility—from air to water—can be managed by the Smart Home.

Phones

A hundred years ago, no one had a telephone. In the 21st century, not only does nearly everyone have a telephone (there are still some weirdos out there who are holding out) but many of us have multiple lines coming into the house, cellular telephones, and cable modems, so our computers don't tie up the telephone line.

As integral as these devices are to our everyday lives, there are still some hurdles to be negotiated when it comes to telephony and Smart Homes. While this may seem like a great place to start, there is precious little standardized telephone connectivity for Smart Homes. However, it is still an important area for consideration. In fact, many Smart Home systems can be managed using the telephone as an interface. As such, we'll take a look at the issue surrounding telephones, your options in choosing one, and how to connect them in Chapter 12.

Integration

Now that you've got all these pieces of your Smart Home in place, it wouldn't be much of a Smart Home if you couldn't manage everything from one central location. This will, most likely, be from your computer keyboard. However, when you're sitting in front of the fireplace, wanting to listen to music and dim the lights while activating the security system and shutting the garage door, do you really want to get up, go to your computer, and do it? Of course not.

What you want is a way to do it right from where you're sitting—you want to use a remote control. Sure, every time you buy a TV, DVD player, or stereo, the remote claims to be a universal remote, but they never are. As such, you've probably got five or six "universal" remote controls on your coffee table and the last thing you want is yet another remote control. The good news is that if you get a kicked-up enough remote control for your Smart Home, you can manage everything in the house (even your TV and DVD player) from a single, truly universal remote. The bad news is you'll need a holster to carry your new best friend around with you wherever you go.

For the times when you want to manage your system via computer, every facet of your Smart Home can be managed from a web browser if you use the appropriate Smart Home software, like HomeSeer, as shown in Figure 1-4. Smart Home integration and setting up your remote control are covered in Chapter 15.

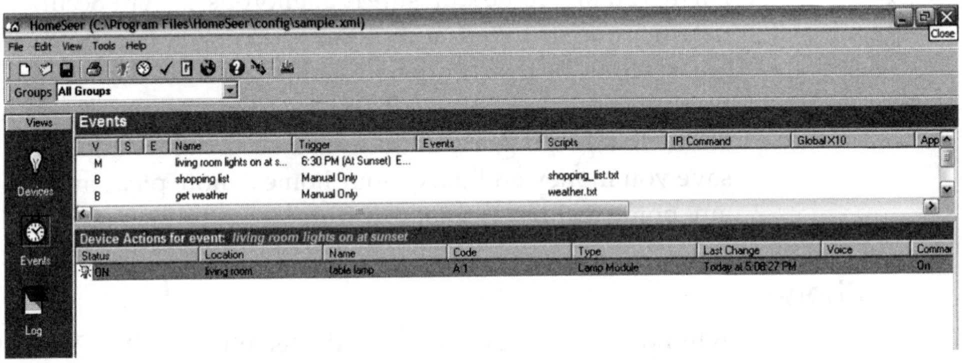

Figure 1-4
HomeSeer allows you to monitor your Smart Home from any web browser.

Now, having said everything we've just said, it's important to take a step back and be a little pragmatic. We don't mean to blow up your skirt with unrealistic expectations of what you can do with a Smart Home. The Smart Home is not going to load your dishwasher for you (yet), your Smart Home is not going to walk your dog for you (yet), and your Smart Home is not going to get your kids to pick up their rooms (probably ever).

As cool as a lot of Smart Home projects are, it's important to realize that the industry is still somewhat fragmented and there are no clear standards for everything yet. The most predominant standard is X10, which we will use to demonstrate different Smart Home projects throughout this book. In spite of a lack of standards, there is still a lot of very useful and fun stuff you can do with Smart Homes.

Chapter 2

Smart Home Design

Tools of the Trade

Blueprint or floor plan of your home
Pencil
Tape measure
Ruler

Before you whip out your credit card and start buying Smart Home components, it's a good idea to sit down and figure out what exactly you need, and how exactly you will get everything to work and play together.

This chapter focuses on two areas of understanding important to Smart Homes. First, we talk about the standards you can expect to deal with in the world of home automation. This covers such basics as X10 and an explanation of the various types of cabling you'll encounter. The second area covers how you can best design and plan for your Smart Home so you can buy gear you need that will coexist happily with other Smart Home products.

Standards

In order for everything in your Smart Home to work together, there has to be some sort of standard. If everything was left up to the whims of manufacturers, products simply couldn't work together. It's a lot like trying to put the air filter for a 1988 Ford Mustang into a 1997 Jeep Wrangler—because the manufacturers have done their own thing, the parts simply aren't compatible (unless you have a box cutter and a roll of duct tape). However, thanks to standards, some products are capable of working together.

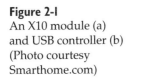

Standards

Standards encompass such things as communications protocols (like X10 and the Internet Protocol), and they also include hardware such as telephone jacks and coaxial cable. Understanding these products will help you appreciate how they work in conjunction with your overall Smart Home design and construction.

X10

No, X10 is not the tenth installment in the *X-Men* movie franchise (at least not yet, anyway). X10 is a communications language that allows your home appliances to be managed via the existing electrical wiring, without having to string new cabling.

Basics

X10 communicates across your home's 110V electrical wiring system. X10 modules simply plug into an electrical outlet or are hardwired into the home wiring system, like those modules used for light switches and X10 electrical outlets. Next, an X10 transmitter is plugged into an electrical outlet. This transmitter is used to send control information to the X10 module. The transmitter can be something very basic or, if you want more complex control of your Smart Home and have specific actions in mind, the controller can be connected to a computer. A USB X10 controller that links to a computer allows the computer to manage the X10 devices. Figures 2-1a, 2-1b, and Figure 2-2 show these various X10 devices.

Figure 2-1
An X10 module (a)
and USB controller (b)
(Photo courtesy
Smarthome.com)

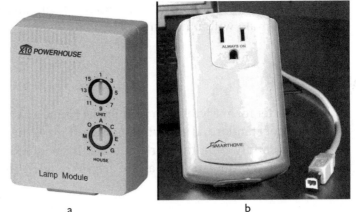

a   b

The X10 signal moves through your home's electrical wiring to control the sundry devices connected to your X10 system.

Figure 2-2
A stand-alone X10 controller module (Photo courtesy Smarthome.com)

If you've got a house full of X10 gear, how—you might be wondering—do you keep all the devices straight? After all, if your computer sends out a signal to turn on your X10 device, what keeps it from turning everything on? On each X10 receiver is a pair of dials. One dial selects letters from A–P (called the *House Code*), the other numbers from 1–16 (called the *Unit Code*). All total, you can have 256 (16 × 16) different X10 devices.

TIPS OF THE TRADE

Stretching Out X10 Addresses

Even though you can have 256 *unique* X10 addresses, you aren't limited to 256 X10 devices. If you want two or more devices to turn on, turn off, dim, or brighten simultaneously, you need only set the X10 addresses so they are the same. Not only will this help you stretch out your X10 addressing, but it can also save you some setup and management headaches. If you want two lamps in the living room to be in sync, simply set them to the same address rather than having to monkey around with additional X10 programming. Of course, if you have two lamps sitting right next to each other that you want to operate simultaneously, you need not even buy two X10 devices—just plug them into a power strip that is connected to the X10 receiver.

Why It's Cool

X10 is a great deal for you because it utilizes existing home wiring as the infrastructure for your Smart Home projects. Obviously, this makes the task of installation dramatically easier, since you don't need to pull wire specifically to run your various Smart Home devices.

X10 Costs

X10 modules and devices tend to be pretty inexpensive (you can get some for less than US$20). Naturally, there are more expensive X10 devices you can buy if you want, but you needn't break the bank buying X10 modules. In fact, even the less expensive ones provide more than simple ON/OFF functionality—they provide the functions of higher-end models, including DIM and BRIGHTEN.

Not only are they inexpensive and easy to use, they are also easy to manage once they're in place. Of course, the management of your X10 devices will depend largely on what you are using to control them. A stand-alone device, like the one shown in Figure 2-2, will provide basic features; however—as we'll demonstrate later in this book—by hooking your computer to a compatible controller, you'll be able to set up some intensive home automation projects.

Limitations

There are some issues that can work to impede the functionality of X10. Most of the time, you can expect to have your X10 devices working just fine. However, because these devices communicate across your home electrical wiring, there are a couple of problems that can occur:

❏ **Noise**   The first obstacle that can create problems with X10 devices is noise on the wiring. This noise comes from running appliances, generally those with motors. Such appliances include vacuum cleaners, exercise equipment, refrigerators, dryers, and so forth. Other sources of line noise are high-tech devices like laptop power supplies, big screen TVs, and so on. To ameliorate noise problems, a simple filter can be plugged in between the outlet and the offending appliance. Such filters include the Leviton plug-in noise filter, which retails for US$34.99.

❏ **Picking sides**   The other issue has more to do with how your house is wired, rather than an inherent flaw with X10. Your home is wired in two different phases—that is, there are two different 110V "sides" of your home's electrical system. If your X10 transmitter is on one side and the receiver is on another side, the X10 signal cannot be received. Often, the signal is bridged through a 220V appliance (where two 110V circuits come together—like a washing machine, for instance). When this condition is not present, you needn't call in an electrician to start rewiring your home. Help is only US$99.99 away in the form of a SignalLinc phase coupler. This device acts as a bridge between your home's two phases, as shown in Figure 2-3.

Figure 2-3
Houses are wired in two "phases."

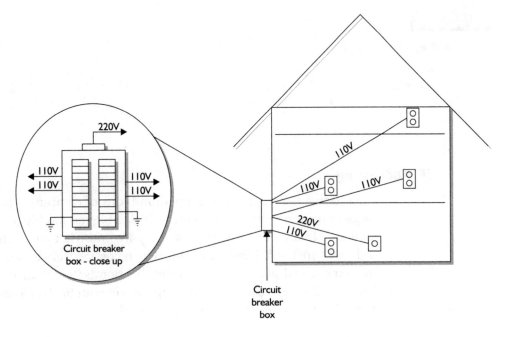

❑ **Neighbors**   Another issue to be cognizant of is if your neighbors have X10 gear, you run the risk of your X10 components being run by your neighbors, and vice versa. A good, albeit somewhat expensive, solution for this problem is to have an electrician install a *noise block* just before your circuit breaker.

IP

There are a number of languages that computers use to talk to one another. These languages are called "protocols." Macintosh computers use AppleTalk to communicate; PCs use anything from NetBEUI to IPX/SPX. Since each type of computer uses its own way to talk with other like computers, it used to be downright difficult to get the computers to talk to each other. However, in addition to nonstop *Star Trek* debates and the latest surreptitious photographs of Brad and Jennifer, the Internet has provided something else—a common protocol. Thanks to the Internet, we have the Internet Protocol (IP). This protocol allows computers to connect to the Internet, surf the Web, and do all the other stuff that we take for granted on the Internet (e.g., checking out the latest on Brad and Jennifer and telling that doofus in Florida that he's all backwards on his Captain Janeway/Borg Queen theory).

HEADS UP!

IP and the Smart Home

So what does this all this Internet stuff have to do with Smart Homes? Thanks to IP, computers have a common way to communicate, and they don't even need the Internet to do it. By using IP, computers in the home LAN can communicate amongst themselves. It's a good idea to use IP, especially if you plan on sharing an Internet connection, or just for the sake of sheer simplicity, as IP has become the de facto networking protocol.

IP Addressing

The Internet is a huge community of millions of computers holding billions of pages of information—and it's only getting bigger and bigger. Internet designers had to figure out a way for you to easily find what you want. To that end, IP addresses are used. These numbers, which you've probably seen here and there, are four sets of digits separated by decimal points (like 192.168.1.1, for example). These are the addresses that the computers in your Smart Home will have to use to be able to connect together in a network.

IP Address Format

Every device on your home LAN (indeed on the Internet itself) must have a unique IP address. There's no getting around this rule, because IP addressing is what ties your network together. IP addresses are 32 bits long and divided into four sections, each 8 bits long (called *octets*).

On the Internet, IP addresses must be unique. That is, every network must have its own unique network address and all the devices within it must have their own unique device or host addresses. Within a private network—like your home LAN—your individual devices must still have unique IP addresses, but they need only be unique within your home. Consider the two home networks shown in Figure 2-4.

Figure 2-4
IP addresses on private, home networks need not be unique, except for the routers which connect to the Internet.

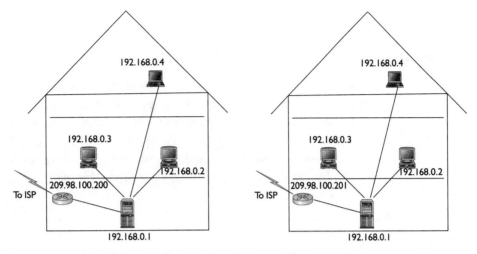

As the figure shows, devices on the two separate networks can have the same IP addresses—the servers can be the same, the printers can be the same, the computers can all be the same, except for the router. Since they are private networks and do not interact directly, there is no device conflict. Neither LAN is even cognizant of the other's existence. The routers, however, will have different IP addresses because they have to interact directly on the Internet.

However, two computers on the same network, as Figure 2-5 shows, cannot have the same IP address. If two devices share the same IP address, there will be a conflict and the device added to the network last will not be recognized.

Figure 2-5
Two devices on the same network cannot share an IP address.

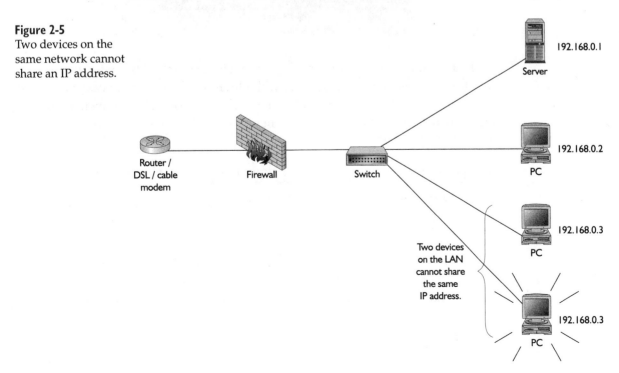

We'll talk more about setting up your home LAN in Chapter 4.

Cabling

There are a number of ways in which components of your Smart Home can be wired together. Depending on the application and the needs, you can find yourself using different types of cabling. For instance, video signals are best transmitted across coaxial cabling, while computer networks utilize twisted-pair wire.

This section examines the different types of cabling you're likely to encounter when building and augmenting your Smart Home.

Coax

Coaxial cable is the cable you screw into the back of your DVD player and TV. If you're like most Americans, you've probably had a small aneurysm trying to figure out in which way coaxial cable connects between the TV, DVD player, VCR, satellite decoder, TiVo, and so forth.

Coaxial cable (popularly known as *coax* cable) is used to transmit radio frequency (RF) signals, such as television and radio signals. As Figure 2-6 shows, there are two components on a chunk of coax cable.

Figure 2-6
Coaxial cable

In the center is a piece of copper wire that is surrounded by an insulating material. This is then enclosed by a mesh shield. Finally, this is all encased in a final insulating layer. Note that coaxial cable is believed to have been invented in Germany in 1884 by Ernst Werner von Siemens. At the time, there was no known application for it.

Comparison   There are two major types of coaxial cable used in homes:

❑ **RG-59**   In most video installations, you'll find this grade of coaxial cable. This is usable—but not ideal—for video networks, cable, and satellite TV connections.

❑ **RG-6**   This is the highest grade and quality of coax cable. It offers the best protection from interference and is best for your video distribution needs. RG-6 is thicker and heavier than RG-59 cabling, but it offers less signal loss at higher and lower frequencies, which is especially important when connecting to digital cable or satellite applications.

The big difference between RG-59 and RG-6 cabling is a matter of signal quality and the cabling's ability. Basically, RG-6 cable is capable of carrying video signals cleaner for much further differences. Naturally, that comes with a cost, but only a small one—1,000 feet of RG-59 coax cable costs about US$89.99, while the same length of RG-6 cable costs about US$109.99.

Making the Connection   To connect your coax cables to various devices, one uses an *F connector*. An F connector comes in male or female versions. The female connector is the type seen on the back of your television or DVD player, and the male connector is the type that screws or plugs in to your coax-connected component. Figure 2-7 shows an F connector.

Figure 2-7
Coax cable with an F connector

Twisted Pair

You use twisted-pair cabling every day, but the name might not pop out and bonk you on the head. The general category—twisted-pair—is used for both telephone and computer networks. It is simply pairs of wires twisted together and encased in an insulating sheath.

Twisted-pair cable is used for a number of Smart Home functions. The cabling is usually 22 or 24 gauge, depending on the function. It is used for

- ❏ Security systems and sensors
- ❏ Speaker wire
- ❏ HVAC systems
- ❏ A/V controls
- ❏ Computer networks
- ❏ Telephones

Twisted-pair wire comes with different numbers of wires, depending on the type you buy. The number of wires in the cable will depend on how many systems you need to connect.

Twisted pair comes in two flavors:

❏ **STP (shielded twisted pair)**   A two-pair cabling medium encased in shielded insulation to limit electromagnetic interference of signals.

❏ **UTP (unshielded twisted pair)**   A four-pair cabling medium not encased in shielding. UTP is used in most computer networks.

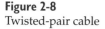

Shielded vs. Unshielded

The more tightly twisted the copper wire strands, the less likely there will be interference or signal loss. STP has only two twisted pairs, but compensates with its shielding. UTP has no shielding, but compensates with an extra pair of wires. Because UTP is fast, reliable, and inexpensive, it has become the predominant type of cabling used in computer networking. Use of the more expensive STP is limited to environments made hostile by high levels of electromagnetic interference—this probably won't be your home unless you live by an electromagnet factory.

Figure 2-8 shows some strands of twisted-pair cable.

Figure 2-8
Twisted-pair cable

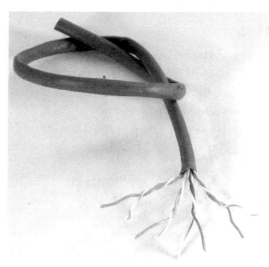

Cabling Specifications   Table 2-1 explains the five categories of unshielded twisted pair specified by an international standards organization called TIA/EIA

(Telecommunications Industry Association/Electronics Industry Association). These cabling specifications are important in that the rate at which data can be reliably transmitted is determined by a combination of factors:

❏ How tightly twisted the copper wire is

❏ The quality of the cable's copper

❏ The type of insulation used to encase the cable

❏ The design and quality of the cable connectors

In Table 2-1, Cat 3 and 5 represent the lion's share of twisted-pair networks today. Cat 3 is predominantly used for telephone networks and security systems, while Cat 5 has the lock on computer networks.

Category	Cable Description	Cable Application
Cat 1	Traditional telephone cable	Not usable for computer networking; no longer installed for telephones
Cat 2	Four twisted pairs	4 Mbps, not recommended for computer networking
Cat 3	Four twisted pairs with three twists per foot, rated up to 16 MHz	10-Mbps Ethernet and 4 Mbps for token ring; also used for new telephone cabling
Cat 4	Four twisted pairs, rated up to 20 MHz	16 Mbps, used for token ring
Cat 5	Four twisted pairs with eight twists per foot, rated up to 100 MHz	100 Mbps, used for Fast Ethernet; fast becoming ubiquitous in networked buildings
Enhanced Cat 5 (a.k.a. Cat 5e)	Four twisted pairs with eight twists per foot, but made of higher-quality materials and rated up to 200 MHz	Rated up to twice the transmission capability of regular Cat 5
Cat 6	Four twisted pairs with each pair wrapped in foil insulation; whole bundle wrapped in polymer	Rated up to six times the transmission capability of regular Cat 5

Table 2-1
Categories of Twisted-Pair Cabling

Cat 3 cabling is used for telephone systems and not generally for computer networks. However, Cat 3 cabling is appropriate for networks operating at 10 Mbps. If you have a home computer network that is running at 10 Mbps, you'd be okay using Cat 3 cabling. That having been said, Cat 3 is really only useful for telephone networks, and you'd be better off with Cat 5 cabling for any home computer networking as it will allow for some future expansion.

HEADS UP!

Cat 5 Cabling

When running cat 5 cabling, it's a smart idea to keep it away from fluorescent lighting and AC wire, which can cause interference.

Jacks   To connect your Cat 3 and Cat 5 cabling, you'll use one of five connectors, depending on your need. Registered Jacks (RJs) have the same basic look—like telephone jacks. In fact, the common, everyday telephone jack is called an RJ-11 jack. Other variations on the jack make it wider so more wires or positions can be utilized. Depending on the number of positions, there are different uses for the jack and the wiring. The following are the types of jacks you will run across when making your Smart Home:

- ❏ **RJ-11**   This type of jack accommodates four wires, although only two wires are used for a single telephone line connection.
- ❏ **RJ-14**   This jack seats four wires, for a two-line telephone connection.
- ❏ **RJ-25**   This jack holds six wires, for a three-line telephone connection.
- ❏ **RJ-31X**   This jack holds eight wires and is used in security systems.
- ❏ **RJ-45**   This jack holds eight wires and is used for computer networks.

Speaker Wire

When connecting your remote speakers to the stereo or other audio source, there are two different types of cabling you will encounter:

- ❏ **In-wall**   This is the cabling that is strung through the walls to connect your audio source to outlets in each remote location.
- ❏ **Patch cabling**   This stretch of wiring is used to connect the outlets with the speakers. This can be the same wiring used in-wall, or you can use another type that has been precut and preconnectored.

TIPS OF THE TRADE

Get Good Speaker Wire

The old chestnut "a chain is only as strong as its weakest link" should be heeded when installing speaker wire. When you install speaker wire (or any cabling for that matter), you should try to buy the best stuff you can. Since you'll be burying it in the walls, it's not something that can easily be replaced and upgraded, as you might find yourself doing in the future with better stereos or speakers. When you are able to afford a new system, including "RoofRecker 4000SUX" speakers, you don't want to have to mess around with replacing substandard cabling simply to accommodate your new acquisition.

Additionally, when you install speaker cabling, be sure to find a brand with a slight twist to it. As cable is strung in long runs, it can act as an antenna and cause interference with the signal you want to pump through those wires.

If you step into any Radio Shack, you'll be assaulted by all the different types of audio cable out there. To demystify it (at least a little), there are a couple important things to look for when selecting your cabling:

- ❑ **Gauge**   This is the thickness of the cabling. Just to make things more confusing, the gauge scale works backward—that is, 16-gauge is actually thicker than 22-gauge wire. As a rule, the thicker gauges will yield better results. A good thickness to shoot for is 16-gauge wire. Thicker wire promises better quality, but it's a bear to pull through the walls. Sixteen-gauge offers a good balance of both quality and maneuverability.

- ❑ **UL rating**   In-wall cabling is rated for its safety and quality by the Underwriter's Laboratories (UL). Look for cabling that has been rated at least a class two or class three (UL CL2 or UL CL3).

Fiber Optics

Fiber-optic cabling is a glass or plastic cable encased in a protective sheath. It's the stuff used in super high-powered computer and telephone networks. It's starting to pick up some steam with home applications, but not a whole lot. At this point in time, there isn't a whole lot of call for fiber-optic appliances, but don't let that stop you from planning for the future.

If you are going to run some cabling, it might be worth your while to throw a run of fiber in there, too. Even though the applications aren't out there en mass yet, it would stink to have to rerun your cabling simply because you didn't run any fiber.

All-in-One

All-in-one cable is certainly worth your attention. All-in-one cable is exactly what the name suggests. It is a bundle of six cables, two each of three different types.

All-in-one cable includes

❏ Two cat 5E cables (for computer, telephone, and security networks)

❏ Two RG-6 coaxial cables (for audio and video distribution)

❏ Two fiber-optic cables (for future applications)

Depending on how the cables are bundled together—either encased in a PVC jacket or in a spiral wrap—the cost for 500 feet of all-in-one cable is US$528.95 or $488.95, respectively. Figure 2-9 shows some examples of all-in-one cable—however, there are many other configurations available.

Figure 2-9
All-in-one cable
(Photo courtesy
Smarthome.com)

Wireless

This being the 21st century and all, you shouldn't *have* to run cabling, if you don't want to. If you think back to the first remote controls, they provided functionality but they were still tethered to the television or VCR via a length of wiring. Now, of course, remotes are wireless devices that clutter coffee tables around the world. As more and more devices are capable of transmitting a signal wirelessly, you might not need to bother stringing cable for some of your projects.

RF

Wireless computer networks predominantly use a protocol called 802.11, with different variations on the protocol for different speeds. The 802.11x LAN is based on an architecture that is very similar to the design of cellular telephone networks. Wireless LANs (WLANs) operate by connecting an *access point* to the server (see Figure 2-10), while client computers are fitted with wireless networking cards. These cards can be fitted for either a desktop or laptop computer. Some computers come with wireless capabilities built in.

Figure 2-10
A wireless computer
network

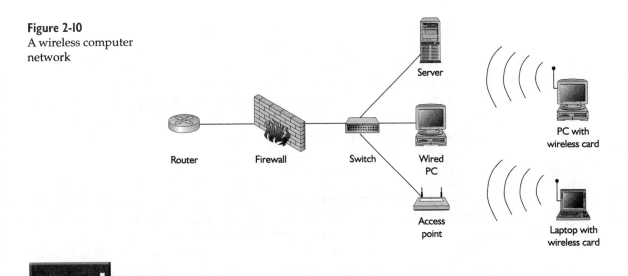

HEADS UP!

802.11x Signals

802.11x signals can operate at distances of up to 300 feet.

There are two types of 802.11x networks that are relevant to our discussion here:

- ❑ **802.11a**   Using this specification, devices transmit at 5 GHz and send data up to 54 Mbps. Although the speed is very good, the range of 802.11a devices suffers, because they are limited to a 60-foot range.

- ❑ **802.11b**   Using this specification, devices transmit at 2.4 GHz and send data up to 11 Mbps. This was the first commercially available wireless network. The speed wasn't great, but it made it possible to connect devices without being tethered by Cat 5 cabling.

- ❑ **802.11g**   This is the latest incarnation of the wireless specification. It handles data communications at speeds of up to 54 Mbps and utilizes the same frequency as 802.11b devices. Because this is relatively new, look for prices on 802.11b gear to drop in price.

HEADS UP!

802.11 Variations

There are other alphabet soup variations of the 802.11x standard (802.11c, 802.11d, and so forth up through 802.11i). The rest of these variations really don't have anything to do with home computer networks and get rather technical. Let's do us all a favor and not discuss this any further.

The price gap between these technologies isn't too broad, actually. The cost of an 802.11a wireless network card is about US$65, an 802.11b wireless network card is about US$50, and the 802.11g card is about US$70. The 802.11b access points cost about US$80, while 802.11g access points will run about US$120. Also, if you happen to have existing 802.11b gear, new 802.11g stuff will be compatible with it. Don't expect your 802.11b card to start chugging away at 54 Mbps, but at least you won't have to buy all new gear.

Infrared

The other type of wireless connection you will encounter in your Smart Home construction is infrared (IR). IR devices are most popularly remote controls, although some computers are set up with IR connection devices.

While RF signals can be up to 300 feet away (or more under ideal conditions) and even be separated by walls, IR requires a line of sight between the two communicating devices, and there is also a limited range. There are a number of products that you can use to extend the range of your remote controls, and to even use them in one room while the signal is carried over to another device and retransmitted to the end device.

Design Basics

An important starting point when designing your Smart Home is to figure out what exactly you need and want in your Smart Home. It is worthwhile to list out all your Smart Home goals, needs, and wants, and then develop a plan for implementation.

This isn't just an important step when deciding how much you are willing to spend, but it is also important when deciding if you're going to go whole hog on your plan or implement your Smart Home projects in a phased manner.

Family Members' Input

It's easy to sit back with a pad of paper and your dreams, then start jotting down your vision for the Smart Home. However, once you've created your dream list of Smart Home projects, do yourself a favor and talk with your family members about the project. It's a good idea to include their input for a number of reasons.

First, understanding their needs and wants may open up new ideas for your Smart Home. It may not even be on your radar screen to install a magnetically sealed smart doggy door. However, talking with your significant other might reveal that need.

Second, involving family members adds an element of excitement for the project and might smooth over any rough edges toward their acceptance. For example, your son might think it's stupid to fish cabling through the walls and wire the rooms of the house. However, if he understands that he'll be able to watch TV in his own room, without having to battle mom over whether he gets to watch MTV or she gets to watch the Lifetime channel, he'll come on board pretty quickly.

Security

There are several different types of sensors that can be connected to your security system. Sensors include the following:

- ❑ Motion
- ❑ CO
- ❑ Glassbreak
- ❑ Open door/window
- ❑ Smoke

Take into consideration how these detectors and sensors are to be used in your home and where they are to be placed. For example, will you place a smoke detector on each level (you should)? Will you place motion detectors covering each door, or will open door sensors be sufficient?

Next, you should decide how you want to be notified if one of the sensors is tripped. Will it be enough for you to have the monitoring company notified if the alarm is tripped, or do you want an e-mail sent to your office, or a text message sent to your cellular telephone? You could also have cameras set up outside that can be monitored over the Internet to show who is coming and who is going.

HEADS UP!

Call the Police

You should also take into consideration your local police department's response guidelines. There is likely a city ordinance in place that explains how many times the police department will respond to false alarms. After that number is exceeded, subsequent alarms will result in a bill from your friendly neighborhood public safety department.

Lighting

When planning Smart Home lighting, there are two ways in which lights can be set up and configured. One is by hardwiring the light controls, and the other is by using the existing wiring (using X10, for example). Hardwiring is more reliable, but it is also twice as expensive. In this book, we're utilizing X10 controls for many of our projects. X10 allows for easy installation, setup, and coordination with other Smart Home controls and devices.

To a degree, lighting schemes and plans go hand-in-hand with security. That doesn't mean when an intruder breaks into the house that the lights are automatically dimmed for his or her comfort. What it means is that certain lights are wired with motion detectors to come on when movement is detected. For instance, a popular lighting fixture is used on the exterior so when motion is detected, a floodlight comes on. This does not need to be connected to the security system (otherwise, the police would come running every time the neighbor's cat decided to go out for its midnight constitutional). In this context, security simply means that if any motion is detected, the light comes on. This could be a benefit if you are getting out of your car at night and need a little light, or if you want to know if someone is outside.

TIPS OF THE TRADE

Paths

Another use for Smart Home lighting, and one that needs to be planned out, is for the creation of *paths*. In Chapter 9, for example, we'll be demonstrating a lighting project in which someone getting out of bed in the middle of the night will have a path illuminated—at a specific level of dimming—so that all the lights in the house need not come on at full intensity. This allows the late night bathroom visitor not to have to worry about turning on lights, nor will he or she have to turn them off because they will be preset to deactivate after a specific amount of time.

You could establish a *path* for any purpose in your Smart Home. For instance, if you like watching movies in your family room after the rest of the clan has gone off to bed, you could establish a path between your family room, up the stairs, down the hallway, and into your bedroom. This wouldn't require you to turn on or off any lights and the light wouldn't be so bright that everyone in the house is woken up once you've finished *Die Hard With a Vengeance*.

Data Networks

Depending on the complexity of your home LAN, you might want to perform an extensive Cat 5 wiring project. By connecting your home computers (the one in your den, the one in Johnny's room, the one in the kitchen, and so forth), sharing resources is much simpler. In fact, it makes nothing but sense to consider your home computing needs and plan for them. For instance, do you have only one printer? Do you want to share files between your computers? Do you want to share an Internet connection? If you answered "yes" to any of these, then a home LAN should be in your plans.

HEADS UP!

Future-proofing

Along with your telephone network, you might consider stringing Cat 5 cable throughout your home. It isn't just to accommodate the equipment you already have, but to prepare for the equipment you don't know about yet.

A concern for wireless networks comes in the realm of security. Unless caution is taken when setting up these networks, it is possible for someone to park outside your house with a wireless network card plugged into a laptop computer and access your home LAN. In fact, there are people who make a hobby of so-called *war-driving*. That is, for the sheer fun of it they drive up and down through neighborhoods looking for unsecure wireless access points they can tap into. We'll talk in Chapter 4 about specific security measures you can take to bolster your wireless network.

Telecommunications

Since telephone systems are very important in our lives—not only for the sake of making voice calls, but also to connect to the Internet and hooking up the satellite dish—this is an area of Smart Home design that needs to be considered with much attention to detail.

Given the importance of telephone systems, it's a good idea—if you don't have phone jacks in every room of your house—to think about adding that to your short list of projects. One of the main problems with telephone wiring in homes is that it doesn't lend itself to future expansion very well. If you're building a house from scratch, it is a good idea to have the telephone wiring *home-run* rather than *looped*.

Home-run (also known as a *star*) wiring is shown on the left in Figure 2-11. Wiring comes into the house and is split into separate connections to various telephone jacks. A looped system, shown on the right side of Figure 2-11, runs the line from outlet to outlet, splitting the signal at each stop. Loop systems (also known as *daisy-chains*) are less expensive than home-run systems because less cabling is used, and you don't need to invest in a punch-down block.

Figure 2-11
Home-run versus
loop wiring

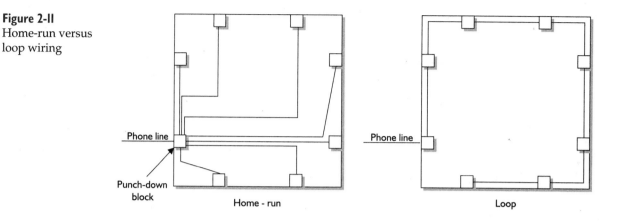

The benefit of the home-run system is one of reliability and flexibility. For instance, if there is a breakdown at any point in the loop system, everything after that point will fail. In a home-run system, if one of the connections fails, the others will still function properly.

A/V

After a hard day of setting up your Smart Home for telephony, data networks, and so forth, don't you just want to unwind in front of the TV or the stereo? Why not do it in your bedroom so you can relax on the bed while watching *Deuce Bigalow: Male Gigolo*?

Take the time to plan not only where you expect audio and video signals to be distributed, but also anticipate where else they might be needed in the future. Along with the other types of cabling you're running, it might be a good idea to locate some extra speaker wire and coax cable that run to other rooms that you don't have immediate plans to wire.

TIPS OF THE TRADE

Think Outside the Box

Also, think about any other applications for audio/video distribution that you might want to implement. For example, if your son has a TV in his room—and you don't mind violating his privacy—maybe you want to set up a distribution system going *from* his room so you can monitor his viewing habits. That is, you can flip on your own television to make sure he's not watching *It Came from Hell IV: Orgy of Blood*.

You wouldn't start building a house without a blueprint and an understanding of what materials you need. Even though adding some smart functionality to your home isn't exactly the same thing in terms of its scope, it's still important to know what you're doing before you start doing it. Take some time to understand what you want and what you need from your Smart Home before you get rolling.

❏   Did you make a list of your Smart Home projects?

❏   Have you considered your family members' wants and needs?

❏   Have you checked city ordinances about how often police will respond to false alarms before they start sending you a bill?

❏   Have you planned any paths?

❏   Have you considered which rooms will need which type of cable fed to them?

Chapter 3

The Cost of a
Smart Home

Tools of the Trade

A list of your Smart Home projects
Calculator
Smart Home catalogs

If you're the CEO of a big company (at least one who hasn't been indicted yet), you can leaf mindlessly through any number of Smart Home catalogs, picking and choosing those projects you want to trick out your home. However, if you're a normal person, paging through Smart Home catalogs might start with a quick look at what a certain product does, then immediately scanning down to the bottom of the ad to figure out if you can pay for it.

The good news is that most Smart Home projects are quite affordable. Many projects can be started for less than US$100. Naturally, however, when you start adding more and more functionality to your Smart Home, the costs will rise. The good news is, it's easy to get started. Plus, if you use X10 compatible equipment (as we will be doing in this book), it is simplicity itself to add more modules and more functionality. You can either do this as you decide to add more projects or as money makes itself available.

In this chapter, we'll help sort through the financial issues related to Smart Home construction. First, we'll talk about determining what you need for your home and look at evaluating both your home and your specific needs. Next, we'll take a look at your budget and how to find some common ground between how much you can spend, and how much you want to spend. Finally, we'll examine some sample Smart Home projects and see how much they cost, in addition to finding some bargains.

What Do You Need?

The first step in figuring out how much your Smart Home project will cost is to determine what it is, exactly, you need. There are two components to this process:

- ❏ Understanding your home
- ❏ Understanding your wants and needs

It is necessary to understand these two issues because each one presents different scenarios for products and cost.

Evaluate Your Home

There are two ways in which Smart Home components can be added to your home. First, and probably the most likely scenario, you could be adding Smart Home devices to an existing home. As such, you probably want to avoid stringing up a lot of wiring (although it is certainly possible, if necessary) and favor simple, plug-in solutions. X10 (which we'll cover in more depth in Chapter 4) utilizes existing home wiring to send messages to various appliances. This is a less costly option than installing new wiring. However, some solutions (like security systems and quality audio and video distribution) will require new wiring to be installed.

The other scenario is that you are lucky enough to have new construction and can add your projects before sheetrock is hung and paint is slapped on the walls. Both scenarios present their pros and cons.

Renovating an Existing Home

Obviously, it is much easier to wire a new home than to go into the walls and start pulling cable through an existing home.

TIPS OF THE TRADE

Running Cable

An easy—albeit costly—way to run cable between rooms in an existing home is to hire a contractor who is capable of doing a cable run. If you decide to go this route, look for someone who is experienced in running telephone or security systems. This will be helpful in that you won't have to worry too much about having to rip into walls—although that might have to happen in some cases, depending on your home's design.

If you are a staunch do-it-yourselfer, a spool of Steel Fish Tape can help run cable through walls, plastic, or metal conduit. This gadget costs US$59.95 for a 100-foot spool, or US$49.95 for a 50-foot spool. If you're going such a route that you need to run cabling, you might want to consider future-proofing your Smart Home by installing all-in-one cable (described in greater depth in the next section).

The best solution, when buying components for a Smart Home, is to buy items that can be used with your home's existing wiring. Such products that employ the X10 protocol, for example, can be used throughout the home because X10 uses your existing electrical wires to transmit its signals. Naturally, however, if you want to connect whole house audio or video, or need to build a wired local area network (LAN), it might be necessary to run cabling. However, there are some solutions that will enable you to use existing wiring to deliver these services. For example, the Leapfrog Home Network System (as shown in Figure 3-1) allows you to watch video from your DVD, VCR, or satellite using existing phone lines. This product costs US$149.95.

Figure 3-1
Leapfrog Home
Network System
(Photo courtesy
Smarthome.com)

Adding to New Construction

Of course, the easiest and cleanest way to prepare your Smart Home is to do it from scratch. That is, if you're building a new house, you can plan your Smart

Home needs while planning the rest of the home. At this stage, it is easy and cheap enough to install various types of wiring after the walls have been roughed in but before the sheetrock is put in place. It might even be worth your while to consider future-proofing your new home by installing different types of cabling.

Wiring for the future might sound expensive, but it really isn't too bad. When you consider all the different types of cable that are bundled together, you're making a good investment in your Smart Home's future.

All-in-one cable includes the following:

- ❏ Two category 5E cables (for computer networks)
- ❏ Two RG-6 coaxial cables (for audio and video distribution)
- ❏ Two fiber-optic cables (for future applications)

Depending on how the cables are bundled together—either encased in a PVC jacket or in a spiral wrap—the cost for 500 feet of all-in-one cable is US$528.95 or US$488.95, respectively.

HEADS UP!

Looking into the Smart Home's Crystal Ball

It's hard to say what, exactly, will be the premiere application for fiber optics in the Smart Home. At this point, fiber optics are useful for audio and video connections, as well as extremely high-speed LANs.

Evaluate Your Needs and Wants

As we observed in Chapter 1, no one *needs* their lighting system connected with a voice recognition system. No one *needs* audio and video pumped throughout their entire house. Having said that, there are certainly a number of projects you want to do. Before slapping down some money at the Smart Home shop, it's a good idea to understand what you need, exactly, so that you buy the right products.

You might find yourself looking for components to serve a specific need. Take time to understand your entire Smart Home project before jumping in and buying a single item. Make a list of all the facets of your project, and then evaluate which ones you'll implement first. From there, it's time to start looking at the products available in the marketplace. For example, there are any number of proprietary devices out there that will serve your needs just fine. However, by buying a light dimmer that isn't compatible with your other Smart Home needs, you'll wind up spending more money in the long run. It's a good idea to take a look at your entire needs first, then buying specific products.

Costs

For most of us, this is really where the rubber meets the road when considering Smart Home projects. How much a project costs is really a determining factor as to whether it will be accomplished or not. But don't let sticker shock scare you away from a project you're really keen on. There are ways you can achieve a desired project, but it might mean dialing down the scale of the project; delaying gratification until you have the money to do it; or doing some research and finding the project somewhere less expensive.

In this section, we'll talk about budgeting—comparing the costs of various Smart Home projects—and give you a few resources for tracking down Smart Home gear. Like many technical projects, you can often get 80 percent of your desired functionality for 50 percent of the total cost. That is, a minority of the features—because of physical constraints, for example—can comprise the majority of the total costs.

Budgeting

There are a couple ways to approach the concept of building a Smart Home. One is to do everything piecemeal. This means when you get the itch for a certain project (automatic sprinklers, for instance), you whip out your credit card and scratch. This is certainly a realistic approach to building your Smart Home, and it allows you to add on based on your own financial position and what you next deem to be necessary as you consider your project list. Having said that, we recommend against a piecemeal approach simply because you'll wind up spending more money in the long run, and you're likely to have a bunch of systems that don't work together.

The other way to approach your Smart Home is to look at it as a whole. Jot down the projects you want to accomplish, order everything, then hook it all up in one rush of technohome pleasure. This has the disadvantage of being the most expensive up-front option. On the other hand, in the long run you will experience better operation of your Smart Home components, because you will have bought them with interactivity in mind. Also, even though buying a couple dozen items at once is more expensive than buying an item or two, it will be less expensive in the long run. This is because you'll spend less on shipping and you'll spend less trying to ensure that everything works well together. Further, the fact that you'll have compatible systems that work together is an even more important cost consideration—if you buy the proper component at first, then you won't need to buy something new to fit in with a different system.

TIPS OF THE TRADE

Getting Help from the Bank

If you are building a new home and adding Smart Home capabilities, it is possible to finance a number of components with your mortgage. The addition of cabling, keypads, switches, panels, and so forth can all be included in your mortgage. This is a good way to pay for your Smart Home infrastructure, because it needn't take an immediate hit on your wallet; rather, it can be a grain of sand on the beach that is your house payment.

A good place to start with a large project that you intend to phase in is to start with the core. That is, you might want to start with a central computer system or security system first. From there, additional components can be added at a later time. By starting with a core system, it is easier and more economical to add components in a logical manner than to start throwing things together willy-nilly.

Of course, the size of your Smart Home endeavor will be limited by the size of your wallet. Unless you're the Sultan of Brunei or Warren Buffet, cost is a huge consideration when purchasing Smart Home gear. To decide how much to spend, you have to establish how much you can realistically afford. If need be, you can piece together the project bit by bit. However, if finances force you to do this, be sure to keep an eye on future expansion and consider your potential projects when buying new gear. For example, you might place wire for an in-wall speaker while you are running a motion detector. Or perhaps you will put off finishing the basement for a season so you can do another home automation project while the ceiling down there is exposed.

Comparing Smart Home Projects

Like anything else we buy, purchasing Smart Home components can be expensive or it can be cheap. Think of it like going to a car dealership. The brand-new models are out front, shining in the sun under the pennant streamers and giant inflatable gorilla. As you move toward the back of the lot—where fewer and fewer salesman storm you—you find that the cars are a little older, a little less shiny, and a little less expensive. There are two different kinds of cars for sale—both provide the same basic function (transportation), but they offer different amenities by way of features.

The same is true of anything you buy, and it is also true of Smart Home components. That's not to say that Smart Home retailers are going to try and sell you stuff that is used or ineffective, but there are different models with different features.

For example, as shown in Figure 3-2, Sony sells a five-component universal remote control for US$39.99. This is a bare-bones remote that allows simple control of five devices with no frills. On the other end of the spectrum, Sony also sells the Universal Remote Commander, as shown in Figure 3-3. This looks a lot like a tricorder from Star Trek fame (circa *The Next Generation*). It's got a touchscreen that can be edited for your own personal preferences. It's also got the preprogrammed codes that its US$40 brother has, but it is also capable of learning from other remote controls. Further, it can control 18 devices and will remember 45 macros—all for US$199.99.

Figure 3-2
Sony's
five-component
universal remote
control (Photo
courtesy
Smarthome.com)

Figure 3-3
Sony's Universal
Remote Commander
(Photo courtesy
Smarthome.com)

Is the Universal Remote Commander better than the five-component universal remote (heck, Sony doesn't even love it enough to give it a cool name)? Sure it is! It's got a customizable touchscreen and can control every appliance in yours and three other Smart Homes—plus it looks like something Captain Picard used to chuck at Data whenever he got obstinate. It's top of the line. That having been said, however, you might not want to invest almost US$200 in a remote control.

The point of all this is, unless money is no issue, there needs to be a balance struck between Smart Home component functionality and price. If you decide that the Universal Remote Commander is just too cool, to stay within your budget other components might have to be downgraded. This is largely a balancing act between "want" and "need" with the fulcrum resting on "budget."

Sample Projects

Blah, blah, blah. We've shot a bunch of information at you about costs, needs, and so forth. Not that all that information isn't useful, but let's put some dollar signs to various Smart Home projects so you can get a taste for what things cost. First, let's take a very easy, sample project and see what the price tag looks like. This won't be a barn burner or anything, just something nice and easy. Next, we'll add a couple of components to the project to make it a little more interesting—and to jack up the price a smidge. Finally, let's look at a whole house implementation and look at the dollar signs associated with that sort of project.

For this exercise, we've chosen some projects from the *Smarthome, Spring 2003* catalog. None of these projects include any sort of tax and shipping (which will vary depending on where your purchases must be shipped). Also, you might also find these products locally. As such, we're using a constant source for the sake of an apples-to-apples comparison.

Something Simple

A first, easy project is to simply control a single light in your home. To do this, we'll buy two products: first, we need an X10 controller (more on X10 in Chapter 4) for your computer, and then we need an X10 compatible dimmer switch.

Sure, you could just as easily stop by Home Depot with US$20 and pick up a dimmer switch that you control manually. However, the benefit here is that this particular light will be able to be set on a schedule to come on and go off as you see fit.

HEADS UP!

A Few Assumptions...

For this project, we're making a couple of assumptions. First, we're guessing that you have a computer with an open Universal Serial Bus (USB) port. Since it's a simple project, and won't be constantly used, you won't need a computer dedicated solely to dimming a single light. Also, we're not figuring in costs for things like tools or connection supplies.

Note that many products, like the Decora Dimmer Switch, come with their own connection hardware, but depending on the project, you might find yourself at the hardware store buying wire nuts.

Table 3-1 sums up the price for each component along with the project's total.

The total cost for this project comes in just a couple cents short of US$55. It's not a bank breaker, and the inclusion of the X10 controller leaves the door open for additional expansion. You'll be able to turn a single light on and off, do some rudimentary dimming, and that's about it. Pretty cool, but just the tip of the iceberg.

Item	Cost
Powerlinc USB X10 controller	US$34.99
Decora Dimmer Switch	US$19.99
Total	**US$54.98**

Table 3-1
Product Costs for a Simple Light Dimming Project

HEADS UP!

The Software Is Included
The software needed to run this project is included with the Powerlinc USB Controller.

Kicking It Up a Notch

The next project is a little more advanced in its scope. We're taking the project from the previous example (a room dimmer) and adding three more pieces to it:

❏ Heavy Duty appliance module, which will be connected to the water heater. At a prescheduled time, the water heater will automatically be turned off, saving water heating costs. It will be reactivated at a preset time.

❏ An exterior motion detector. Not only will this light fixture turn on exterior lighting when motion is detected, it is linked with a couple of your interior lights, letting you know—inside—that something has tripped the detector outside.

❏ Wireless motion sensor. Used for indoors, this sensor (used in tandem with an RF base receiver) will turn on lights in a room when someone enters the room. Connected to the X10 module, a schedule can be set up to set varying levels of dimming.

This project allows more functionality to the Smart Home's lighting features. Not only will it allow you to control lighting levels and apply them to a schedule, but now the system is sensitive to motion and will activate when someone either enters a room, or passes by the sensor, outside the home.

Item	Cost
Powerlinc USB X10 controller	US$34.99
Decora Dimmer Switch	US$19.99
220 Heavy Duty X10 Appliance Module	US$20.95
Leviton DHC X10 Motion Detector	US$64.95
Wireless X10 Motion Sensor	US$18.95
RF Base Receiver	US$24.99
Total	**US$184.82**

Table 3-2
Product Costs for a Four-item Home Automation Project

This project is pretty heavy on lighting, but each piece adds its own unique functionality. In addition to the ability to manage lighting levels in a single room as the first project provides, we are now able to turn on some security lighting outside when a motion sensor is activated. Additionally, the component we've selected—a Leviton DHC X10 Motion Detector—will also turn on an X10 device inside the house, letting you know that someone (or at least the neighbor's cat) is outside.

A similar idea is carried indoors with the Wireless X10 Motion Sensor. When connected with the RF Base Receiver, someone entering a room will activate the lights. Additionally, when connected to the X10 controller, a schedule can be set up that will establish different levels of lighting in the room.

Finally, we have a nonlighting component for this project. By connecting a 220V heavy duty X10 module to the water heater, money can be saved by turning off the heater when no one's home. Coming in at less than US$185, this project provides some concrete functionality—not only is the "isn't that cool" level pretty high, but it provides some solid cost savings and security. There's no wiring expense since we are using X10 for this entire project.

All-out, Full-home Automation

Our last example shows the tendrils of home automation worked into virtually every facet of daily life. In addition to the products introduced in the first two examples, this final project adds more overall functionality to the Smart Home (including a security system), along with some conveniences (like whole house audio and video). This project requires a number of additional pieces:

❏ **Computer** Since the project is going to be comprehensive, it's necessary to have a computer dedicated solely to home automation needs. This is a computer that will be kept separate from the rest of the household (located in the basement, probably).

❏ **Security system**   The earlier projects added some elements of security (namely, motion-detector-enabled lights), but they weren't security systems per se. This project adds an HAI OmniPro II security system. Connected to the system are five pet-sensitive passive infrared (PIR) motion sensors and two door sensors.

❏ **HVAC**   The system also adds a thermostat that can be managed either at the system's computer or via a web interface.

❏ **Motorized drape controller**   The addition of the motorized drape controller is not only pretty cool to see operate, but it also manages the opening and closing of the patio door drapes so that sun is let in to warm the house in the winter and kept out to keep the house cool in the summer. The end result is a cost savings in heating and cooling costs.

❏ **Home entertainment**   One of the costlier parts of this setup is the whole house distribution system for audio and video. The system sends video signals to five televisions while the audio system transmits to four sets of speakers. In one room, the audio and video can be changed, remotely, by using the Powermid remote extender. Note that we haven't included the price of additional television sets or speakers in this cost estimate.

❏ **Pet door**   Pet doors might not sound like something especially Smart Homish—however, the door we're installing (the Dog Mate Electromagnetic Door) provides a little magnet to hang around Fido's neck. This magnet acts as a "key" so when he approaches the pet door, it automatically unlocks.

❏ **Voice recognition and web interface**   Sure, having a Smart Home is cool enough, but it's even cooler—and more utilitarian—if system status can be checked and managed remotely. By implementing the voice recognition and web interfaces, it will be possible to check the Smart Home from school, work, or anywhere with a computer or telephone.

HEADS UP!

No Need to Break the Bank

Taking a look at Table 3-3, you can see that we have a lot of stuff—US$4,675.60 worth—but not nearly as much as we could have included. The point of this exercise wasn't to list each and every item listed in the Smarthome catalog; rather, it is to show you what different projects would cost.

Item	Cost
Powerlinc USB X10 controller	US$34.99
Decora Dimmer Switch	US$19.99
220 Heavy Duty X10 Appliance Module	US$20.95
Leviton DHC X10 Motion Detector	US$64.95
Wireless X10 Motion Sensor	US$18.95
RF Base Receiver	US$24.99
Computer	US$500.00
Dog Mate Electromagnetic Door	US$79.99
Hal 2000	US$249.99
OmniPro II Controller	US$1,249.99
HAI Web-Link II Software	US$279.99
OmniStat Single Stage Thermostat	US$139.99
Twin PIR Motion Sensors	5 @ US$41.99 = US$209.95
Magnetic Contact Switch	2 @ US$3.99 = US$7.98
Multiroom video distribution system with modulators	US$199.99
RG-6/U Quad Shield Coaxial Cable (1000 feet)	US$179.99
Powermid Remote Extender	US$52.99
Motorized Drape Controller	US$89.95
NuVo Simplese Audio Distribution System	US$999.99
Speaker wire (500 feet)	US$249.99
Total	**US$4,675.60**

Table 3-3
Product Costs for a Whole-Home Automation Project

Finding Bargains

There are certainly some home automation projects that will induce sticker shock. But don't let the price of some projects scare you away, entirely. There are a couple ways you can save some money and still find what you want:

❏ **eBay**   You can find anything, short of the Holy Grail, on eBay (www.ebay.com). Anyone who's never heard of the World Wide Web's premier auction site will probably also be fascinated by such things as sliced bread, fire, and the wheel. If it's ever been made, someone's bought it and is selling it on eBay. If you can tear yourself away from the auctions for complete collections of "Mama's Family," you might be able to find the gadget for which you're looking. Oftentimes, companies sell products on eBay that are overstocks—meaning you might get a deal on a brand-new product. Don't take this as a glowing endorsement of eBay or other online auction sites, however. There are plenty of sleazebags out there who want to rip you off, so be careful in your dealings. Some tips for buying items from eBay:

❏ *Always read the product descriptions completely before bidding.* This is a simple way to avoid problems later on. Is the product new or used? Is it X10 compatible? Is it in good condition? These are things to check for in the product description.

❏ *E-mail the seller and ask questions about the product that aren't answered in the product description.*

❏ *Don't jump too fast.* Do your research: Are there other products for sale that you might be able to get cheaper? Are these products truly less expensive than you can get from a retailer? If the current bid on a thermostat is only US$5 less than you can get it from a retailer, you might be better off getting it from a retailer rather than a private individual.

❏ *Check the seller's feedback rating.* Before you place even one bid, read what other buyers have had to say about their transactions with the seller.

❏ *Make sure you know how much shipping and handling will cost.* There might be two auctions for the same item; however, one seller will ship it to you for half as much as another seller. Find that out before deciding which seller's product to pursue.

❏ *Avoid counterbidding.* Remember the movies where someone goes into the auction hall to bid on the Monet, only to have the price jacked up by a competitor? It happens all the time on online auction sites. If you find yourself in the middle of a bidding war, you're really not getting the best price for something—you're probably setting the stage to overpay for the item.

❏ *Use a credit card, whenever possible.* If there is a problem with your purchase, it will be easier to ameliorate it if the payment is coming via credit card than if the seller has already cashed your check.

❑ **Shop around**   There are a number of online resources for home automation products. Do the smart thing and look around a little before buying something. You might find that one seller offers that X10 module for US$5 less than another. Some online retailers worth your attention include these:

 ❑ **SmartHome**   www.smarthome.com

 ❑ **GadgetHome**   www.gadgethome.com

 ❑ **Fernbrook**   www.dnet.net/frnbrook/

 ❑ **Smarthomecatalog**   www.smarthomecatalog.com

 ❑ **Homecontrols**   www.homecontrols.com

 ❑ **Radio Shack**   www.radioshack.com

 ❑ **Smarthomeusa**   www.smarthomeusa.com

Building your Smart Home can be expensive, but it doesn't have to be. If you take the time to research your Smart Home projects, looking for both deals and the best way to implement them, you can have a Smart Home that doesn't break the bank.

❑ Did you compare different solutions for your Smart Home project to find the one that best matches your need?

❑ Did you plan all your projects at once so they can be phased in as money comes available?

❑ Did you shop around for the best deal?

Chapter 4

Designing and Building the Smart Home LAN

Tools of the Trade

Home computers
Switch
Router
Firewall
Printer
Cat 5e cabling
X10 Controller
X10 Controller software

For a really integrated Smart Home, the core of the system will be a local area network (LAN). Not only is this LAN necessary for your Smart Home controls, but it is also useful for simple acts of computing. As we noted in Chapter 1, it's likely you already have a computer (most people do, especially those wired enough to want to build a Smart Home). You might also want to connect several computers if yours is a multicomputer home. The advantages of a home LAN are plentiful—from Internet connection sharing to file sharing to printer sharing. Not only can you share resources, but you can also dedicate individual computers to specific functions, like running a security system or serving as a music jukebox. Also, depending on the size of your Smart Home project, it may make the most sense to buy a computer dedicated solely to the management of your devices.

Of course, a LAN is not a requirement for a Smart Home—you can perform any number of functions without a LAN. However, if you want to add deeper layers of functionality and integration, a LAN is a good thing to include.

In this chapter, we take a look at a Smart Home LAN and discuss the various components you can expect to encounter, along with the pros and cons of sharing a high-speed Internet connection. At the end of the chapter, we'll walk you through the steps of connecting your Smart Home LAN along with the heart of your Smart Home devices, an X10 Controller.

Components

In any home LAN, there are a number of devices you can expect to come in contact with. Some of these devices (like client computers) you are probably already familiar with, especially if you utilize a network at work. Other components, like switches and routers, may be new to you. However, if you do use a network at work, there's a good chance you're connected to these devices but wouldn't necessarily be aware of them (they're probably locked away in that room only the computer folks go into).

First, we'll start with some of the components you're likely acquainted with: clients. From there, we'll take a closer look at two devices crucial to networking and connecting a network to the Internet: switches and routers.

Clients

Clients are any devices that are used for input or output purposes. That is, these are the devices that connect to the network and either take in information or present it for the user's consumption. These devices are such things as client computers and printers.

Client PCs

For this discussion, let's examine the schematic in Figure 4-1. This illustration shows a sample home LAN. The computer you will likely have the most contact with is a client device. As Figure 4-1 shows, this home LAN uses three client computers—one in the home office, one in the family room, and one laptop.

Figure 4-1
Client computers are
those your family
members will use for
their computing tasks.

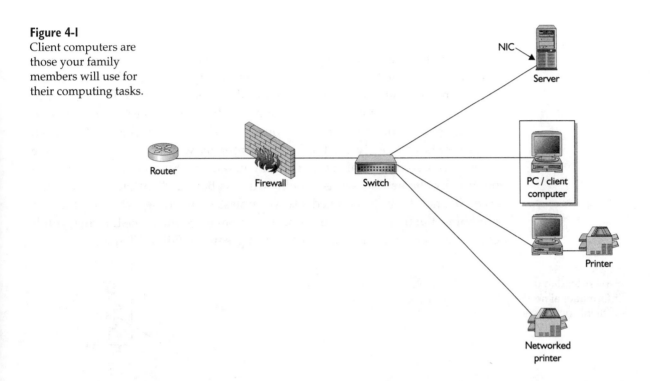

These computers are the ones that family members will use for their daily computing needs. For instance, these are the computers that will be used for homework, for accessing the Internet, and for other common computer usage tasks. Windows-based computers are the most common, although you could also use a Macintosh or a combination of the two just as long as a common protocol is used for communication.

HEADS UP!

If you need a refresher on protocols, flip back to Chapter 2.

In this example, the two desktop PCs are tethered to the network using Cat 5e cabling, while the laptop is connected to a wireless connection—but really any combination of the two is acceptable. You could just as easily utilize wireless cards on all three computers. However, as we noted in Chapter 2, wireless is fine if you're downloading something from the Internet, but if you are transferring large files, expect wireless's 11 megabits per second (Mbps) connection to be about nine times slower than a hardwired connection.

Servers

The next device, highlighted in Figure 4-2, is a server. Servers are computers dedicated to tending to the needs of their client computers. Servers manage the connections between client computers and their connections to the Internet. In large companies, it is not uncommon for multiple servers to be used to attend to the management of hundreds or thousands of client computers. However, unless you have a really big family, you probably won't need more than one server. Plus, you'd probably be just fine if you ran your Smart Home software on one of your clients that served double duty as both a client machine and the server. It's not likely you'd need a server unless there are several computers in your home, but if you decide to connect your Smart Home to the Internet, you'll need a web server. We'll talk about that in greater detail in Chapter 7.

Figure 4-2
Servers tend to the informational needs of client computers.

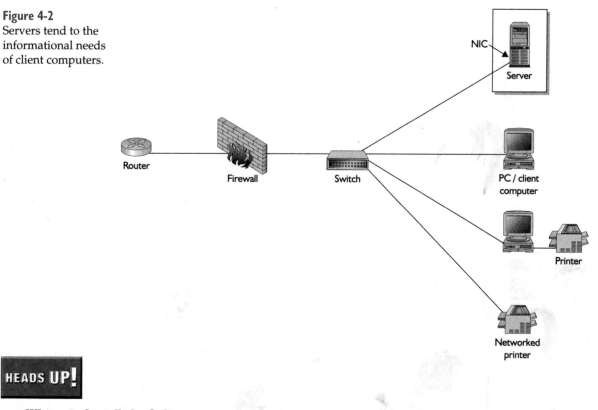

HEADS UP!

Where to Install the Software

In our example, it is the server on which the Smart Home software will be installed. However, Smart Home software could just as easily be installed on client computers, or a lone computer.

NICs

If you look on the back of a wired, networked computer, you'll see a piece of Cat 5 cabling, terminated with an RG-45 connector (remember, it looks like a fat phone connector), and plugging into the computer. This cabling is plugged into a *network interface card* (NIC). The NIC is the interface (as the name suggests) between the computer and the network.

In older computers, this card had to be purchased separately and installed, however NICs are pretty much standard equipment on computers now—you have to specifically request that they not be installed on your machine if you are so inclined. There are different types of NICs that employ different communications technologies. The most popular is *Ethernet*.

TIPS OF THE TRADE

Purchasing Inexpensive NICs

Ethernet NICs are inexpensive (you can get a good one for US$10, but you can occasionally find a deal where you get the card for US$10, then get a manufacturer's rebate for US$10), which makes them very popular both in business and in home applications. In fact, the devices you'll buy to connect with your network are likely to be Ethernet-based, so it is not only a good option; it's also your only option.

Ethernet used to run solely at 10 Mbps, but now the prevalent speed for these networks is 100 Mbps. There are Ethernet implementations that run at 1 Gbps and 10 Gbps, but their price hasn't brought them into the home networking arena.

Printers

There are a number of styles of printer—bubblejet, color, and laser—that offer different functionality. You were probably able to get a bubblejet printer for a buck when you bought your computer. However, the glory of a home LAN is that you needn't save the cover of the Fourth Quarter Earnings Report onto a floppy and run upstairs and print it out on Jimmy's color printer while he's running downstairs to print out his term paper on your laser printer. If you are networked and the printers are appropriately set up, you can print your stuff on Jimmy's printer, he can print his paper on yours, and you can meet halfway on the stairwell to exchange the pages.

Printers will be connected to your LAN in one of two ways—as the printers in Figure 4-3) show. They can either be connected to the network through another computer, or they can be stand-alone devices.

Figure 4-3
Printers can be shared on a home LAN.

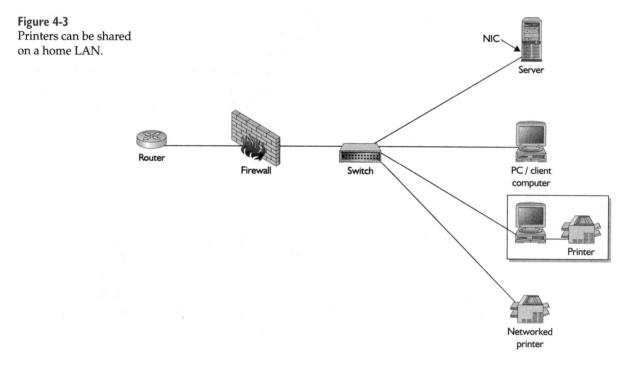

Connected to a Computer   This is probably the most common way to connect a printer to the network. The printer is connected either via a parallel cable (it's a really wide plug with a couple dozen connectors in it) or a universal serial bus (USB) cable. You'll see parallel connectors used on older printers, while newer printers will offer both (and sometimes only USB connections).

HEADS UP!

Beware Human Error

Once the computer is properly connected to the network, the printer can be shared by others on the network. The only downside to shared printers is one of human interaction— if there isn't communication between the people sharing the printer, you can find yourself with a minor headache. For instance, you might have loaded photo paper into the printer and before you can start your print job, someone else prints their stuff on it.

Networked   Networked printers have their own NICs, and their own Internet Protocol (IP) addresses. These printers need not be connected to another computer;

rather, the network knows where they are and work sent to that printer is shot directly through. These printers are said to have their own print server. Otherwise, the PC acts as a print server.

Here, again, is another opportunity to use wireless technology, if you are so inclined. Don't have good desktop space for your laser printer? Why not stick it in the corner of the basement with a wireless NIC? With a wireless-enabled, networked printer, it's an option.

Switches

The next network device might be a little foreign to you, unless you've already done some network design and construction. Switches are used to connect all your network devices, as the illustration in Figure 4-4 shows.

Figure 4-4
Switches connect network devices.

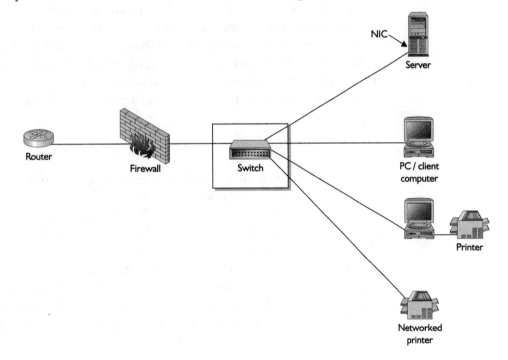

Think of the switch as a steroid-pumped power strip used to share data among all your devices. It is through the switch that you are able to share Internet connections, share files and printers, and check the Smart Home settings located on your server.

There are two ways in which your switch can be connected. It can either be wired, using Cat 5 cabling, or it can be of the wireless variety.

Wired

Wired switches are very common and not very expensive. In fact, you can buy the Linksys EZXS55W EtherFast 10/100 5-Port Workgroup Switch for US$36.88. This gives you connections for five devices, for example:

❑ Input from a router (more on routers later in this chapter)

❑ One server

❑ Two clients

❑ One networked printer

This is just an example and, of course, which devices you connect depends on your needs and what you want to connect to your home LAN.

Of course, even though these devices are reasonably inexpensive, you still have to connect everything with Cat 5 cabling, so there's a little more expense incurred when cabling has to be run through your home, not to mention the headache of actually performing the cable run. On the other hand—and this is the big plus of wired networks—you don't have to worry about interference (unless you run your Cat 5 right next to a power line, so don't do that!) and the speeds are excellent.

Wireless

A wireless switch is more expensive upfront than a wired switch; however, you'll find that current models do a whole lot more than just provide wireless access. For example, the Linksys BEFW11S4 EtherFast Wireless-B Access Point + Cable/DSL Router with 4-Port 10/100 Switch sells for US$75.99. Not only does it provide a switch, but it also adds a router and wireless access point. With this particular model, you can connect four other devices, which is pretty good because it's already got a router and access point included in the device. This example uses an 802.11b device, which only runs at 11 Mbps. Remember, if you decide to go to the next level of wireless connectivity, a comparable switch/ router/access point costs US$40 more but provides 54-Mbps connections.

Wireless Synonym

Wireless Ethernet is also known as WiFi.

Wireless connections sure are nice, but there are also some important considerations when setting one up: namely, placement and security.

Access Point Placement   With a wired network, you need not worry too much about interference from other devices. For instance, running the vacuum cleaner can cause your wireless connection to drop out. Also, even though your wireless-enabled laptop affords you the freedom to go anywhere in your house, you can only be about 300 feet from your access point. After that, you'll lose your connection. Of course, this still beats the pants off a wired connection, which only lets you roam as far at the Cat 5 tether allows. However, when setting up your access point, it is a good idea to bear in mind where your wireless devices will be and whether they will be adequately in range.

Unless you're shacking up with a Rockefeller or a DuPont, you probably don't have the burden of living in a house in which you will be more than 300 feet from your access point. On the other hand, it's a good idea to keep in mind that ductwork, walls, and other elements of construction can conspire against you. Once you set up your network, try and locate your access point as centrally as possible. This doesn't mean you have to move your refrigerator out of the house so the access point can be in the geographical center of your home. However, plan out where you think your wireless devices are likely to be, and where they're likely to be taken, and then plant an access point accordingly. You can certainly keep your access point in the basement, away from the rest of your home if you like, assuming you have a strong enough signal.

TIPS OF THE TRADE

Extend Your Wireless Network's Range

What if you just can't get a good signal and you really want wireless? Easy—just buy a second access point. This doesn't even have to be an expensive model, just a stand-alone unit like the Linksys WAP11 Wireless-B Network Access Point that retails for US$71.99. This extra access point can be used to extend the range of your wireless network, as this illustration shows:

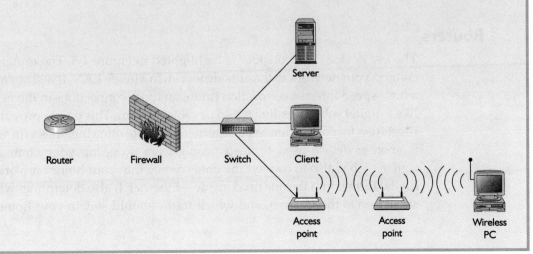

The second access point need not even be plugged into any network devices; it just needs a power source. If you have an outlet in a closet, it can even be installed there if you are so inclined. These extra access points are especially useful if you want to go outside and need more range. You can locate one in the garage and go to town (assuming town is less than 300 feet away).

Security   The biggest concern with wireless networks is their security vulnerabilities. On one hand, they are very nice because they are easy to set up and use. On the other hand, it is this ease that makes them attractive targets for evildoers. All it takes is someone with a wireless-equipped laptop driving by your home to be able to access your network. Happily, however, this problem is easily ameliorated.

Wireless Equivalent Privacy (WEP) is a security protocol that you establish on your wireless access point. This is a code that you establish on the access point and then enter into your wireless-enabled devices. This code is used to encrypt the data being transmitted and provides the key to decrypt incoming transmissions. Without the code, it is very difficult for anyone else to access your network.

HEADS UP!

Security Starts with You

WEP is a double-edged sword. First, it's easy to use—you simply enter a valid code in both devices. However, people tend to be lackadaisical and don't take the two minutes to establish the code.

Another way to avoid wireless invasions is by setting up your access point so that it doesn't broadcast its name. The act of broadcasting a name can be an invitation to hack into your network. Do yourself a favor and avoid any problems that stem from someone being able to access your network because of a backdoor that can easily be nailed shut.

Routers

The last device we'll consider is highlighted in Figure 4-5. The router is used to connect your network to the outside world. In a home LAN, it will be connected to a high-speed Internet connection (more on those connections in the next section) like a digital subscriber line (DSL) or cable modem. This device provides a single IP address for connection to the Internet and quite often includes a firewall, which is another device used to keep people from accessing your home LAN. The router's job is also to convert the data coming into your home network from one digital format into the one used inside—Ethernet. It also determines which traffic should go to the Internet, and which traffic should stay in your home.

Figure 4-5
Routers connect your
home LAN to the
Internet.

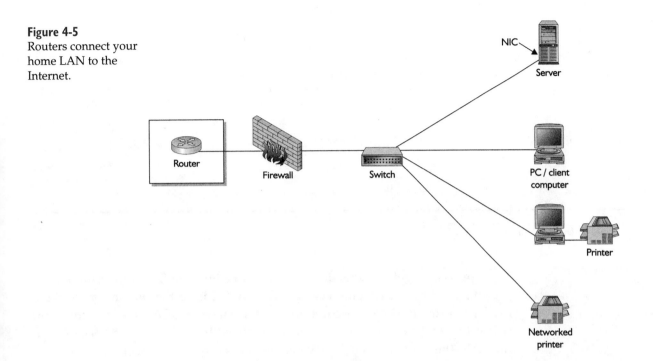

You might feel your head and wallet throbbing simultaneously with the
thought of having to buy a switch, router, access point, *and* firewall. These devices all sound expensive, singly, so four of them must be bank breakers. As we
mentioned in the switch section, it is possible (and very popular) to buy devices
that cram all these tools into one box loaded with flashing red, green, and yellow
lights. Table 4-1 compares some combination devices, the various features they
include, and their price.

Product	Features	Ports	Price
Linksys BEFSR41 EtherFast Cable/DSL Router	10/100 Mbps wired Router Switch	4	US$59.99
Linksys WRT54G	54 Mbps wireless 10/100 Mbps wired Access point Router Switch	4	US$129.99

Table 4-1
Some All-In-One Home LAN Devices

Product	Features	Ports	Price
Linksys BEFW11S4	11 Mbps wireless 10/100 Mbps wired Access point Switch Router	4	US$75.99
Netgear FVS318NA	10/100 Mbps wired Switch Router Firewall	8	US$99.95

Table 4-1
Some All-In-One Home LAN Devices *(continued)*

To put it all together, consider the picture in Figure 4-6. This shows three components in our Smart Home LAN. On the left side of the picture is the cable modem. In the middle is a combination switch/firewall/router. On the right side is the wireless access point. The high-speed Internet signal comes in from the cable, then into the switch to which the access point is connected. In this case, the server and client computers are located elsewhere in the Smart Home, because they are able to connect via WiFi connections.

Figure 4-6
Components of the
Smart Home LAN

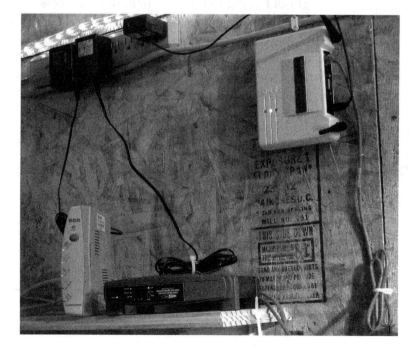

High-Speed Internet Connections

There are a number of ways in which you can connect your home LAN to the Internet. At first blush, you might be wondering, "Why on Earth do I need to hook up to the Internet just to make my lights go on and off?" Well, to be honest, you don't *need* to. You can manage your Smart Home just fine without hooking up to the Internet. However, being able to connect is useful for a couple of reasons.

First, you probably want to connect to the Internet anyway, just for the sake of being able to check out web sites, send e-mail, and all the other stuff Internet connectivity provides. You can do this well enough with a dial-up connection, but if you connect with an analog modem (at 56 kilobits per second (Kbps)), you won't be able to download information as quickly as if you used a DSL or cable connection.

Second, if you want to manage your Smart Home over the Internet, you'll need an "always-on" connection, such as DSL or cable. In this case, a dial-up connection isn't ideal because your telephone line will have to be tied up to ensure that your LAN will be accessible remotely. A high-speed connection is also important for such Smart Home functions as remote management, security, and surveillance.

This section examines your options for high-speed Internet connectivity, along with the pros and cons of high-speed always-on connections.

Types

There are three main ways to get a high-speed Internet connection at your home. These methods are all known as *broadband* connections. These connection types, which you've probably heard of, are listed here:

- ❏ DSL
- ❏ Cable
- ❏ Satellite

Let's take a closer look at these connection types and examine which might fit best with your own particular wants and needs.

DSL

DSL stands for digital subscriber line. As the name implies, DSL also runs digital signals over copper wire. DSL uses sophisticated algorithms to modulate signals in such a way that much more bandwidth can be squeezed from the existing last-mile telephone infrastructure.

DSL is an inherently asymmetric telecommunications technology. What this means is that data can be moved much faster downstream (from the local phone carrier to your home) than upstream. There are several types of DSL; two are important to this discussion:

❏ **aDSL**   Asymmetric DSL, a two-way circuit that can handle about 640 Kbps upstream and up to 6 Mbps downstream.

❏ **DSL Lite**   Also called G.Lite, a slower, less expensive technology that can carry data at rates between about 1.5 Mbps and 6 Mbps downstream, and from 128 Kbps to 384 Kbps upstream. The exact speeds depend on the equipment you install.

DSL's inherent asymmetry fits perfectly with the Internet, where most home users download far more data than they upload.

The key fact to know is that DSL requires a special piece of equipment called a DSL modem to operate. It's the DSL modem that splits signals into upstream and downstream channels. The major difference with DSL Lite is that the splitting is done at the telephone switching station, not in the home or small office.

HEADS UP!

Location Matters

To use most DSL circuits, you must be located no farther than about four or five miles from the telephone switching station.

Cable

A cable modem connects to an existing cable television feed through a cable modem, then to a router or an Ethernet network card in the computer. Though cable modems and dial-up modems share a common functionality, the two are very different devices—primarily in the realm of speed. Dial-in modems top out at 56 Kbps (and that's only when ideal circumstances permit—expect to get connection speeds less than that). Cable modem downloads range from 384 Kbps to several million bps, depending on the service provider and the package purchased.

HEADS UP!

Cable Modem Speedbumps

Cable modems are nice because they use one of the more prevalent home utilities—cable connections—as a transport medium. Unfortunately, one of the biggest problems with cable modems is that you wind up sharing your speed with the neighbors. If you are the only one on the block with a broadband cable connection, you should experience some pretty good speeds. However, whenever a neighbor jumps on the cable bandwagon, expect your speeds to drop, proportionally. For example, if you and another neighbor have cable modems, if you are ever on at the same time, you'll only experience half the speed that you used to enjoy before. If three of you are on at the same time, your speeds will only be a third of when you're on alone.

Satellite

If cable or DSL aren't options and you still feel the need for speed, you need look no further than the heavens. Companies like Hughes Network Systems offer satellite delivery of Internet content. Much like the 18-inch dishes bolted to the sides and roofs of millions of houses for digital television and movies, these services utilize the high-bandwidth broadcasts to deliver high-speed Internet access. Data can be sent both ways and the only requirement is a clear view of the southern sky.

Pros and Cons

High-speed Internet connections have a number of benefits, but they also have a number of disadvantages.

Speed

Probably the most useful and utilitarian aspect of these connections is right in their names—high-speed. These connections are ideal because not only are you able to download web pages and such at high speeds, it is also beneficial to be able to control your Smart Home functions without long delays caused by slow connections. Furthermore, if you have a camera connected to your Smart Home and you wish to monitor it over the Internet, a high-speed connection is necessary for good image quality and transmission rate.

Always-On

The other great aspect of broadband connections is their sheer availability. Of tentimes, these types of connections are known as *always-on* connections, because you can always be connected to your Internet service provider (ISP). This is ideal for your Smart Home management, especially if you plan to do it over the Internet. With an always-on connection, it's a simple matter of entering your Smart Home's IP address to check your home and make whatever changes you might deem necessary.

Security

With broadband connections, there is a heightened risk of security breaches, if you are not careful. DSL and cable connections are more open to hacking, unlike dial-up connections. This is bad enough if some sleazoid accesses your home LAN, but it's even worse if the hacker is able to alter your home controls.

Happily, it's easy enough to put solid security measures in place. The first place to start is by utilizing your computer network's built-in security features, including ensuring passwords are used wherever possible. Also, this is when a firewall comes in handy. The firewall is a line of defense protecting your network from the outside world.

Firewalls aren't necessarily expensive items to employ. You can get freeware or shareware firewall products like Tiny Personal Firewall (www.tinysoftware.com) or Sygate personal Firewall (www.sygate.com). Also, as we noted earlier, if you buy a multipurpose device—like an all-in-one router/switch/firewall—you don't have to buy multiple devices.

Expense

When you sign up with an ISP for a dial-up account, you can get access for anywhere between US$10 and US$25 per month, depending on the company and the number of hours you plan to use. However, pricing schemes ramp up sharply when you have a broadband connection—generally about US$30 per month more. There is a question you must ask yourself, in the context of both your Internet access and Smart Home needs: "Is a high-speed connection worth that extra charge?"

Availability

Maybe the biggest hurdle involved with broadband connections is their availability. This is a problem with both DSL and cable connections. If your neighborhood is not wired for cable, or the cable company does not offer cable connectivity, then you can forget a broadband cable connection. The availability of DSL is even more austere. In order to qualify for a DSL connection, you must be within a few miles of the central office.

HEADS UP!

What Is a "Central Office"?

The central office is that little nameless shack on the corner where the telephone company van always seems to be parked.

Happily, however, satellite connections make the prospect of broadband more available. The only thing you need for a satellite connection is a clear view of the southern sky.

The X10 Connection

X10 is a great way to provide functionality to your Smart Home. These devices can be managed with stand-alone devices; however, for greater control, X10 Controllers connect with your home computer or LAN and allow you to manage a multitude of details.

To connect your home LAN with your Smart Home gear, you need some special equipment to interface between the two. For this book, since we're using X10 gear, we need an X10 interface and the appropriate software. The last section of this chapter will show you how to connect this piece of hardware to your computer, then how to install the requisite software so you can start managing the X10 components of your Smart Home.

The Hardware

There are two types of X10 Controllers that you can use to manage your Smart Home. There are stand-alone controllers that simply plug into the wall. These look just like key pads that sit on your desk, coffee table, or night stand. However, since this chapter is all about computer integration, let's take a closer look at X10 Controllers that operate via your computer.

Controller Types

Within the realm of X10 Controllers, there are two different types that you can plug into your computer. The first plugs into your computer's RS-232 serial port. This port is the wide, trapezoidal plug on the back of your computer. This connection is most common with older X10 devices, but—depending on the age of your computer—you might need to find an X10 Controller with a serial interface. The downside of the serial connection is that it is extremely slow, but unless you have a lot of X10 stuff going on at once, you needn't worry too much about whether your serially connected X10 Controller can handle it.

The more popular and modern X10 Controller is a USB-based device. This device simply plugs into an open USB port on your computer. USB is rather user friendly and your computer should recognize the new device right away. This streamlines the whole setup and installation process considerably.

5 MINUTES

Setting Up

In this example, we're using Microsoft Windows XP, but the steps will be similar on other versions of Windows that recognize USB devices (namely, Windows 98se and later).

1. After unpacking your X10 Controller, the first step is to plug it into an outlet near your computer. As Figure 4-7 shows, plugging the X10 Controller (in this case, a PowerLinc USB Model 1132U) is as simple as plugging anything into an open outlet.

Figure 4-7
Plugging the X10 Controller into an open electrical outlet

HEADS UP!

Power Strips and X10 Controllers Don't Mix

Do not plug the X10 Controller into a filter or a power strip. These devices will prevent the X10 signal from propagating to your X10 devices.

2. Next, boot up your computer and ensure that all running programs have been turned off.

3. Connect the USB cable (pictured in Figure 4-8) to an open USB port.

Figure 4-8
Connect the X10
Controller's USB
cable to an open
USB port.

TIPS OF THE TRADE

Locating a Good USB Port

Many modern computers have USB ports on the front of the computer as well as on the back. This allows for easy connection and removal of devices like digital cameras, personal digital assistants, and so forth. Since your X10 Controller is likely to be plugged in all the time, it's a good idea to locate a port on the back of your computer so the cable will not be in the way.

4. After a few seconds, the computer will display a message indicating that it recognizes the new device.

5. Windows should have a copy of the appropriate drivers already installed; however, if they are not installed, you should use the CD-ROM that came with your X10 Controller and install them. If no drivers have been included with your X10 Controller, go to the device manufacturer's web site—they are commonly provided there.

HEADS UP!

USB Hub Considerations

Most X10 USB controllers get their power to operate from the computer. As such, if you use a USB hub to share components, you'll need to use a powered hub.

Software

It isn't enough just to install the hardware, as easy as it was. Now, in order to control your X10 devices, you must also install software that tells the X10 Controller what you want it to do. There are a number of software packages for managing your X10 Controller and devices, and we'll go into more depth with a very useful application—HomeSeer—in Chapter 15. However, for the sake of getting the controller up and running, let's look at some other software.

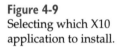

Along with our PowerLinc USB X10 Controller, we received a CD-ROM containing two pieces of X10 software: the Home Control Assistant for PowerLinc Limited and the Home Control Assistant for PowerLinc Plus. To install either of these products, follow these steps:

I. Put the CD-ROM into your computer's CD- or DVD-ROM drive.

2. The pop-up menu (shown in Figure 4-9) will appear. Select the appropriate software you wish to install.

Figure 4-9
Selecting which X10 application to install.

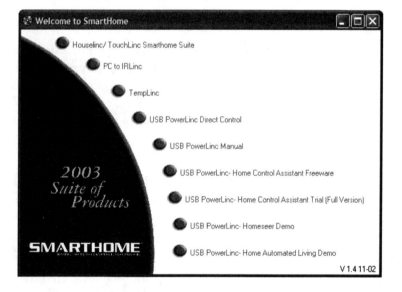

Getting to Know Your X10 Controller Software

The HCA PowerLinc Limited application offers limited control of your X10 devices and is really meant to get a flavor for your X10 Controller, or to run just a couple devices. If you want more control, and you like the HCA PowerLinc program, the HCA PowerLinc Plus program offers full features, but you are limited to a 30-day trial unless you care to buy it.

3. You might be prompted to provide your Windows CD-ROM to complete the installation of the software.

At this point, the software is installed and ready to control your Smart Home's X10 devices. There are additional setup steps involved to control specific devices. We'll explain those steps as we encounter them in subsequent chapters. This represents the basic steps required to install the particular software provided with the PowerLinc USB X10 Controller. Other controllers and other software packages will require a different setup procedure, which will be provided by the manufacturer.

HEADS UP!

Using X10 Software

For a more in-depth explanation about how X10 software is set up and controlled, flip ahead to Chapter 15.

A home LAN is not a necessity in a Smart Home, but it is a good thing to have. First, controlling your X10 devices will be much easier with a solid computer system. Second, if you have multiple computers and a high-speed Internet connection, building a home LAN is a great way to share the Internet connection. Taking the time to develop your home LAN is a good foundation on which to build your Smart Home.

TESTING 1-2-3

❏ Are your clients connected to a switch?

❏ Is your high-speed Internet connection protected by a firewall?

❏ Is your X10 Controller installed?

Part II

Smart Home Safety Systems

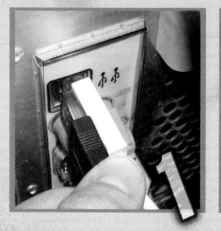

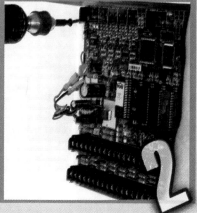

Chapter 5
Security Basics

Tools of the Trade

Blueprint or floor plan of your home
Ruler
Tape measure
Wire cutters
Masking tape
4-wire, 22-gauge security cabling
Fish tape
Permanent marker
Crimper
Butt splice connectors

Over the next two chapters, we'll take a look at security systems for your Smart Home. We'll talk about how to install your security system and its various components in Chapter 6, but first we need to introduce the cast of characters. This chapter examines the role of security systems in your Smart Home. We'll examine a number of the sensors you can add to your system to serve your various safety and security needs. Then, we'll talk about how to go about planning your security system. Finally, we'll explore issues germane to installation preparation by covering wiring fundamentals.

Security Systems

The first section of this chapter examines the various components that are used in home security systems. First, we'll look at the pieces that come together to make your security system—from consoles to sensors to wiring, among others. Then, we'll drill down even deeper and talk about the various types of sensors, what they do, and how you can use them in your Smart Home project.

Components

When you buy a security system, you don't just swing by the mall and pick up a box containing "a security system." Security systems are not "one size fits all" affairs; rather, they are pieced together based on the needs and wants of the individual Smart Home owner. These systems contain a number of components, each serving unique functions.

Control Panel

The core of the security system is the control panel. This is where the guts on the security system reside. Consider Figure 5-1. This is the control panel of the Omni II security system by HAI. This is the security system we'll be installing in the next chapter.

Figure 5-1
Omni II control panel

HEADS UP!

Placement Considerations

The control panel sits in a quiet, out of the way—yet secure—place in your home and all the other security system components connect to it. A popular place for the control panel's location is in a basement or utility room. Obviously, you don't want to locate the box somewhere outside your security perimeter, because it would be easy to access and deactivate.

The control panel is the device that connects the security system's sensors, consoles, sirens, and video cameras. When considering which control box to purchase, there are a number of factors to be juggled. In addition to the age-old consideration of cost, you must also be cognizant of how large your security system will be and then purchase a panel with enough connections. For example, the Omni II system allows 16 *zones*. A "zone" is the terminology for the sensor that controls a specific area (like a door or window) or a function. Even though this system is capable of handling 16 zones, if we ever decide to expand the system, we need not go out and buy a new control box. Rather, HAI manufactures a module that can be installed onto the Omni II, providing up to 48 zones. Other systems provide capability for more or fewer zones.

Some control panels even allow for the addition of wireless expansion modules. This allows the control panel to communicate, wirelessly, with various sensors. These are good to use if you have problems running cable to a particular location.

Sensors

The devices that will be used to trigger an event are sensors. Conventionally, when thinking about home security we only consider motion detectors or window and door sensors. However, in your Smart Home, you can connect all kinds of devices to your security system.

For instance, you can install a water sensor and place the sensor next to your sump. If the water ever overflows onto your basement floor, the signal can be tripped and you can be made aware of the problem. We'll talk about some specific types of sensors you can connect to your security system later in this chapter.

Wiring

To connect your security system sensors to the control panel, you run a length of shielded, 4-wire, 22-gauge security cable. This cable contains four wires, which is sufficient to connect most components of your security system. Some devices (like open door/window sensors) will use two wires, while devices that require a power source (like a smoke detector or a motion detector) will use three or more wires. The wires handle both the signals from the control panel and power. The shielding is a protective layer that prevents interference from affecting the signal.

Figure 5-2 shows a close-up of the cabling and Figure 5-3 shows a 500-foot spool of the security cabling we used for our security system, obtained from a local home improvement store for about US$35.

Figure 5-2
Four-wire, 22-gauge security cable

Figure 5-3
A 500-foot spool of security cabling

HEADS UP!

Using More

If you are going to use components that require more wires, you can also opt to run 8-wire, 22-gauge security cable.

Installation Concerns   Wiring for your various sensors and components are home-run from the control panel in your equipment room to the sensors, consoles, sirens, and so forth. However, there are some considerations to be aware of when installing your security cabling.

First, be sure you select the most direct route between the equipment room and your sensors, being mindful of any obstacles. For instance, will you need a few extra feet of cabling because you have to negotiate around a heating duct?

HEADS UP!

Take It Easy

When you pull cable, make sure it's coming off the spool easily and not getting kinked or hung up on anything. If you pull too hard, you'll be likely to damage the cabling; then, you'll wind up having to rerun the cabling.

If you are installing cabling in new construction, cable is pulled to each location by drilling a ½-inch diameter hole in the wall studs. At this point, the cabling should also be secured to the studs so that it is not accidentally pulled out of the wall.

However, if you are retrofitting a completed home, it's easy enough to run your cabling through the basement or attic to your various locations. Again, once the cabling has been placed, it is a good idea to anchor the cabling to a stud to avoid the wiring being yanked out of the wall (if possible without ripping out the drywall).

Splicing   When you connect your components to the cabling, there's no plug that makes for easy connectivity. Rather, you'll have to splice your wires together. An easy, common sense method for splicing wires is to trim back the insulation, twist them together, and wrap them with black electrical tape. Regrettably, the fire marshal doesn't see it that way, and prefers a more urbane way to connect wires.

When connecting two lengths of cabling (maybe you ran out halfway through a run and had to reconnect) or a sensor or other component to a cable, the approved method is to use a *butt connector*. These are small metal and plastic sleeves into which the two wires are inserted, then pinched down tight using a crimper. Butt connectors are selected based on the gauge of the wire and usually come a dozen or so per package (though you can find them in many size packages). Take a look at Figure 5-4, which shows how wires are spliced properly.

Figure 5-4
Splicing wires using butt connectors

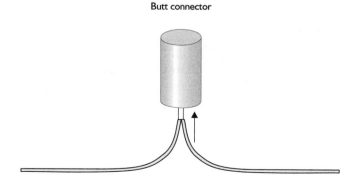

Butt connector

Wires to be spliced are inserted
into the butt connector, then pinched
together using a crimper.

Connecting to Sensors   Once you've reached the cabling to the sensors or other components, the connection method is identical to that when splicing wire. Connecting wires together, whether splicing cable or connecting components, follows a similar process because the sensors routinely come with a set of wires already attached.

TIPS OF THE TRADE

Pay Attention to the Colors

It's also critical to pay attention to which colored wire you're connecting your sensors. For instance, the cabling we used for our security system utilized four wires: red, black, white, and green. This color scheme was present in some of the sensors we connected (at least to some extent—red and black tended to be present, and once in a while there was white), but oftentimes there was a rogue color with which we needed to deal. For instance, our cabling consisted of red, white, black, and green wires. However, a sensor might have come from the manufacturer (as did our siren) with red, white, and yellow wires.

There isn't anything magical about these wires. If you connect red to black, it will still work fine, assuming you know to connect the black wire to the correct post. Back to our siren example: Since red and white were present, we simply connected the green wire of the cabling to the yellow wire of the siren, made a note of it for future reference, and went on with our business.

Your sensors might also have ports with tiny screws in them. In that case, connection couldn't be simpler (assuming you have the right size screwdriver). You simply loosen the screw, insert the wire clockwise around the screw, and then retighten the screw.

Consoles

When you step through the front door and your alarm starts whining or chirping, it is deactivated by punching a code into the console or keypad. Like the one shown in Figure 5-5, the console is the user interface with your security system.

Figure 5-5
Security system
console

HEADS UP!

Another Interface

If you are using a security system that interfaces with your computer, then the computer is, naturally, another user interface.

The console is used to turn your security system on and off, check the status of zones, add new users, and other administrative functions. For instance, the console used with the Omni II allows the temperature to be displayed from all the temperature sensors.

Sirens

There's no better way to scare off burglars and annoy your neighbors than by connecting a siren to your security system. Sure, it's gratifying enough to know that when your security system has been tripped that the police will show up with their pistols drawn and bloodthirsty K9s straining against their leashes, ready to chomp on a perp. However, a siren gives the burglar a head start, making the whole apprehension a little more sporting. The siren we're using for our Smart Home project is shown in Figure 5-6.

Figure 5-6
A siren can be
activated by a sensor
being tripped.

Cameras

If you want to survey your domain without ever having to leave the comfort of your easy chair, you might consider attaching video cameras to your security system. These cameras can either be part of a closed circuit display, or they can be connected in conjunction with our Smart Home's LAN. By connecting to the computer system, you can monitor your home from your home office, or if connected to the Internet, from a remote location such as at work.

HEADS UP!

How to Choose a Camera

The factors in play determining what type of video camera you'll get include whether the camera is black and white or color, what resolution is available, its field of view, and whether it has a motor to sweep across a range.

Sensors

Your control panel is certainly an impressive (and expensive) collection of microchips, flashing LEDs, and wire. However, to make the security system work, you need to be able to detect various activities. There are a multitude of sensors that you can add to your security system to monitor all sorts of goings on. The most common are the motion sensors and the open door sensors, but there many other things you can monitor.

TIPS OF THE TRADE

Normally Open or Normally Closed

Sensors are said to be *normally open* or *normally closed*. This refers to the contacts inside the sensor and describes the state of the sensor. For instance, a sensor that is normally closed is one that is always seen by the system as being closed. When it is opened, it goes into a not ready state, and trips the alarm. This type of sensor would be used on doors or windows. These points of entry are typically closed, so when they are opened, the alarm is tripped. The point of whether a sensor is normally open or normally closed is to indicate the normal state of the sensor. Sensors can be purchased for a number of applications in either the normally open or normally closed state.

Motion

Motion sensors are devices used to detect movement in the area on which it is trained. Motion sensors communicate with the control panel, sending a signal whenever motion has been detected. If your security system is monitored by a third party, the signal from the control panel is sent to the monitoring service.

There are two main types of motion detectors: PIR and Dual TEC. Also, if you have a pet, there are some sensors that can keep Fido from setting off the works.

PIR Passive infrared (PIR) motion sensors sense a change in background temperature. When someone enters the room, the background (or *ambient*) temperature changes. This change is detected by the PIR sensor, and a message is sent by the sensor to the control panel. Figure 5-7 shows a PIR sensor.

Figure 5-7
PIR motion sensor

When installing PIR motion sensors, you can avoid false alarms by making sure the sensor does not have these:

❑ Hot or cold air blowing on it

❑ Sunlight or reflected sunlight on it

❑ Intermittent heat sources nearby

❑ Pets that are likely to wander into the sensor's field of vision (more on pet immune systems in a moment)

Dual TEC A Dual TEC motion sensor uses two different ways to detect motion. In addition to detecting ambient temperature changes (like a PIR sensor), it also uses Doppler to detect a moving mass. A Dual TEC sensor only sends a message to the control panel if it senses *both* a change in ambient temperature *and* a moving mass. By the way, if *Doppler* sounds familiar, that's because it's the same technology meteorologists use to "predict" the weather.

**TIPS OF
THE TRADE**

Animal Immunity

If you have a pet, buying sensors that are animal immune will save a head-ache every time Rover or Ruggles strolls across the living room. Animal immunity is able to sense between the family pet and human beings and can be built into both PIR and Dual TEC sensors. Animal immune sensors are rated for pets between 25 and 100 pounds, depending on which sensor you purchase.

Glassbreak

Glassbreak detectors are sensors that connect to glass doors, windows, skylights, or any other glass-covered point of entry. In essence, glassbreak detectors listen for two sounds to determine whether glass has been broken. First, the sensors listen for the nonaudible to humans "flex" sound that a window makes just before it breaks. Then, it listens for the sound of the window breaking that we can hear. If both of these sounds are detected by the glassbreak sensor, a message is sent to the control panel. Glassbreak detectors can be purchased based on the glass type, size, and thickness, as well as the range at which they can sense glassbreaks.

CO

Carbon monoxide can come from such sources as a failing gas stove, a furnace, a fireplace, or a water heater. After fires, carbon monoxide poisoning causes the greatest number of accidental deaths. Whether you choose to connect this sensor to your security system or not, you should be sure to install a number of these detectors. Figure 5-8 shows a CO detector.

Figure 5-8
CO sensor

Smoke

Smoke sensors are akin to the smoke detectors that have been keeping us safe for years. The only difference between these sensors and the round modules on every level of our homes (you do have one on every level of your home, don't you?) is that these sensors are connected to the security system control panel. When smoke is detected, a message is sent to the control panel and the alarm is tripped.

Open Door/Window

A door/window magnetic contact is a two-piece unit, as shown in Figure 5-9, that consists of a reed switch and a magnet. The reed switch is mounted to the wall, for instance, and the magnet is mounted to the door or window frame. When the door or window is opened more than a couple inches, the contact is broken and a message sent to the control panel.

Figure 5-9
Open door/
window sensor

Water

Water sensors, like the one shown in Figure 5-10, sit on the floor and are used to detect the presence of water. For example, you could place a water sensor next to your sump. If the water sensor detects water coming over the top of your sump, it sends a message to the control panel indicating that there is trouble.

Figure 5-10
Water sensor

WaterCop, shown in Figure 5-11, is a specialized type of water sensor. In this case, it is used to detect whether your washing machine is overflowing. WaterCop is connected to the water pipes going into the washing machine and another sensor is located on the floor. The presence of water on the floor not only triggers the sensor, but it causes the valve to shut off, stopping more water from flooding onto the floor.

Figure 5-11
WaterCop water sensor (Photo courtesy Smarthome.com)

Temperature

Temperature sensors do just what their name suggests: they sense temperature. You can install these sensors inside or outside. These sensors aren't going to detect a burglar, but they can be important when you are trying to integrate certain behaviors of your Smart Home.

Outdoor Infrared Beam Sensors

These sensors create an invisible fence around your yard. A transmitter is positioned at each corner of your yard with a receiver positioned on another corner. This creates an infrared boundary that, if the beam is broken, sends a signal to your control panel to take action. Maybe you just have an exterior light set to activate, or maybe you are tired of the neighbor kids throwing beer cans in your yard, and you want the neighborhood to wake up the next time they do it. Beam sensors are weatherproof, and even manage to maintain 99 percent of their functionality in crummy weather.

TIPS OF THE TRADE

Combination

Like the all-in-one devices we talked about in the last chapter for computer networking, security systems are able to combine two or more sensors into one unit. For instance, Smarthome sells a combination PIR and glassbreak detector for US$69.99. If either of the sensors is tripped, a message is sent to the control panel. Combination sensors are good solutions if you want to add more functionality to your system but don't have any more zones available on your control panel.

System Design

Now that you understand the more prevalent sensors and components of security systems, let's look at how you can connect all these components to make a security system to fit your needs. First, we'll talk about evaluating what you need in your Smart Home, and then we'll cover overall system design.

30 MINUTES

Evaluating Needs

Before heading off to the store and picking up a bag of sensors and some security cabling, it's a good idea to understand your needs. This will help you when you do decide to go to the store—you'll know what types of sensors you need and how many spools of cabling to pick up.

Points of Entry

The first place you should look at are your so-called *points of entry*. This is anywhere someone can get into your home, or other places you wish to secure. For example, consider the blueprint in Figure 5-12. This is the sample blueprint we'll use as an exercise for planning our Smart Home's security system.

Figure 5-12
Locate your home's
points of entry.

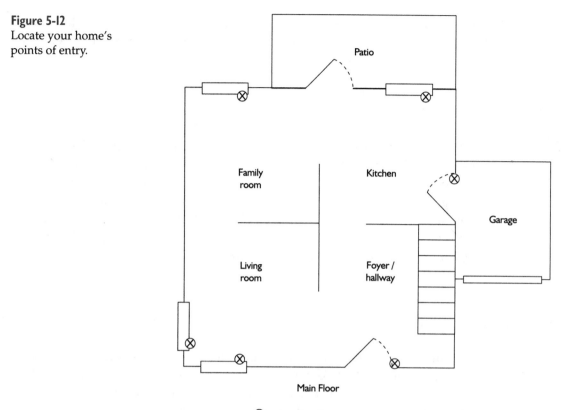

= Locations for new sensors

You'll notice there are three doors (a front door, door to the garage, and a patio door) and four windows on the main level that we're planning. Since all of these are points of entry, we're going to install open door/window and glassbreak sensors at these locations.

TIPS OF THE TRADE

Outside the Smart Home

Don't limit yourself to points of entry that just serve the home, however. In our project, we're also installing open door sensors on the garage door and an open door sensor on an exterior gate. You might not want to bother with setting off an alarm if the gate is opened, but—when linked with the rest of your Smart Home system—you can set it to turn on exterior lighting, or send a message to you that someone has opened your gate. Additionally, the garage door may or may not be connected to an alarm. However, a more likely use of the garage door sensor is to let you know, after a certain time, if the door is open. This will help you from forgetting and leaving the garage door open all night.

Danger Zones

If someone is able to get into your home, it's now the job of the motion detectors to make you aware. Danger zones are areas that you want covered by your motion detectors. Again, consider our blueprint shown in Figure 5-13.

Figure 5-13
Danger zones are policed by motion detectors.

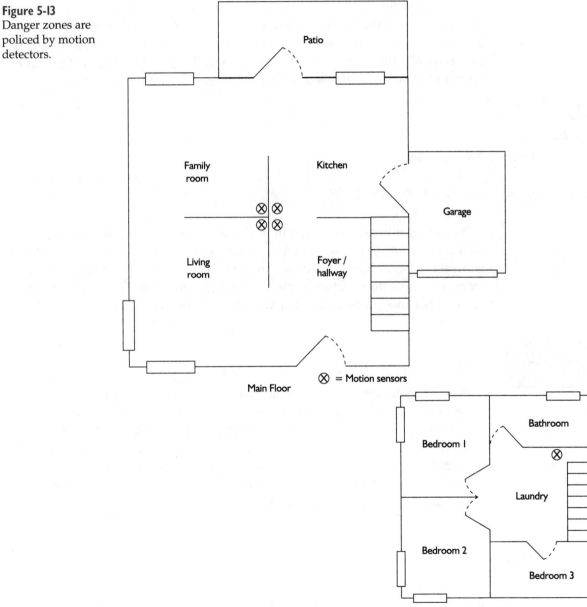

In this example, we're showing the areas in the house where we want various sensors located. Placement and positioning of the sensors is important so that intruders can be detected as soon as they enter a room, not when they're halfway out of the house lugging your TV along. Locate the sensors so that they cover any doors or windows.

Additionally, you'll notice that most of the motion detectors are located on the main floor of the home. Examining the second floor with the bedrooms and bathroom, there is only one motion sensor that covers the stairwell. This is because when family members get up in the middle of the night to visit the littlest room in the house, they need not worry about turning off the alarm.

HEADS UP!

Sensor Placement Considerations

Remember, even if you're locating the sensors to monitor a window, you must ensure that the sensor isn't in a location where there is direct sunlight.

Our danger zones aren't just in the house—they are also outside. But these aren't only going to be installed for security reasons. They're also important for general safety. An X10-compatible motion detector light can not only activate to scare away intruders, but it can also help when your Aunt Tilly makes an unexpected visit and needs to find her way up the sidewalk after dark.

TIPS OF THE TRADE

The Convenience of Smart Home Lighting

In addition to sensors used for intrusion detection, we're also installing some sensors for convenience. We've located a motion sensor on the stairwell to the basement so that the light automatically comes on whenever the door is opened. Likewise, if we wanted to install a sensor in the upstairs hallway, it could be programmed to turn on the light to a dimmed level whenever someone steps into the hall. This, again, is for convenience sake and need not trip the klaxons.

System Size

Once you've decided how many sensors you need, you must also take into consideration where you wish to locate your control panel and where you want to install consoles, along with other miscellaneous sensors (like temperature, water, CO, smoke, and others). As soon as you understand how many sensors you will have, it's time to find a control panel that will accommodate that number of sensors.

For example, we'll be installing the Omni II system in Chapter 6. This system, as we already noted, is able to monitor 16 zones and will interface with our X10 devices. This is fine, because it accommodates our monitoring needs. However, what happens if we decide to add more sensors to the home? In the case of the Omni II, we can add a module that will increase the number of zones threefold. This is an important consideration when designing your own Smart Home security system. Will you have enough room in your control panel to suit your current needs? How well does the control panel of your choice handle future expansion?

Designing for Needs

The next step in designing your Smart Home security system is to actually sit down and figure out how it will all come together. This section examines how you can, ultimately, get what you want and what you need to work together in your Smart Home.

Mapping

The first step, as we already demonstrated, is to make a map of your home. This is an important step and one you should not skip over, mainly because it will give you a good sense of the size, scope, and complexity of your project. Ideally, you'll map the interior and exterior of your home wherever you plan to install sensors or any other security system hardware. If possible, a copy of your home's blueprints would be an excellent source from which to start, because it will already have the exact measurements of your home listed.

Next, indicate where you want your control panel, sensors, sirens, CO detectors, water sensors, smoke detectors, consoles, and everything else to go. In Figure 5-14, we have another home blueprint, this time with all the various components indicated on it. You'll note that there is also a legend accompanying the components and a number listed next to each component. This is important for later identification of your cables and sensors.

Figure 5-I4
Map out the locations of all your security system components

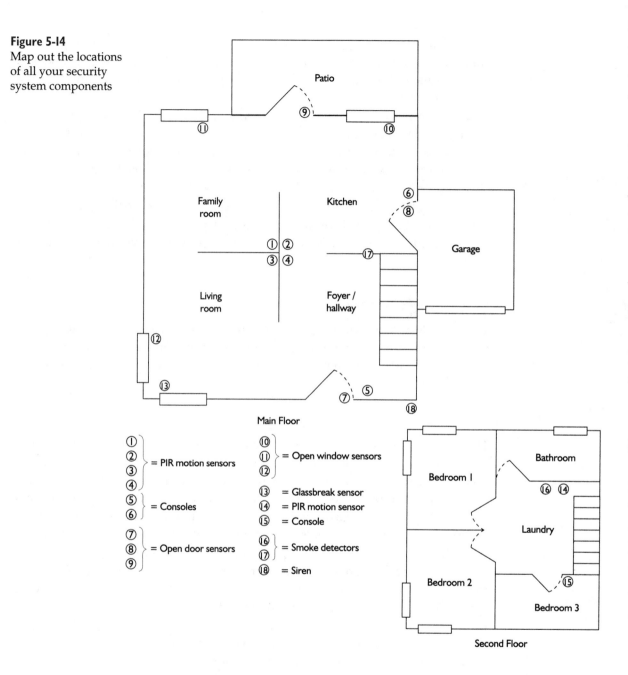

At this stage, you should not only worry about where the motion sensors should be placed, but also consider where you want to place other components. Table 5-1 lists common placement suggestions for various security system components.

Component	Location
Control panel	Any out-of-the-way location within your home's security perimeter, like a basement or utility room. It should be located someplace dry.
Consoles	Near the commonly used doors and in the master bedroom so the alarm can be activated and deactivated when you enter or leave the house, or when you go to bed at night or wake up in the morning.
Motion detectors	Covering areas you wish to protect that can't be avoided by an intruder.
Open door/window sensors	On entry or accessible windows and doors you wish to monitor.
CO detectors	In your living areas, especially by gas-burning appliances.
Glassbreak sensors	Near windows and plate glass doors you wish to monitor.
Smoke detectors	On each level of your home and in each bedroom.
Cameras	Wherever you wish to monitor activity.
Sirens (indoor or outdoor models)	Indoor sirens should be placed high within the home so the intruder cannot easily access them. Outdoor sirens can be installed in the soffit or in the attic, next to a ventilation grate.
Water	In areas where water is likely to start coming into the home—for instance, next to the sump or washing machine. If you have a place in your home where you've experienced water damage in the past, it might be a good idea to locate a sensor there so you'll know if trouble is starting.

Table 5-1
Security System Component Placement Tips

Cable Runs

Once you've planned out the locations of all your security system components, you need to measure how much cabling you'll need to run between the control panel and the component, then purchase and install the cabling.

Planning   If you're using a map that's to scale, you should be able to measure out how much cabling you'll need for each run between the control panel and the component. However, don't just rely on the map, do a reality check first. Take a look at where you'll be running the cable and look for any obstacles. Are you going to have to maneuver around a bunch of pipes or ductwork? If so, how much extra cable will you need for that particular run? Once you've got an idea of how much cabling you need, add an extra foot or two to the number (this will provide enough working cable length during the trim-out stage) and jot it down next to the sensor on your blueprint.

TIPS OF THE TRADE

Buy It by the Spool

When you've marked down the lengths for all the sensors, add up all the runs and then buy the appropriate amount of cabling. At a home improvement store, you can either buy it by the spool (it normally comes in spools of 500 feet) or you can buy specific lengths and pay by the foot. It might be most convenient to simply buy the spool—you're going to need a lot of cable, plus you don't want it to get tangled up.

Pulling Together   Measure out your runs of cable and cut them to the length you need. Now is a good time to go back to the map. Locate where cables are likely to run together, at least for some duration. It's best to run these cables together for the sake of both efficiency and ease of installation. If you collocate your cables, it will also be easier to anchor them to the studs or floor joists, *en masse*, rather than individually.

Also, if you are going to be pulling cable into an area that is likely to be expanded, now is the time to add an extra run of cable or two for the sake of future-proofing.

Marking   The old chestnut "an ounce of prevention is worth a pound of cure" is very true with security systems. When you have a dozen or so runs of cable coming to your control panel, it's a little late to decide then what each piece of cabling is for. You can ameliorate this problem *before* pulling the cable by marking a number or some other indicator onto each end of the cable.

HEADS UP!

Make Your Mark

If you remember back to Figure 5-14, when we jotted a number next to the security system components, this was to identify the proper cabling later. Without taking the time to mark the cabling now with a permanent marker at both ends, you'll spend a lot of time scratching your head later, trying to decide which cable is which.

Protecting and Hiding   Since we're installing our security system in an existing home (as many of you are likely to, we imagine), hiding the cable is an important consideration, but not something that is especially easy to do. To run the cable without having it out in the open, we're going through the basement ceiling to feed various components on the main floor. This is an easy way to handle your own installation, especially if you have an unfinished basement, or can snake cabling through the attic.

If your basement is finished and does not accommodate easy installation of cabling, it might be necessary to utilize fish tape (which can be difficult, but not impossible). There are also wireless sensors you may wish to consider that don't necessitate drilling holes in anything.

TIPS OF THE TRADE

Fish Tape

Fish tape is a flexible, steel wire that can be threaded through a wall or floor. When the tape comes through the other end of the wall or floor, the cable to be run is attached to the tape, then retracted back through the wall. This sounds simple enough, but lining up the fish tape so it comes out in the desired location is part skill, part art form, and part luck.

Protecting your cabling is also an important consideration. Not only does locating it in the wall keep it from being an eyesore, it won't get tripped on, nor will the family dog chew through it. Protection is also important for cabling that's been placed out of sight. If you locate your cabling near electrical wires or other sources of interference, it's a good idea to buy shielded security cabling. Frankly, shielded cabling only costs a little more (if at all) than unshielded, so you should probably get that anyway. Generally, avoid running security cable next to power cabling to avoid interference. If you must, make sure you cross electrical cabling at 90-degree angles.

Testing   Before connecting your system sensors to the control panel, it's a good idea to test the cable for shorts, ground faults, and opens. Testing is performed after the cabling has been pulled and checks for any damage that might have occurred during installation. There are two ways to check the integrity of your cabling:

❑ **Continuity**   The first test requires that you twist the ends of two sets of wires together. For instance, in the security cable we pulled, there are red, white, green, and black wires. To perform the continuity test, twist the red and white wires together, then twist the green and black wires together (as shown in Figure 5-15). Next, connect a multimeter to the wires on the other end of the cable run. Select the 0 to 100 ohms resistance range, then place one test lead on each conductor at the end of the cabling. A reading of more than 2.8 ohms per 100 feet of cable indicates that there is damaged cabling.

HEADS UP!

Multimeters

A multimeter can be picked up at home improvement or electronics shops for less than US$20.

Figure 5-15
Continuity testing

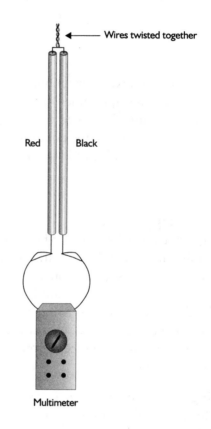

Wires twisted together

Red   Black

Multimeter

❏ **Battery**   The more popular method for checking the integrity of cabling is to connect a 9-volt battery to the cable, using alligator clips. Then, using the multimeter, set the detector to a DC voltage of 20V. Measure the voltage coming out of the battery for a baseline reading (it's rare that the voltage will be precisely 9V). Next, place one test lead on each conductor end, then measure the voltage. If the voltage difference is more than .5V for every 100 feet, the cable is damaged or defective. Figure 5-16 illustrates this. The battery method tends to be the more popular, chiefly because the ends of the cabling need not be twisted together.

Figure 5-16
Battery testing

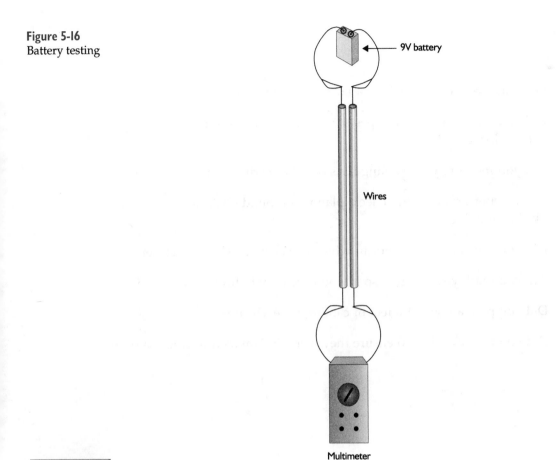

9V battery

Wires

Multimeter

HEADS UP!

Don't Do this...

As with any trade, installers have their own "shortcuts" that have developed over time. One such shortcut eliminates the multimeter from the battery method. Instead, installers simply touch the ends of cable to their tongues. Naturally, we're not endorsing this method (not only is it unsafe, but how can they tell the difference between 6.5V and 8.3V?), but as soon as you heard that a 9V battery was used, this possibility had to have popped into your mind.

Now that you know the cast of characters for home security systems, turn the page to Chapter 6 and we'll start drilling holes in things (including a very expensive maple floor!), pulling cable through them, and connecting wire after wire after wire.

❏ Did you analyze your points of entry and danger zones?

❏ Did you figure out which types of sensors you'll need in various locations?

❏ Did you measure your cabling runs on a home diagram?

❏ Did you perform a reality check, planning around obstacles, like heating ducts?

❏ Did you note on your blueprint which cables will run to which sensors?

❏ Did you mark your cabling so it would be easy to find later?

❏ Did you plan a few extra feet of cabling for each run?

❏ Did you test the wires to ensure they weren't damaged during the pull?

Chapter 6

Designing and Building a Security System

Tools of the Trade

Wire stripper

Crimping tool

Drill

Level

Staple gun

Rounded staples

Butt connectors

Hex wrench

Screwdrivers of various sizes and head shapes

Mounting screws

Wall anchors

RotoZip

In Chapter 5, we introduced you to the various components that you can expect to see in a home security system, and talked about some wiring topics. Now it's time to put all of these components into play.

In this chapter, we're demonstrating security system installation using an Omni II from Home Automation Inc. (HAI). Don't worry that the steps are too unique to this particular system that they won't apply to whatever system you install. The steps and processes are similar between all types of security systems. Naturally, however, you should perform a reality check to make sure that your system does not require any special installation steps.

Omni II

There are a number of good security systems out there, and they all work—basically—the same way. For our Smart Home project, however, we will be using the Omni II home security system. It retails for US$1,229.99.

The Omni II system coordinates lighting, heating, air, security, and messaging based on a schedule you establish. It comes with several standard modes, like Day, Night, Away, and Vacation. Further, it can accommodate customized schedules—for instance "Home From Work," "Movie Night," or "Catnap"—that set the temperatures, lights, and security to customized levels for those particular settings.

The system utilizes a variety of sensors in a coordinated effort to adjust lighting, appliances, and thermostats. Sensors, such as temperature and security, are used to monitor a wide range of environments and actions. The system is X10 compatible, which allows devices beyond the confines of the Omni II system to be integrated. For example, if an exterior motion detector senses movement outside, then not only can an exterior light be turned on, but so can a light inside the house.

The system is programmed and controlled either through a console or via a home computer. Additionally, one can use a palmtop computer to access the Omni II settings (as shown in Figure 6-1). The included console shows system status and allows control and scheduling of various attributes of the Smart Home, including lighting, security, and temperature.

Figure 6-1
Controlling
the Omni II via
palmtop computer

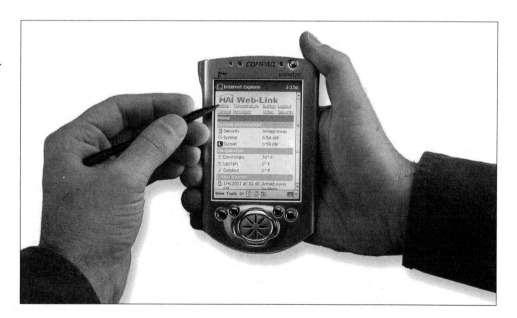

Further, the Omni II has a built-in serial interface that allows for connection to the Internet via HAI's Web-Link II, personal computer, touch screens, voice recognition, and home theater controls. Additionally, the Omni II can be accessed via telephone (either within the home or calling in to the system) to allow additional accessibility. When an event is triggered, a built-in digital communicator can send alarms to a central station and up to eight additional telephone numbers for voice notification.

The Omni II is geared for homes and small businesses and is the middle child of HAI's Omni home security line (sandwiched between the OmniPro II and the Omni LT series). For comparison's sake, Table 6-1 shows these different systems and what they offer.

	Omni Pro II	Omni II	Omni LT
Household Square Footage	3,000+	1,000-3,000	Up to 2,000
Thermostats	64	4	2
Consoles	16	8	4
Scenes	128	64	16
Lighting	256	64	16
Security	16	16	8
Expanded Security	176	48	24
User Codes	99	16	8
Programming Codes	1,500	500	100
Warranty	Three years	Two years	Two years
Price	US$1,699.99	US$1,229.99	US$619.99

Table 6-1
Comparison of Omni Security Systems

Control Panel

The control panel is the heart, soul, and guts of the home security system. Installing the panel can seem daunting (after all, it's a big, heavy, expensive piece of electronics that you're mounting to a wall with a couple screws and a prayer). However, taking the time to understand where to place it, how to mount it, and how it works will help you in the long run.

Installation

We've chosen to locate the control panel in the basement of our Smart Home. This is a good location because it keeps the control panel out of sight, it is in a protected area, and it is collocated with the rest of our Smart Home LAN. Proximity to the Smart Home LAN isn't required; however, it's convenient and handy to have everything positioned together.

Depending on your home, you may or may not have a basement, or the basement simply might not be an option for you. As such, the general rule of thumb is to make sure the control panel is located in a place that is both out of the way and safe—safe from the environment and safe from potential attackers.

The other bonus of installing the control panel in the basement is that when we run cabling to various locations, it is easier to run under the unfinished basement ceiling, then drill through the floor to access the sensors.

You cannot, however, simply place the control panel anywhere you like in the basement. There are important considerations when locating the control panel. First, it's necessary to locate your control panel near an electrical outlet—preferably on its own circuit. That way, if the circuit breaker should pop because you've turned on the dryer, washer, and a half dozen other things, your security system won't have to fall back to its battery power. Our Omni II will require two outlets—one to provide power to the control panel, the other for the X10 interface.

Second, you should locate the control panel in close proximity to your telephone system's punch-down block. The punch-down block is where the telephone line comes into the house and is distributed to phone jacks around the home. This is important because your security system might have to connect to the outside world. For instance, if you decide to have your system monitored, you'll need to connect to the telephone system. Also, our Omni II has a feature that allows it to be controlled through the home telephone.

Mounting

To mount your control panel, follow these steps:

1. Choose a location for your control panel. In addition to the aforementioned placement considerations, you must also decide where on the wall you wish to mount it. Since the control panel is encased in a hefty metal box, fasten the control panel to wall studs so that it will have enough support to prevent it from ripping out of the wall and crashing to the floor.

2. Use a level (as shown in Figure 6-2) to make sure the control panel is positioned properly (you might need a friend to help with this one).

Figure 6-2
Leveling the control panel before installation

3. Using a pencil, mark the location of the mounting screws through the hangers on the back of the unit.

4. Attach two mounting screws into the studs where you made a pencil mark. Screw them in about three quarters of the way. Alternately, you could hang a piece of plywood between a couple studs, then locate the control panel's mounting screws anywhere on it.

5. Place the control panel and enclosure over the screws and let it slide down so it seats properly.

6. Turn the screws until the control panel is held firmly in place, as shown in Figure 6-3.

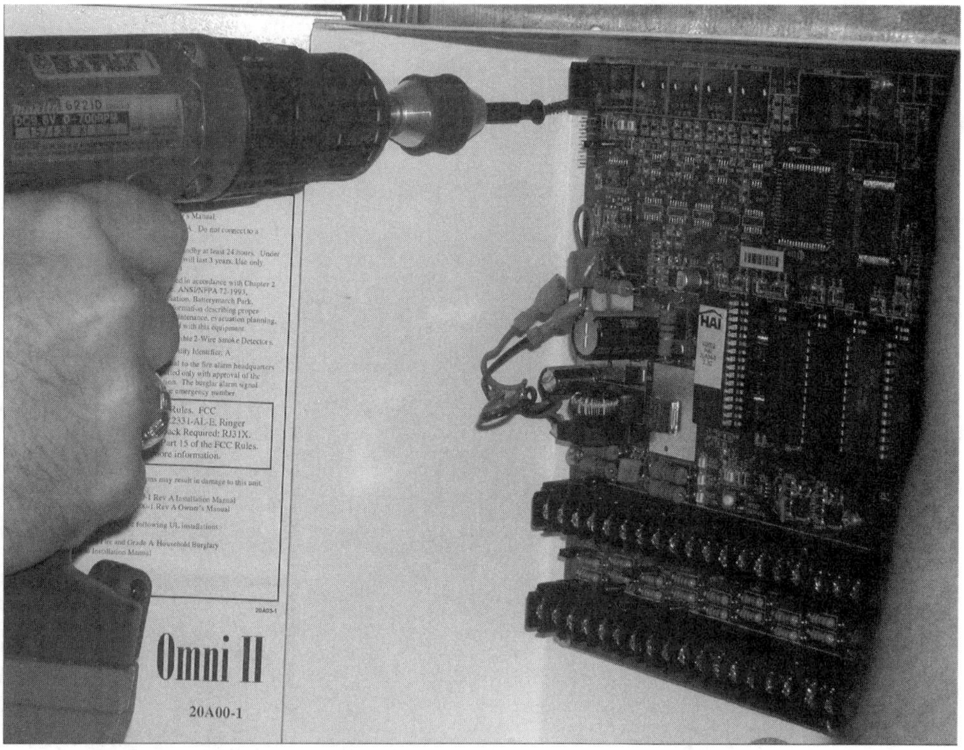

Figure 6-3
Mounting the control
panel to the wall

Terminals

When you look at the circuit board on your control panel, the top portion looks like a circuit board you've seen in everything from computers to microwave ovens. You don't have to concern yourself with what the microchips and capacitors do. However, at the bottom of the control panel are two rows of terminals into which you'll be connecting your sensors, as shown in Figure 6-4.

Figure 6-4
The terminals on your
control panel

— Special functions

— Zone inputs

Special Functions

On the Omni II, the top row of terminals is dedicated to specialized components. For instance, this top row is where the telephone connection is made and where the consoles are connected. It is also in this top row of terminals where 12-volt (V) power and grounding terminals are available. These terminals are used for components that require power; then, other wires from that cable are connected to the lower row of terminals (these are the zone inputs, explained in the next section).

HEADS UP!

Don't Connect Too Many Devices

Read your manufacturer's guidelines to find out how many devices can be connected to a single 12V terminal.

Zones

The bottom row of terminals contains the so-called *zone inputs*. It is on these terminals that two-wire connections are made and the non-power connections of four-wire connections are made. Each zone has two terminals, and (with our base Omni II system) there are 16 zones.

For example, when connecting a two-wire door sensor, one wire would be connected to the first terminal, the other wire to the second terminal. However, when connecting a four-wire sensor—like a motion detector—the power wires would be connected to the power and ground terminals on the top row of connectors (typically red and black), while the other two wires would be connected to the zone inputs on the bottom row of terminals (typically, white and green), as shown in Figure 6-5.

Figure 6-5
Connecting a four-wire component to the control panel

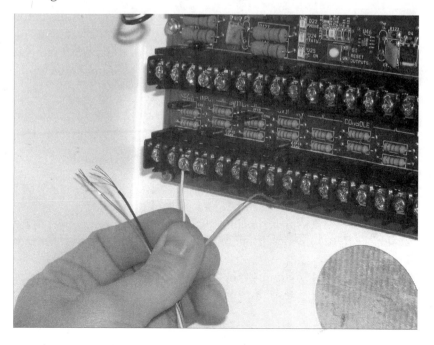

Power

You might be surprised when you open your control panel to find that it doesn't come with a backup battery. If that wasn't shocking enough, you'll be floored to see that it doesn't come with a power transformer either. Many security system control panels don't ship with batteries or transformers, so don't be surprised if you have to incur some extra costs when setting up your security system. The following steps explain how to connect the transformer and battery, once you get them.

2 MINUTES

Transformer Installation

The control panel draws its main power from your home's electrical system and must utilize a transformer to connect.

1. Our Omni II control panel utilizes a Revere model RT-2440SL or equivalent transformer. This transformer supplies 24 volts AC (Vac) and 20 volt-amperes (VA). Your system might use a different transformer.

HEADS UP!

Converting Power with a Transformer

The power transformer redirects power from your home electrical system and converts it into the voltage, wattage, and amperage needed by the control panel. This is a box that plugs into your wall, then connects to the control panel.

2. The control panel must also be grounded before any power is applied. This is accomplished by running a length of 14-gauge wire from the "EARTH GND" terminal of the control panel (on the Omni II, it is the leftmost post on the upper row of connectors) to either a cold water pipe or ground rod.

3. Next, connect the grounding wire to a cold water pipe or a four-foot grounding rod.

HEADS UP!

Grounding Guidelines

Grounding must be done in accordance with the national electric code, ANSI/NFPA 70, which deals with transformer installation.

4. Connect the 24Vac power transformer to the 24 Vac INPUT terminals on the control panel.

1 MINUTE

Battery Installation

The battery for the Omni II should be a YUASA NP7-12 or equivalent (naturally, double-check your own control panel's battery requirements before plunking down the cash for a battery). This battery provides 12V at 7 ampere-hours (AH).

HEADS UP!

Battery Backup for Power Outages

A backup battery isn't needed, but in case your home's power goes out, it's a good idea to have one so you still benefit from your security system's protection. Also, if you don't have a battery, there will be an annoying little light or indicator that keeps blinking, telling you that your backup battery has failed.

When running the wires to the battery, make sure the wires are kept at least 1/4 inch from all other wiring in the enclosure, then connect the black wire to the negative (-) contact and the red wire to the positive (+) contact.

Connecting the Components

In addition to the aforementioned sensors, consoles, and other components, there are other connections that must be made to our Smart Home security system's control panel. These two particular connections are somewhat unique to the Omni II, however they might be required on other systems (depending on the features they offer).

2 MINUTES

X10 Connection

Because the Omni II utilizes X10 technology, we must connect the control panel with an X10 device. In this case, the X10 functionality will allow certain behaviors to occur when sensors are tripped. For instance, when the living room motion detector senses movement, it sends a signal to the control panel, then the control panel activates an X10 capable light. This feature may or may not be present on your security system's control panel. Before connecting various sensors to the control panel, we must first connect the X10 interface.

The Omni II comes with the X10 Power Line Interface and a length of four-wire cable with telephone jacks at each end.

Installation is rather straightforward:

1. Connect one end of the telephone cable to the jack at the top of the control panel's processor board.

2. Connect the other end of the cable to the X10 Power Line Interface device.

3. Plug the X10 Power Line Interface device into the home's electrical system, but not into a power strip that might have a surge protector in it.

5 MINUTES

Telephone

Connecting your telephone to the security system offers additional benefits in the form of extra features. For example, the reason we connect the Omni II to the telephone line is to enable telephone monitoring and control. One can control the security system from any phone inside the home, or call in from any phone outside the home. Additionally, if there is an emergency, the security system gives precedence to outgoing calls for help.

You might be a couple steps ahead of the game if the telephone company has already installed an RJ31X jack. If so, it's simply a matter of plugging the eight-connector telephone cable into the jack, then connecting the red, green, brown, and gray wires to the terminals on the control panel marked "PHONE."

If, however, no such RJ31X jack is present, you'll have to perform some wiring on your own. To connect the control panel to the home telephone system, follow these steps:

1. Locate the punch-down block in your home. This is where the telephone line comes into your house.

2. Connect four wires to the punch-down block (also known as a *66 block*)

3. Connect those wires to the RJ31X jack, as shown in Figure 6-6.

HEADS UP!

Protect Your Phone System from Power Surges

The phone line coming into the house must be connected to a grounded surge arrestor outside the home. This is the telephone company's responsibility. Check the incoming telephone lines. The first place they should go when they enter the home is into a small box on the outside of the home. From that box, a heavy wire should run to a cold water pipe or a grounding rod. If there is no surge arrestor or ground wire, call the telephone company and insist they install one.

Figure 6-6
Connecting your
home telephone
system and security
system using an
RJ31X jack

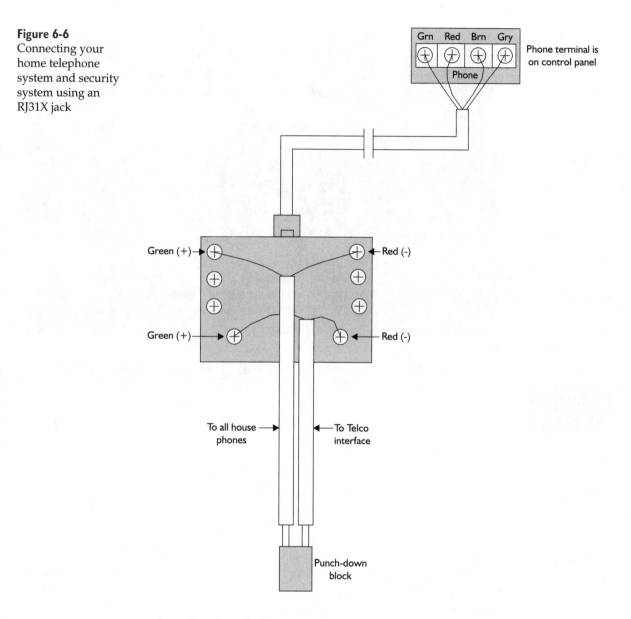

4. Mount the jack to the wall.

5. Once the RJ31X jack is installed, plug the eight-connector telephone
    cable into the jack, then connect the red, green, brown, and gray wires
    to the terminals on the control panel marked "PHONE."

6. The completed RJ31X jack installation should look like the one
    in Figure 6-7.

Figure 6-7
A connected
RJ31X jack

For more information on connecting a telephone jack, flip ahead to Chapter 12.

HEADS UP!

Connecting Without a Punch-down Block

If your home is not equipped with a punch-down block, it will be necessary to connect the RJ31X jack between the home and the telephone company interface at the surge arrestor. Further details on this connection can be found in the manufacturer's installation instructions.

There are a number of other components that we will be connecting to the Omni II security system, including thermostats, temperature sensors, and water detectors. However, we will present the installation of those components in later chapters, along with some nonproprietary solutions for connecting with your Smart Home.

Sensors

There are numerous zones you can monitor with your security system. We've chosen a few of the more popular sensors and components to connect. After we talk about installing these various components, we'll also explain how to connect them to your control panel. You need not make all these connections as you install the various components. Rather, you can spend your time connecting all your sensors, then connecting the wires to the control panel all at the same time.

Connection Steps

In Chapter 5, we talked about the various steps required in the installation of wiring for your security system's components. Now, we'll talk about how to physically place those sensors and how to connect them to the wiring you've already strung through your Smart Home.

Placing Wire

0–? MINUTES

Amount of time required depends on the complexity of your system.

Pulling cabling is a tedious process, but by following the planning steps we presented in Chapter 5, it doesn't have to cause a massive headache. Once you've planned your runs and have measured out the requisite lengths, start in the basement (or wherever your control panel is located). Keep a couple feet of excess cabling near the control panel. This will give you some slack with which to work when you start making connections to the control panel.

Next, run the cable through the walls or along floor joists. You might need to maneuver around air ducts or pipes to get to your location. As you place the cable, it's a good idea to staple the cable to floor joists and wall studs to keep the cable in place, to keep it taut, and to make sure you have enough cable to get to the sensor.

Anchor the cable using a staple gun loaded with rounded staples. The rounded tops will prevent the cable from becoming damaged by the staples. If you are collocating cable, you can buy cable holders that will allow you to anchor multiple runs of cable in a single location. Not only is this more time efficient, but it also saves space along floor joists and wall studs.

HEADS UP!

Staple Guns Save Time

Consider investing in an electric staple gun. This will aid greatly in the anchoring of security cable—unless, of course, you want to develop Popeye-esque forearms. Electric staple guns range in price, but you can find them for as little as US$33.

When you get to your sensor's location, trim back the cabling to a workable amount, strip off the outer insulator sheath, then, using a wire stripper, strip the wires you'll be using. After your sensor has been connected, tuck excess cabling into the hole in the wall.

Placing Sensors

If your sensor comes in two parts (for instance door/window sensors composed of a sensor and a magnet), make sure that you take into consideration placement of both components. For instance, when locating a garage door sensor on the floor, you must ensure that there is also an appropriate place for the magnet and that it can be safely and securely fastened. Affixing the magnet so it barely attaches to the door will present connection problems, plus it is likely to get kicked off when you come in the house.

You must also take into consideration which component will be positioned in a fixed location and which component will be attached to the moving part. For example, let's consider a door/window sensor. The sensor (the part with the wires coming off of it) needs to be mounted to a fixed surface, like the door jamb. The magnet, however, will be placed on the door or window itself. This placement is necessary because placing the magnet on the moving object (the window or the door, for instance) allows the door or window to be opened or closed. If the sensor (the hardwired piece) were located on the door or window, it would only be possible to open the door or window a couple inches, if at all.

Connecting Wire

Depending on the sensor, you will need to connect the wires to the sensor, then to the control panel in a specific manner. In our system, we're using security cable that used four wires, each a different color: red, black, white, and green. The sensors may or may not have these color wires, so when you splice the sensors onto the security cabling wire, it is helpful to make a note of which colors are which so connecting them to the control panel is easier. This is especially important when the sensor is mounted to the wall and the wires are not able to be seen.

Other sensors only utilize two wires and it won't matter which wire is connected to the control panel. As such, it's still a good idea to keep track of which wires from your cable you're connecting to your sensor, but it doesn't matter which one is connected to which terminal on the control panel.

TIPS OF THE TRADE

Develop a Standard Color Scheme

Develop an overall standard for your connections. For instance, if you have many two-wire sensors, make it a point to always use the same colored wires, like red and black, for all your connections. That way, you don't have to remember which wires you used. In our Smart Home project, we use red for power, black for ground, and white and green for zone connections.

To connect two wires together, utilize butt connectors, as shown in Figure 6-8. Then, use a crimping tool to secure the connector, like the one shown in Figure 6-9.

Figure 6-8
Connecting wire using butt connectors

Figure 6-9
Crimping the butt connector

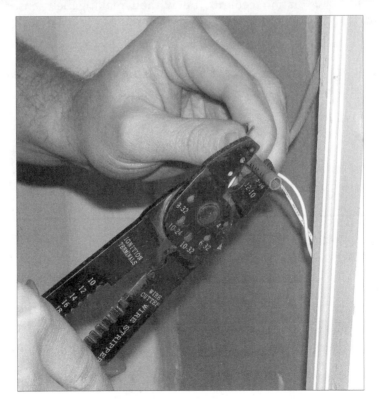

Motion Detector

Motion detectors are a major component of any security system, but they are especially important in Smart Homes. There are many different types of motion sensors that you can use, but the following steps are indicative of general motion detector installation. This particular motion detector is being placed in the garage.

1. Run cabling to the location where you want your motion detector positioned. You might need to use fish tape to run the cabling through the wall.

2. Prepare the cabling by stripping insulation from the cable and the four wires.

3. Remove the back of the motion detector casing. This allows access to the sensor's electronics.

4. Perform any knockouts that are necessary.

TIPS OF THE TRADE

Using Knockouts

Knockouts are scored areas on the sensor's housing that can be "knocked out" so that wire can be passed through. Manufacturers create knockouts so that the customer can install their product, allowing for multiple installation scenarios, but without making their sensor look like a piece of Swiss cheese.

5. Using screws, install the backplate to the wall, as shown in Figure 6-10.

Figure 6-10
Attaching the backplate to the wall

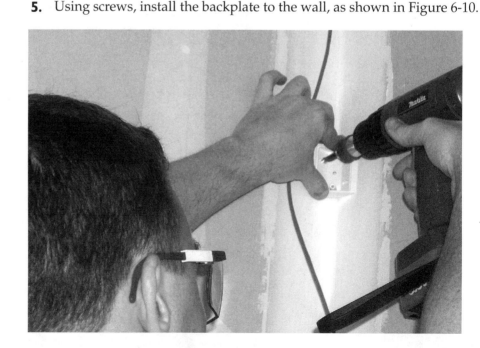

6. Connect the security cabling to the sensor's circuit board. This sensor is being installed in "normally closed" mode. As such, we've made the following wiring connections (this is shown in Figure 6-11):

   ❑ Red to a +12V

   ❑ Black to GND

   ❑ Green to NC

   ❑ White to C

Figure 6-11
Connecting the wires
to the motion detector

7. Ensure the wiring is clear of the cover and internal components.

8. Put the cover back on the sensor.

9. At the control panel, the following connections are made:

   ❑ Red to a 12V terminal

   ❑ Black to a GND terminal

   ❑ White to a zone input terminal

   ❑ Green to the other zone input terminal

Door/Window Sensors

Installing door and window sensors is a very simple task. Since these sensors only utilize two wires, the only difficulty is in fishing the cabling to the location where you need it. After that, it's a simple matter of splicing the sensor into your wiring and making final connections. The following steps enumerate the process of connecting a contact switch on a door or window.

1. Run cabling to the location where you want your sensor and magnet positioned. You might need to use fish tape to run the cabling through the wall.

2. Prepare the cabling by stripping insulation from the cable and two wires.

3. Drill hole through wall or floor (as shown in Figure 6-12).

Figure 6-12
Drilling a 3/16-inch hole to accommodate security cabling

4. Fish cable through wall or floor.

5. Connect sensor to door jamb.

6. Connect magnet to door (shown in Figure 6-13). The sensor and magnet come with an adhesive backing, however we're also using #4 screws to attach the sensor and magnet for additional strength.

Figure 6-13
Attaching the
sensor to the
door and
door jamb

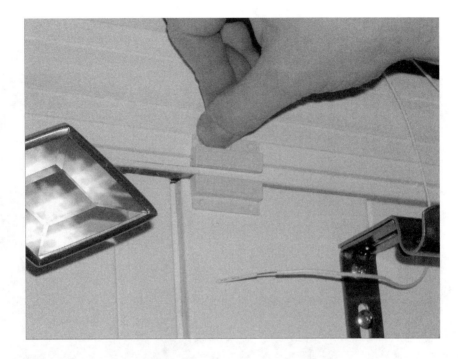

7. Connect sensors to security cabling—with this type of two-wire sensor, it doesn't matter which lead is spliced into which wire.

8. At the control panel, the following connections are made:

   ❏ White to one terminal of a zone input

   ❏ Green to the other terminal of a zone input

HEADS UP!

Standards for Two-color Wiring

Again, we've developed our own standard for wiring two-wire sensors. To avoid confusion with the red and black wires (which are typically used to connect to power sources and grounding), we're using the white and green wires to connect all the door and window sensors.

Even though we're fishing security cabling through the walls and floor, it is inevitable that there are some places where cabling will have to be seen. However, this can be ameliorated by strategically locating your sensors. For example, on the front door of our Smart Home, we were able to conceal the sensor, wire, and magnet.

1. We pried back a piece of molding in front of the door (as shown in Figure 6-14).

Figure 6-14
Prying back molding using care not to mar the wall or floor

2. After drilling a hole in the floor, we continued the aforementioned steps for installing the sensor and magnet.

3. When the sensor and magnet were located in a convenient, unobtrusive location, we were able to replace the molding.

15 MINUTES

Siren

Sirens, strobe lights, or other means (called sounders) to alert you that an alarm has been tripped are easy enough to install, but can be cumbersome to connect just by sheer virtue of their size and shape. If you do install a siren, you might be wise to seek out a second set of hands to help hold the siren while you make connections. The following steps are required when installing a siren:

1. Run cabling to the location where you want your siren positioned. You might need to use fish tape to run the cabling through the wall.

2. Prepare the cabling by stripping insulation from the cable and three wires.

3. Connect your security cable wires to the siren's wires and make the appropriate splices, as shown in Figure 6-15. If the same color wires are not present on your siren that are present on your cabling, be sure to make note of which wires have been connected together.

Figure 6-15
Connecting the siren to your security cable

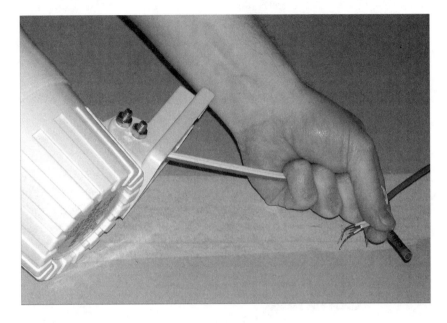

4. Attach the siren to the wall, as shown in Figure 6-16.

Figure 6-16
Mounting the siren to the wall—preferably on a stud for stability

HEADS UP!

Device Mounting Might Require Some Disassembly

When we installed our siren, it was not possible to screw the bracket into the wall as the siren was blocking the top set of screws. As such, it was necessary to unscrew the siren from the bracket, fasten the bracket to the wall, then reconnect the siren to the bracket.

5. At the control panel, the following connections are made:
    ❏ Red to INT
    ❏ Black to GND

This particular connection was made because we located the siren in the garage. If it were located outside, we'd connect the red wire to the EXT terminal. If we had both an exterior and interior siren, we'd connect the black leads from both sirens to the GND terminal and the red wires to the respective INT and EXT terminals.

30 MINUTES ## Consoles

This particular console is being placed by the door leading from the attached garage to the house. Once we pull into the garage, this is the first console with which we'll come in contact. This is the most likely place where we'll deactivate or activate the alarm.

Preparing the Wall

Consoles can be affixed to the wall in one of two ways:

❏ *They can be hung on the wall using screws.* If your drywall cannot hold the console to the wall, or you are not located near a wall stud, then you should consider wall anchors like the ones shown in Figure 6-17. These are plastic sleeves that fit inside a hole you drill, then insert a screw. As you twist the screw, the anchor opens up behind the wall and creates a solid base to which your console will be secured.

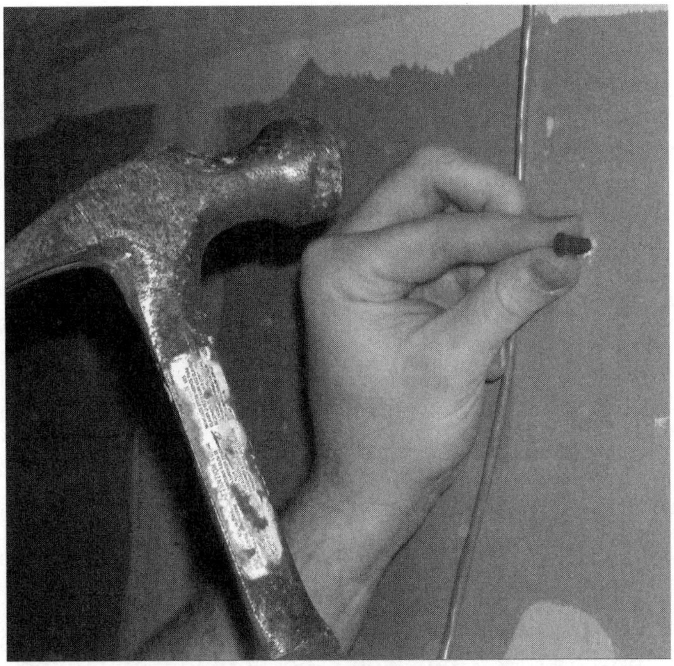

Figure 6-17
Installing a
plastic anchor

❑ *They can be recessed into the wall*. This method is a little more aesthetically pleasing, since you don't have a chunk of hardware sticking out of the wall. However, this method is a little more complex and involved than simply hanging the console on the wall, then going off to have lemonade. A recessed console requires you to place the device where a hole can be cut in the wall and the console inserted.

The method you end up using will depend on the type of console you purchase. The console for our Omni II can either be wall-mounted or recessed. The following steps show how this console installed as a recessed device. However, the only part of installation that applies solely to recessed consoles is the portion where we actually cut into the wall and mount the hardware. Otherwise, the steps are similar for wall-mounted consoles.

Location

Placement is a concern, as we need to ensure it is easily accessible. This is a good opportunity to locate the console at a height convenient for you.

Chances are, if you locate your console at eye level, you will wind up using fish tape to get the security cable from the floor up to the location of the console. Fish tape is simply fed through the hole you drill (if the console is wall-mounted) or the hole you cut in the wall (if the console will be recessed), then the cabling is affixed to the end of the fish tape and pulled through the wall.

Check the Range of Your Control Panel

With the Omni II, consoles cannot be more than 1,000 feet away from the control panel. Check the requirements of your own security system for maximum distances. If your house is big enough to have a console 1,000 feet away, you are probably not reading this book because Jeeves is installing the system for you.

This is more of a factor to consider when installing more than one console. With each console installed, the range decreases. For example, if two consoles are installed, the range for each is 500 feet. If eight consoles are installed (the maximum number allowed), the range is cut to 125 feet.

Cutting

In order to install the console, we have to do a little more damage to the home than we did for the sensors. A 3/16-inch hole here and there isn't so obtrusive. However, when we have to install the console, things get a little messier. Obviously, a 6" × 6" box won't shoehorn into a 3/16-inch hole. As such, we have to break out the RotoZip tool.

Before you cut into the wall, you need to be sure that there aren't any wires already where you'll be cutting. Also, make sure your measurements are accurate because you won't be able to put more sheetrock back where you've cut it.

HEADS UP!

Measure Correctly

Remember the old chestnut "measure twice, cut once."

Installation

Follow these steps to install and connect your security system's console:

1. Locate where you want your console to be placed. A good location is at eye level. Since the model we're using has special mounting equipment that grips the sheetrock, we're locating it away from studs. However, if you will be mounting a wall-mounted console, you might be better off locating the console over a stud for a secure connection.

2. Place the frame of the console against the wall and use a level to ensure that the console will be situated squarely in the wall (shown in Figure 6-18). Once the frame is properly located and level, trace around the outside of the frame with a pencil. Note that this step is not necessary if you are mounting the console on the wall rather than in a recessed location.

Figure 6-18
Using a level to
ensure the console
is straight

3. Using a Rotozip tool (like the one in Figure 6-19), cut out the drywall
where the frame will be placed.

Figure 6-19
Cutting the
appropriate-sized
hole in the wall using
a Rotozip tool

HEADS UP!

You Might Not Need to Cut a Giant Hole in the Wall

If you are wall mounting your console, don't cut out a giant chunk of wall; rather, a 3/16-inch hole should be drilled in the wall instead.

4. Pull the cable through the hole in the wall. This might need to be done using fish tape (as we described earlier); then, line the cable up with the hole on the back of the console mounting hardware.

5. Secure the mounting hardware to the wall. With this particular model, there are special brackets that fan out of the back of the mounting hardware, then hold the hardware to the drywall. Once it has been installed and the cabling pulled through, it will look like Figure 6-20.

Figure 6-20
Installed mounting
hardware

6. Connect the wires from the console to the wires from your security cable. With our console, the available wires are red, black, green, and yellow. As such, we connected all the wires of the console to their color match partner on the cabling. However, we connected the yellow wire

of the console to the white wire of the cabling. With this particular model, we connected the wires of the cabling to the wires of a plug, which will then be plugged into the console.

7. Plug the connector into the console, as shown in Figure 6-21.

Figure 6-21
Plugging the
connector into
the console

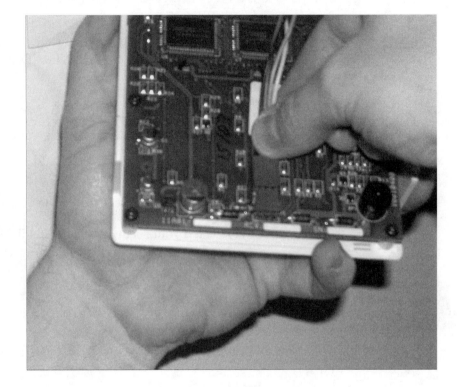

8. Insert console into wall.

9. At the control panel, the following connections are made:
   - ❑ Red to 12V
   - ❑ Black to GND
   - ❑ · White to A
   - ❑ Green to B

Power Up

Once you've connected all your sensors, consoles, and the transformer and battery, it's time to power up the system. The following steps are required on the Omni II system, but are similar to other control panels. Check your security system's installation instructions to ensure you follow the correct power-up procedures.

1. Double-check your work. Make sure everything has been connected properly.

2. Disconnect one lead of your sirens or other sounders.

3. Disconnect the positive lead to the battery.

4. Plug in the transformer. On the Omni II system, we're checking to ensure that the AC ON LED illuminates, the STATUS LED starts blinking after a minute, and the PHONE LED is off.

5. Unplug the transformer.

6. Connect the red wire to the battery.

7. Plug in the transformer (reactivating the system).

8. Unplug the transformer. The system should work on battery power, as indicated by the STATUS LED flashing.

9. Plug the transformer in and secure it to the outlet.

Once you've connected your security system, it will be necessary to program it. In the next chapter, we'll talk about programming your security system.

TESTING 1-2-3

At this point, you should double-check all your security system's connections and components:

❏ Is the cabling secured using rounded staples and free of slack?

❏ Have you made a list indicating how wiring should be connected to the control panel?

❏ Are the splices properly made?

❏ Are your sensors, consoles, and other components securely fastened to the wall or floor?

❏ Are connections to the control panel made properly?

❏ Have the battery and transformer been properly installed?

❏ Is the telephone connection and RJ31X jack installed correctly?

With the grunt work behind you, you are ready to start having fun with your new system.

Chapter 7

Programming the Security System

Once your security system is physically installed, there are a number of ways in which you can manage it. However, depending on the system you buy, you may have more or fewer control options than your neighbors do with their systems. Security systems utilize consoles, telephones, computers, and even web browsers for system management.

Since the last chapter explained how to install security systems, and we used Home Automation, Inc.'s (HAI's) Omni II system, we'll continue by showing how to manage that system using two software packages that allow for the setup and management of the system.

The system can be controlled via a console, but initial setup is very cumbersome. If you've ever tried to program your cellular telephone with someone's name and telephone number, you have a basic idea of the steps required for console programming. Now, however, imagine setting up hundreds of little details from a small keypad. Forget it. The console is great for checking system status and it's what you want to use to arm and disarm the system, but it's a pain for programming. We can ameliorate this headache by utilizing a personal computer. Note that the Omni II also allows for management of your Smart Home via a telephone interface. However, that's a little more advanced and out of the scope of our discussion.

Instead, our system will be set up using HAI's PC Access software package. Then, we'll be able to monitor the system over the Internet, using HAI's Web-Link II application. Naturally, not every security system will allow this level of management. However, since the PC Access and Web-Link II packages allow connectivity with other Smart Home devices (namely, our X10 components), we'll show how these tools are an integral part of our Smart Home. If you elect to buy another sort of security system (or none at all) the following pages should at least give you an understanding of what goes on with computer control of your Smart Home.

From the PC

Controlling the Omni II system from the PC is accomplished via the PC Access software program. PC Access is designed for use with all three versions of HAI's Omni security systems. There are two versions of this software:

❏ **PC Access for Professional Installers**   This version is geared toward professional installers. It allows quick programming and file backup for customer support. It sells for US$164.99.

❏ **PC Access for End Users**   This version is meant for system end users, offering a way to program the automation system and most other features. It sells for US$49.99.

5 MINUTES   Installing the Software

Installing the software is fairly straightforward.

1. Insert the PC Access CD into your CD- or DVD-ROM drive.

2. From the Start menu, select Run.

3. Type *<drive>*:**setup**. For example, if the CD is in your D drive, you'd type **D:setup**.

4. You'll be prompted for your company name (optional) and serial number (located on the back of the CD-ROM envelope).

5. Next, the setup program prompts you for a location where PC Access will be installed. If you're okay with the default location selected by the setup program, click Next. Otherwise, select Browse and find your preferred location.

6. On the next screen, which verifies the information you've already entered, click Next. Installation is complete.

When you start the program for the first time, you'll be prompted for a "security stamp." This stamp can be anything you choose and is only entered the first time you start the program. This stamp is used to encrypt your account files so only you have access to them.

Keep Track of Your Security Stamp
Write down your security stamp and keep it in a safe place. If you have to reinstall the software or if you want to access your files on another computer using PC Access, you will need the security stamp to decrypt your files.

Whenever you start the PC Access software, you'll be asked for the password. The default password is PASSWORD. When you start PC Access for the first time, you should change the password to something of your choosing. This can be done by using Configure | Password.

Record Your Password
Remember your password. Without the password, you will have to reinstall the software to restore the default password.

Connecting to the HAI System

5 MINUTES

There are two ways in which your computer can communicate with your Omni system using the PC Access software: either via a modem or serial connection.

Modem

By default, PC Access is set up to use a modem connected to your PC's COM1 communications port. The modem's settings can be changed using the Configure | Modem command. This allows you to manage such settings as

❑ Communications port

❑ Baud rate (between 75 and 19,200, depending on the capabilities of your modem; however, we're using a 2400-baud rate)

❑ Modem command strings

Serial

Another way to connect to the Omni control panel is via your PC's serial port. It utilizes either an RS-232 or RS-485 connection. To access the serial port, you must use the HAI Model 21A05-2 Serial Cable Kit.

Use RS-485 to Cover Greater Distance

While an RS-232 is the more common connection, use of RS-485 will allow you to connect over a greater distance.

To do this, you connect a serial cable between your computer and the control panel. Change the Com port using the Configure | Modem command. Change the communications port to reflect the serial port, rather than another COM port. For a serial connection, you should set the baud rate to 9600.

Setup

Once the software is installed, it is necessary to set up the software to manage your unique security system. There are a number of attributes that can be managed, ranging from individual access codes to naming specific zones.

1 MINUTE   Files

The first step in setting up your Omni security system is to create a new file. This is done by accessing the File | New command. Next, you'll be presented with a dialog box asking for the name of your file. With that entered, you are presented with a list of the various Omni systems. Since we've installed the Omni II, the radio button next to that was automatically selected.

5 MINUTES   Adding User Codes

PC Access allows you to assign 16 unique access codes. That is, you can give a different code—with different restrictions—to 16 different people (or groups of people). For example, you can assign unique codes to yourself, your spouse, and your children. With everyone having a unique access code, another layer of convenience and security is afforded. In the event someone gives their code away or there is some sort of breach, then everyone doesn't have to remember a new code. You can also set up accounts that are restricted as to when they are allowed to enter the premises. For example, if you have cleaning staff coming in

Mondays, Wednesdays, and Fridays between noon and 2 p.m., you can give them their own, unique code that is only valid on those days and times.

The ability to assign 16 access codes might seem overkill for the home use of this device. However, bearing in mind that the Omni II is geared toward both homes and small businesses, it is possible to give a unique access code to different employees or service providers.

To access this tool, follow Setup | Codes. Once you've started the tool, as shown in Figure 7-1, you can select a user number, then change their code, times of access, and so forth.

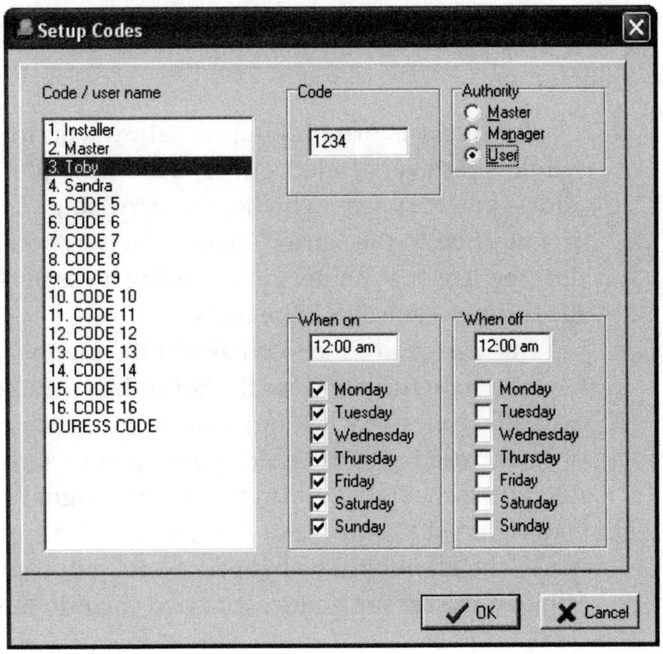

Figure 7-1
Establishing user codes and times of access

Adding Zones/Units

Security systems are like beautiful snowflakes—no two are exactly alike. Your security system will have different sensors and behaviors than your neighbor's system. As such, it is necessary to set up the zones unique to your system and tell the system what type of sensor is connected to each zone.

On the PC Access application, follow Setup | Installer | Zones to access the Zones tool. Once there, you'll see a window like the one shown in Figure 7-2. There are two sets of radio buttons, a list of all the available zones, and a pull-down menu to select which type of sensor is being used with each zone.

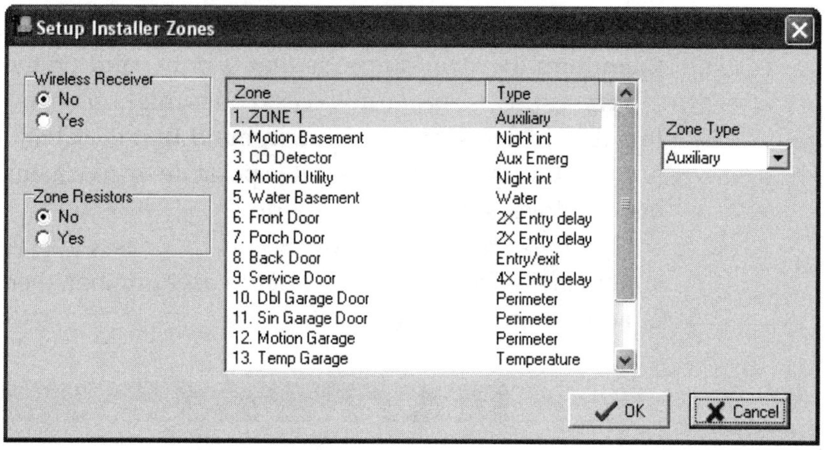

Figure 7-2
Configuring zones
on PC Access

Setup Installer Zones

Wireless Receiver
- ○ No
- ○ Yes

Zone Resistors
- ○ No
- ○ Yes

Zone	Type
1. ZONE 1	Auxiliary
2. Motion Basement	Night int
3. CO Detector	Aux Emerg
4. Motion Utility	Night int
5. Water Basement	Water
6. Front Door	2X Entry delay
7. Porch Door	2X Entry delay
8. Back Door	Entry/exit
9. Service Door	4X Entry delay
10. Dbl Garage Door	Perimeter
11. Sin Garage Door	Perimeter
12. Motion Garage	Perimeter
13. Temp Garage	Temperature

Zone Type
Auxiliary

✓ OK   ✗ Cancel

The two sets of radio buttons allow you to specify whether you are using wireless receivers (select either "yes" or "no"). The other set of radio buttons allows you to specify whether you are using *end-of-line resistors*. These resistors are attached to the sensor's wiring between the sensor and the control panel, near the sensor. Whether you are using these resistors or not, it is important to indicate your choice to PC Access.

This is a good time to break out the plan you drew for sensor placement in Chapter 6. In the center of the Setup Installer Zones window is a list of all the available zones. By clicking on the appropriate zone and then selecting the type of sensor used, you can quickly set up your security system. These settings will determine later what to arm and when to signal a breach. For example, if a sensor is designated as entry/exit and you arm the system, if any of these become not ready, the alarm will be tripped. Some will trip an alarm all the time, like fire. Some of the sensor types supported include these:

- ❏ Thermostat
- ❏ Entry/Exit
- ❏ Perimeter
- ❏ Fire
- ❏ Key Switch

Configuring Communications and Dialers

When an event occurs, PC Access can notify you by calling one of eight telephone numbers you specify. When calling, you can establish a certain message that the computer will speak. Also, it is possible to set up the Omni II to call a central station to indicate there is a problem. The ability to call that central station is managed through the Communicator tool, located by following Setup | Installer | Communicator. The tool is shown in Figure 7-3.

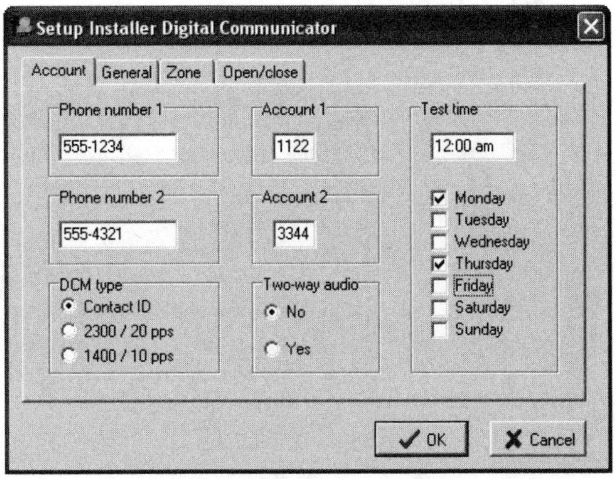

Figure 7-3
Establishing
communication
rules

The Account tab allows you to specify which telephone number (or numbers) will be dialed when a specific condition is met, such as a door being opened, or if there is a freezing danger, or other alarm scenario. It also allows you to establish certain days of the week and times of day during which test calls will be made to ensure system integrity.

The General tab (shown in Figure 7-4) allows you to determine which messages will be sent for miscellaneous conditions, like a low battery on the control panel or a fire. The message numbers shown in these examples are managed using the "Names/Voice" menu selection, which we'll talk about in more detail later in this chapter.

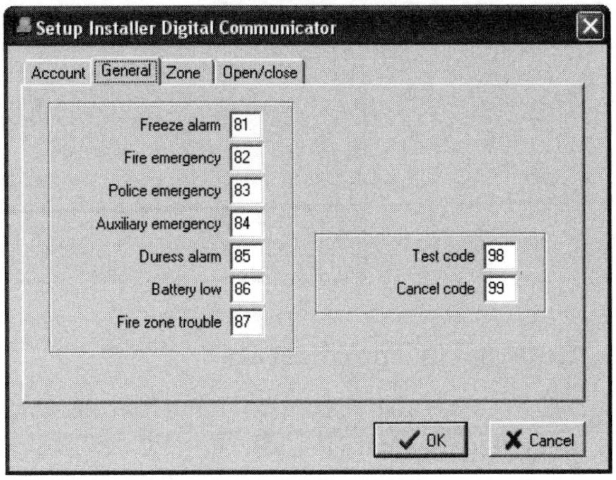

Figure 7-4
The General tab of the
Communicator tool

The Zone tab (shown in Figure 7-5) is used to set up specific messages when a zone alarm is tripped. In this example, there are different numbered messages for zones 1–6. However, we've decided that zones 7–12 can all share the same message when they are tripped. As such, they have the same message number.

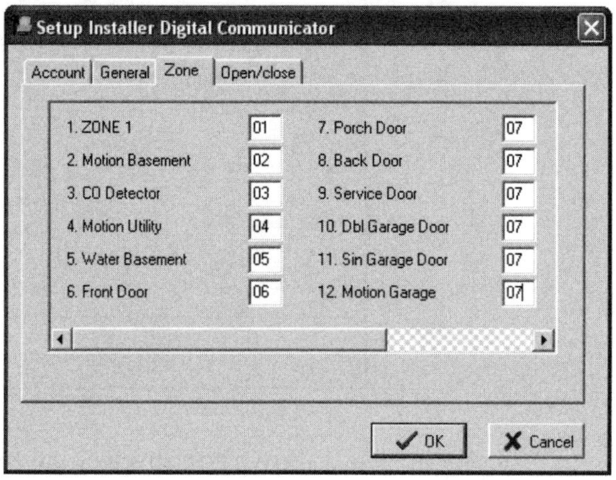

Figure 7-5
The Zone tab of the Communicator tool

The Open/Close tab (shown in Figure 7-6) is used to send a message when someone activates or deactivates the alarm. You can also use this screen to decide whether or not notification needs to be made every time someone comes home.

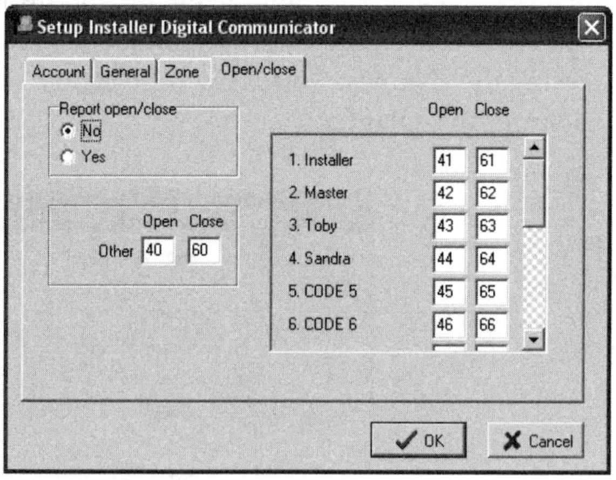

Figure 7-6
The Open/Close tab of the Communicator tool

5 MINUTES

Setting Up Thermostats

PC Access is also used to manage thermostats. Up to four thermostats can be connected to the Omni II and, using PC Access, are managed by using the tool found by following Setup | Installer | Temperature. This tool is shown in Figure 7-7.

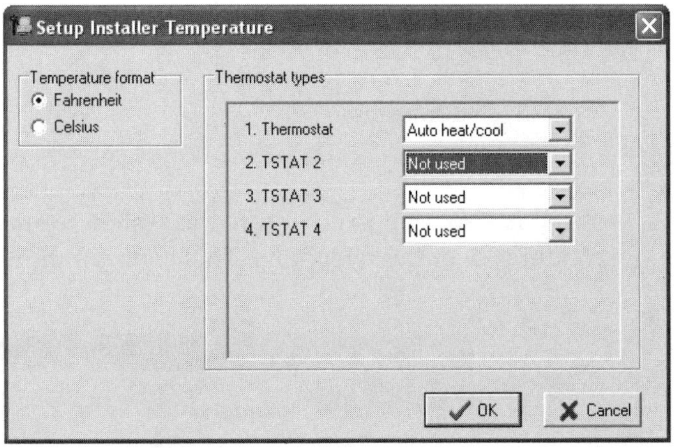

Figure 7-7
Managing
thermostats
using PC Access

First, you can decide which measurement you will use to gauge the temperature: Fahrenheit or Celsius. Next, you are given a list of your thermostats and a drop-down list of the varying types of thermostats that can be managed by the Omni II and PC Access. Those thermostat types are

❏ Auto heat/cool

❏ Heat/cool

❏ Heat only

❏ Cool only

❏ Setpoint only

Naturally, this setting will be made based on what type of thermostat or temperature sensor you've installed.

15 MINUTES   **Giving Zones and Units Names**

By default, PC Access simply identifies its various zones, codes, and so forth with a simple name and numbering scheme: Zone 1, Zone 2, Zone 3, and so forth. It can be confusing and—let's face it—a little less than cool to have to keep referring to things like Zone 1, TSTAT2, and so forth. However, these settings can be changed to customize and personalize your system for easier reading and understanding.

The Setup | Names/Voice configuration page is used to show and modify

❏ Zones

❏ Units

❏ Buttons

❏ Codes

❏ Thermostats

❏ Message names

It is also used to configure the system to speak descriptive names for those features over the telephone. This configuration page is shown in Figure 7-8.

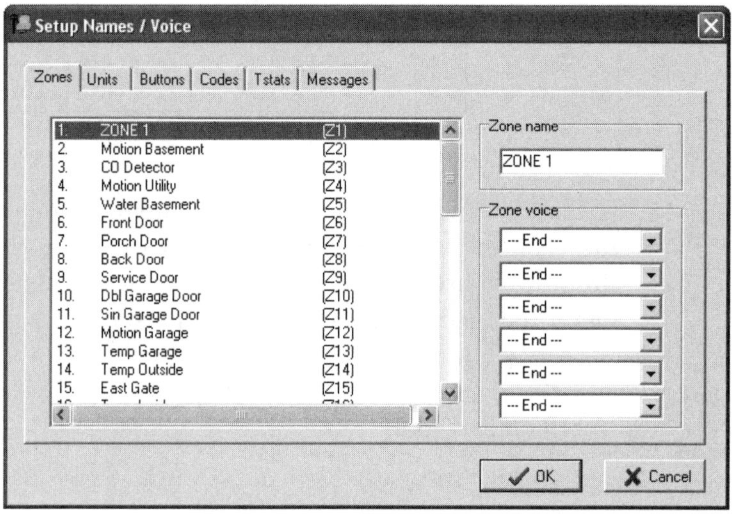

Figure 7-8
Configuring
names and voices

By selecting the appropriate tab and scrolling through the list of names, you can edit the name to provide a customized setting. For example, by default PC Access names all zones "Zone 1" through "Zone 16." However, to be more helpful and descriptive, you can edit the zone to reflect what, exactly, that zone is. Rather than calling the zone "Zone 1," it can be changed to read "Garage Door" or whatever the sensor is monitoring. These descriptive tags will show up on the console and in log messages.

Additionally, you can use this tool to change the message that will be spoken over the telephone. There are six drop-down menus, from which more than 250 words or sounds can be combined. Figure 7-9 shows the message that will be spoken across the telephone when Zone 6 ("Front Door") is tripped.

Figure 7-9
Creating a spoken
message for an alarm

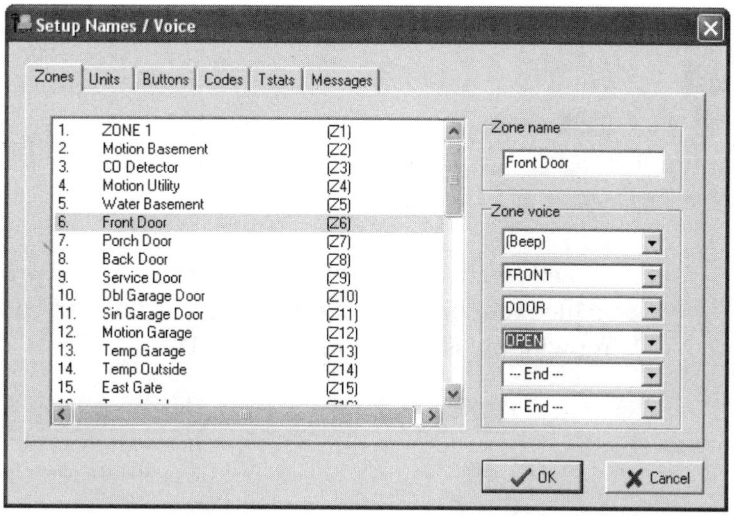

0-? MINUTES

Amount of time
required depends
on the complexity
of your system.

Creating a Program

You don't need to know C++ or J++ or any other programming language to set up a program in PC Access. This tool is located by following Setup | Programs, as shown in Figure 7-10.

Figure 7-10
PC Access's
Programs tool

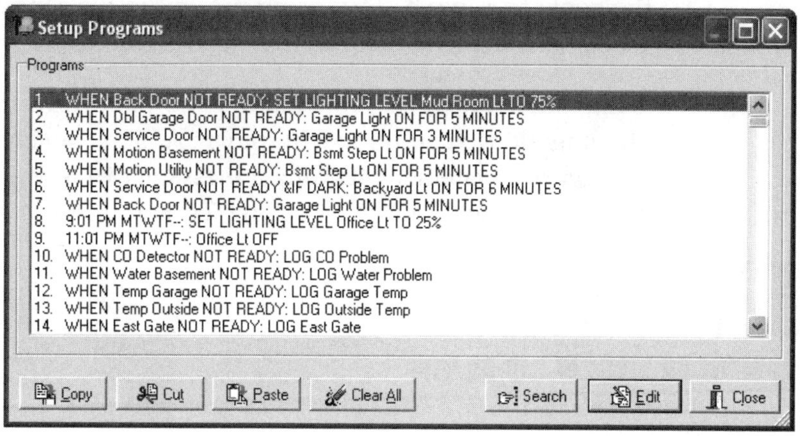

The Programs tool allows you to enter specific conditions that, when met, will trigger a behavior. For example, one program can be set up so that everyday at dusk, exterior lighting comes on. Another program will automatically turn on your interior lighting whenever the security system is deactivated—for instance, when you come home from work. However, you could also set up that program so that the lights will only come on when the security system is deactivated and when it is after dusk.

HEADS UP!

Knowing when Dusk Occurs

So how, exactly, will PC Access know when dusk is? Simply enter your longitude and latitude using the tool located by following Setup | Misc.

Let's walk though how the aforementioned program would be set up. First, on the Programs tool, highlight a blank line and click the Edit button. The resulting window is shown in Figure 7-11.

Figure 7-II
Editing a program

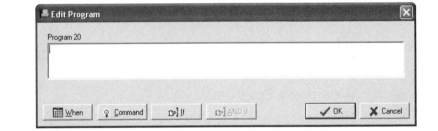

When Click the When button. This offers up a menu of different scenarios, from checking the status of X10 devices, to time of day, to telephones being off the hook, to a low battery being present in the control panel. In our program, we've selected when any security code deactivates the system.

Command Next, the Command button allows you to specify the action the aforementioned condition will spawn. Actions can include arming or disarming the security system, or sending a message to a telephone number. For our program, we've selected "All On," which will turn on all X10 devices.

HEADS UP!

Controlling All Kinds of X10 Devices

Naturally, this example makes the assumption that the only X10 devices we have installed control lights. However, we can use the Control command to specify a certain X10 device and specify a specific level of brightness.

If We could stop there, but PC Access also allows us to add a couple of conditions that must also be met for this action to take place. In this case, we want the lights to come on *only* if it is dark outside. Next, we click the If button. This presents us with a list of conditions, including whether a certain X10 device is on or off, the status of the security system, or just the status of a specific zone. Under the

Misc listing of conditions, we selected "If Dark". There is a second button that requires a second condition to be met for the action to take place. Our completed program is shown in Figure 7-12.

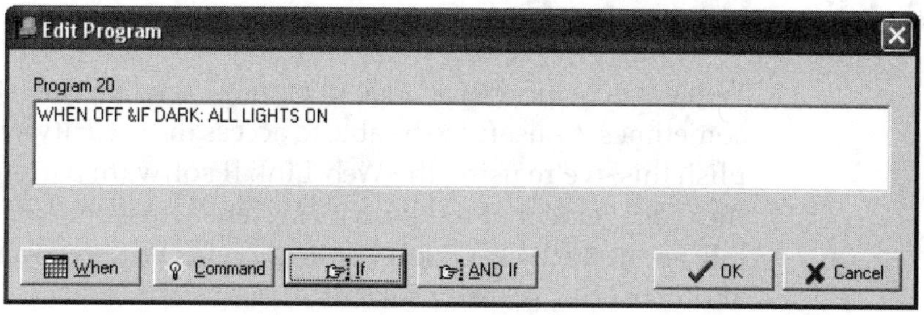

Figure 7-12
A completed program

Figure 7-12
A completed program

The Programs tool also offers the type of cut-and-paste tools that you've probably become familiar with working with any brand of computer. These tools allow you to navigate your program and add, remove, or copy instructions. The Omni II allows for 500 programs to be entered, which should suffice for most homes.

Monitoring

In addition to being able to configure the Omni system via a PC using the PC Access software, it is also possible to monitor the system, checking the temperature, zones, and so forth. By clicking on Status and then selecting the Zones tab, you can check on the status of your zones, as Figure 7-13 shows.

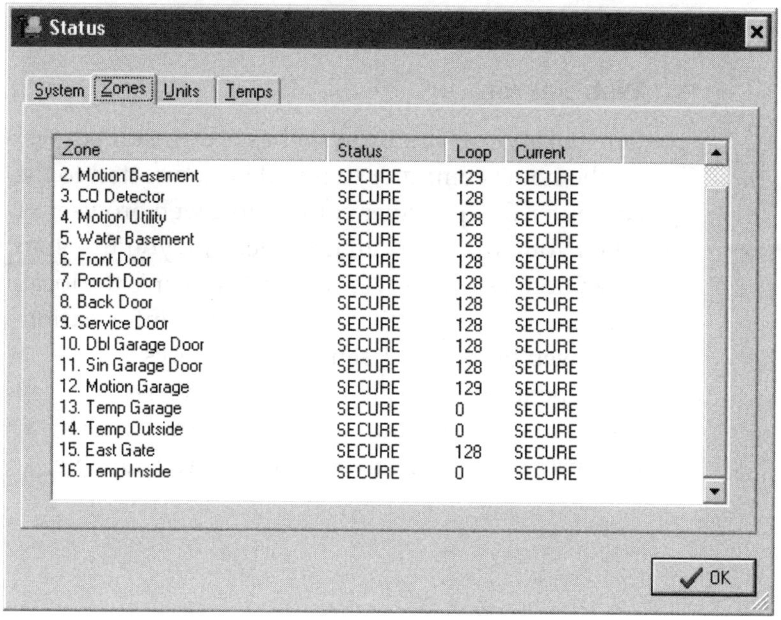

Figure 7-13
Monitoring the Omni
II using PC Access

Additionally, using this window, you can also check temperatures and the status of the system.

Adding Remote Support

While it is helpful to be able to manage a security system via a local computer, sometimes it's useful to be able to access the security system remotely. To accomplish this, we're using the Web-Link II software package from HAI. This allows the management of the security system across the Internet. In this section, we'll talk about the Web-Link II application for Windows and how it is used to set up and manage a security system.

Installing the Web-Link II Server

Unlike the PC Access software, there are a number of components that must be installed in order for Web-Link II to function. For proper operation, we'll need a web browser, web server, and, finally, the Web-Link II software.

30 MINUTES

Web Browser

First, the system requires an Internet web browser to be installed. HAI recommends at least version 5.0 of Microsoft Internet Explorer, but version 5.5 or later is preferred. Because it utilizes certain features only available on Internet Explorer, other browsers are not recommended. The most recent version of Internet Explorer can be downloaded directly from Microsoft at www.microsoft.com/windows/ie.

10 MINUTES

Web Server

Once an appropriate browser has been installed, Web-Link II needs a web server on the home computer that will be connected to the Internet. A web server is a computer that provides content to a web browser via the Internet. For instance, when you visit www.smarthome.com, you use your web browser to connect to Smarthome's web server. The web server is the location of Smarthome's catalog. It is the web server that transmits the information you're searching for; then, your web browser presents and displays it.

Depending on which operating system you're using, there is likely a web server available to you. Table 7-1 lists the various flavors of the Windows operating system and which web servers are available.

Operating System	Web Server
Windows 98 and 98SE	Personal Web Server (PWS)
Windows NT Workstation	PWS
Windows NT Server	Internet Information Server (IIS)
Windows 2000 Professional/Server	IIS
Windows ME	Not Supported by Web-Link II
Windows XP Home Edition	Not Supported by Web-Link II
Windows XP Professional	IIS

Table 7-1
Web Servers for Various Microsoft Windows Operating System Flavors

We simply don't have the space here to explain how these various web servers are installed. Typically, however, if these web servers are not already installed on your system, they are included on your Windows CD-ROM and can be installed as supplemental Windows applications.

Table 7-1 represents the web servers that come with your Microsoft Windows OS. You can also download third-party web servers, like the Abyss web server (www.aprelium.com). However, Web-Link II has only been tested with Microsoft web servers.

Installing the Application

5 MINUTES

Installing the Web-Link II application is rather straightforward:

1. Insert the HAI Web-Link II compact disc into your CD- or DVD-ROM drive.

2. Select the Run command from the Start menu.

3. In the Run dialog box, type *<drive>*:**setup** (where *drive* is the letter of your CD- or DVD-ROM drive).

4. Follow the instructions provided on the screen.

Logging In

1 MINUTE

In order to log in to the security system, you must provide additional information beyond just username and password. Here's what you need to do:

1. Ensure that the PC Access software is not using the serial connection to the security system, because it takes over the serial connection for operation.

2. Start the web server. Normally, this is automatically started when Windows starts, but if it does not, you should start it manually.

3. Start the web browser and enter the address of the web server followed by **"/web-link"**. There are three scenarios in which you can connect to the web server:

❑ From the server: http://localhost/web-link

❑ From a client on your home LAN: http:// [followed by the computer name or IP address of your network interface card]/web-link

❑ Over the Internet: http:// [followed by your Internet IP address or hostname]/web-link

Once Web-Link II is started, you must log in using a valid username and password. The first screen that appears shows the Login dialog box. Enter the following information:

1. Specify the NAME and corresponding CODE of a user on the Omni II system. The NAME corresponds to the name of a "Code" on the controller. The CODE is the code associated with that name. (For example, Dave 1111). These names and codes can be checked on the PC Access software.

2. Indicate which start page you wish to use for Web-Link II. The drop-down list provides the available Web-Link II. The "Home" page is the default.

3. If you don't want to go through all the username and password steps, you can check the "Remember Password" check box. This will store your login information on this particular computer. If you attempt to log in on another computer, you will be prompted for your login information.

4. Click the Login button to start Web-Link II.

5. When finished, click the "Logout" button on the top right of the page. If you don't log out before closing your browser, or if you surf away from Web-Link II to visit another web site, you cannot log in to Web-Link II using the same username for at least seven to ten minutes.

Figure 7-14
Web-Link II
home page

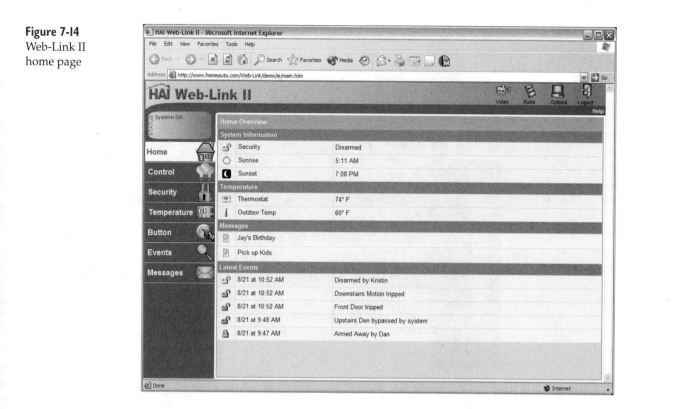

Overview

When you start Web-Link II, you get a snazzy overview of your system's status, as shown in Figure 7-14.

Details on the home page include the security system's status, time of day, sunrise and sunset times, interior and exterior temperature, messages, and the last five events to have occurred. But beyond simply showing these details, clicking on one of them allows you to manage elements of it, although not to the degree that you get with the PC Access software.

For instance, clicking on the security setting allows us to select a new status for the security system, as shown in Figure 7-15. By checking this remotely, we can tell if we forgot to set the security system—or maybe we forgot a delivery was going to be made today, so we can deactivate the alarm remotely, then reactivate it once the delivery has been made.

Figure 7-15
Checking the security
system's status

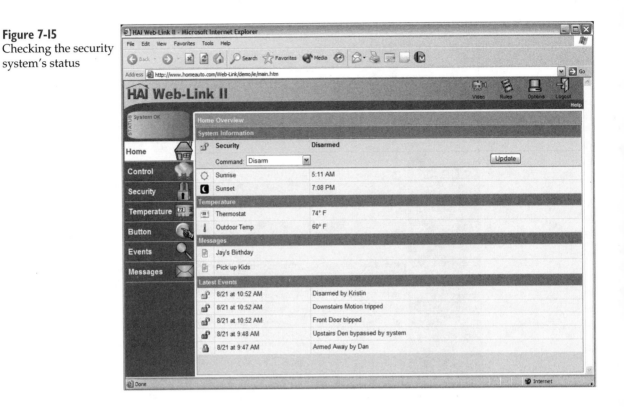

Along the left side of the page are buttons for accessing various pages for your Omni II security system. Those buttons are

❑ Home (the home page)
❑ Control
❑ Security
❑ Temperature
❑ Button
❑ Events
❑ Messages

We won't go into the function of each of these buttons. However, we'll give an overview of some of the more important ones as they relate to our discussion of remote management.

Viewing Events

You can set up your Web-Link II software to track all sorts of information about your system and what has been going on with it. Want to know when someone came home? Curious about when various sensors were tripped? The Events button, along the left side of the screen, is used to view the various events that have occurred on your system. For example, the screen in Figure 7-16 shows the date, time, and what event occurred.

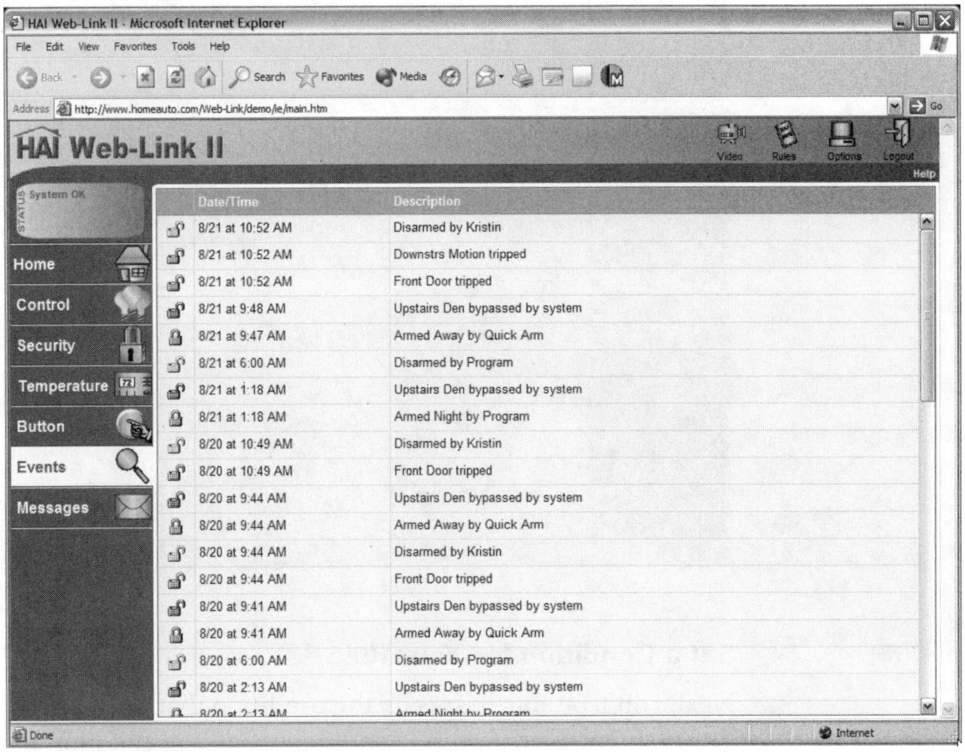

Figure 7-16
Viewing the most recent events

This page shows the most recent 50 events.

Setting Up Rules for E-mail Notification

In the PC Access program, we were able to establish rules within a program that, given certain behaviors, would cause another device to activate, deactivate, or send a message. The same behavior is possible in Web-Link II; however, in this case, the actions will spawn either an e-mail to be sent or the event to be captured on video (assuming a web camera is pointed in the right spot).

The following explains how to set up a new rule and how Web-Link II will make a notification if the rule has been broken. To create a new rule, select the Add Rule button (shown in Figure 7-17) or right-click an existing rule and select Create New Rule from the context menu.

Figure 7-17
Clicking the
Add Rule button
to add a new rule

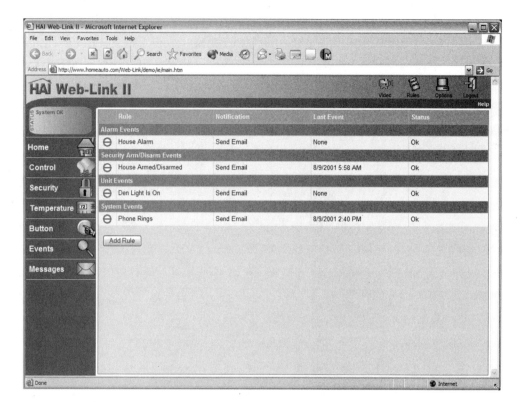

5 MINUTES

Set a Condition for Your Rule

Next, you'll be able to specify the condition that must be met for your rule to be violated. There are several conditions that you can monitor:

❏   Alarm is activated

❏   All On/Off commands issued

❏   Battery power changes state

❏   Button execution occurs

❏   DCM changes state

❏   Phone line changes state

❏   AC Power changes state

❏   Security is armed or disarmed

❏   Unit changes state

❏ X10 command issued

❏ Zone changes state

Once you've established what condition must be met, you select your method of notification: either send e-mail or record video.

Send E-mail

From the drop-down list, select e-mail notification. Then, you'll be required to enter the following:

❏ **E-mail Name**   This is the e-mail address where a message will be sent.

❏ **SMTP Server**   This is the SMTP server from which the e-mail message will be sent.

HEADS UP!

SMTP Defined

SMTP stands for Simple Mail Transfer Protocol and is used to send e-mail.

❏ **Send the e-mail message in HTML format**   Checking this box will allow the e-mail to be sent in the HTML format and include such information as

❏ Event details

❏ System information

❏ Temperatures

❏ Latest events

HEADS UP!

Gathering SMTP Information

The SMTP server is likely to have the same domain name as your ISP. However, if you don't know what it is, you can get this from your ISP. If you are adventurous, you can set up this PC to be an SMTP server as well.

Figure 7-18 shows an example message generated by Web-Link II and sent using HTML.

Figure 7-18
An HTML e-mail
message generated
by Web-Link II

```
Web-Link Notification: Back Door opened

 File   Edit   View   Tools   Message   Help

  Reply   Reply All   Forward      Print    Delete    Previous    Next    Addresses

 From:     Web-Link.Notification.Server @buddy.siteprotect.com
 Date:     Friday, June 06, 2003 4:49 PM
 To:       toby@velte.com
 Subject:  Web-Link Notification: Back Door opened
```

Web-Link Event Notification

Event Details:

Date:	6/6/2003
Time:	4:49 PM
Description:	Back Door opened

System Information:

Area #1:	**Disarmed**
Sunrise:	5:26:00 AM
Sunset:	8:54:00 PM

Temperature:

Thermostat:	71.6° F
Temp Garage:	68.9° F
Temp Outside:	64.4° F

Latest Events:

6/5/2003 8:08:00 PM	East Gate logged
6/5/2003 7:31:00 PM	East Gate logged
6/5/2003 3:36:00 PM	Garage Temp logged
6/5/2003 3:35:00 PM	Garage Temp logged
6/5/2003 3:34:00 PM	Garage Temp logged
6/5/2003 3:32:00 PM	Garage Temp logged
6/5/2003 3:30:00 PM	Garage Temp logged

1 MINUTE

Record Video

If you choose, you can elect to record video of the event. It is likely this option would be used if you already have a video camera pointed at a sensor you wish to monitor. For example, if you are wondering about whether your dog is sleeping on the couch when you're at work, a motion sensor in the living room being tripped can cause video from that area to be recorded. To set up video recording, from the drop-down list select Record Video. Then, you'll be asked to enter a couple pieces of information:

❑ **Record Duration**   Enter the duration (in minutes) for the record operation. Video can be recorded up to 720 Minutes (12 hours)—assuming you have enough hard drive space.

❑ **Channel to Record**   Select the channel to be recorded from the drop-down list. Note that "Channel to Record" is only displayed if you have a TV tuner installed and Channel Changing is Enabled.

5 MINUTES

Controlling X10 Devices

In the preceding chapter, we connected a bunch of gadgets that were hardwired directly to the security system. However, one of the reasons we decided to get the

Omni II system was because of its ability to interact with X10 devices. We were able to control them using PC Access, but we also have the ability to manage them remotely using Web-Link II.

To access the various X10 devices we have installed, it's simply a matter of clicking the Control button on the left side of the Web-Link II screen. This will call up a screen like the one shown in Figure 7-19.

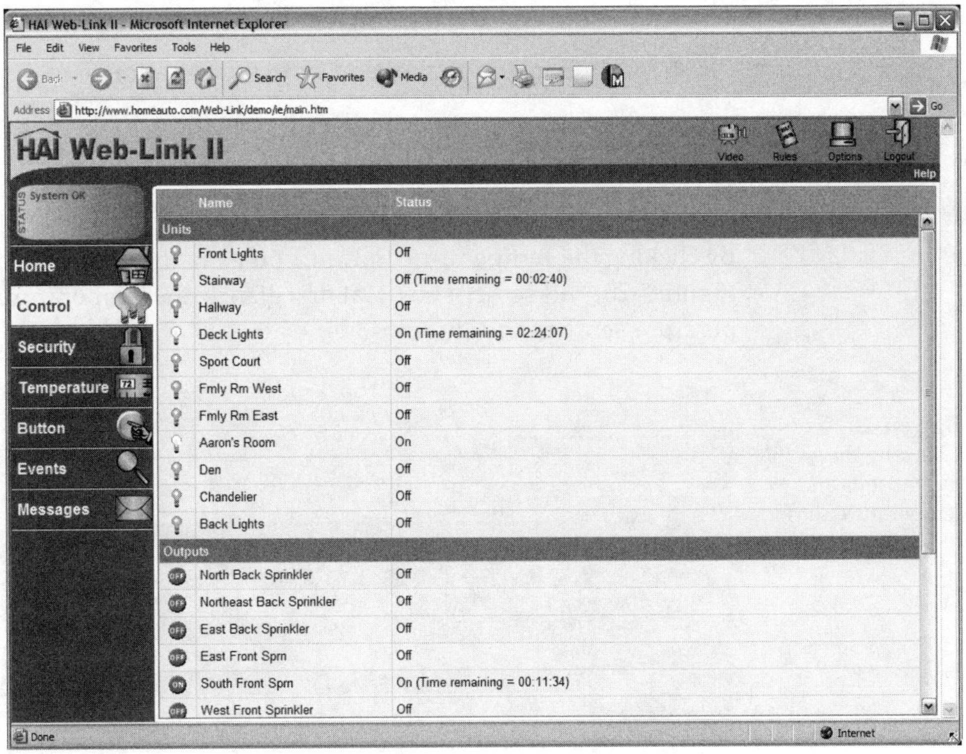

Figure 7-19
Accessing X10
devices

The Control page displays the status of all named units in the system and allows for their control. The status of each unit includes these:

❑ On or off with any remaining time until a program is executed

❑ Dimmed or brightened with any remaining time until a program is executed

❑ Level

❑ Ramp rate and time (which is only available with advanced lighting-control lighting)

To change any unit, follow these steps:

1. Select the item to control from the list by left-clicking it with your mouse (you can also right-click it, which will present its context menu).

2. Select the desired command from the list.

3. For those commands that require more information (such as the rate at which an appliance will be ramped up to a certain level), an edit box will appear for additional input.

4. Choose a duration period from the Duration list.

5. Click on the Update button to send the command to the controller.

5 MINUTES

Controlling Thermostats

By clicking the Temperature button, you generate a screen like the one shown in Figure 7-20. This screen shows, at first glance, the temperature from all your temperature sensors and thermostats.

Figure 7-20
Checking the thermostats and temperature sensors

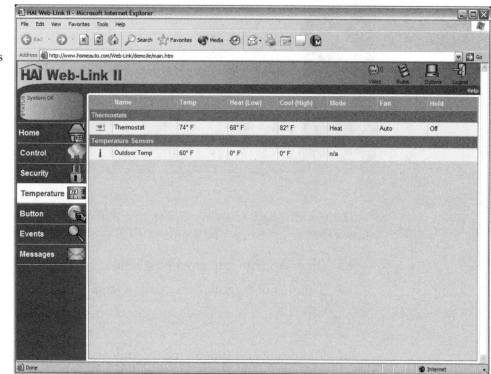

To control a thermostat or temperature sensor, simply follow these steps:

1. Select the thermostat or temperature sensor to control from the list by pointing to it using your mouse pointer.

2. Left-click on the desired unit or right-click to display its context menu.

Changing the Thermostat, Remotely

By right-clicking on a specific thermometer or thermostat, the context menu allows you to raise or lower the heat and cool settings in 2-degree increments.

3. Select the desired command from the list. (This is shown in more detail in Figure 7-21.)

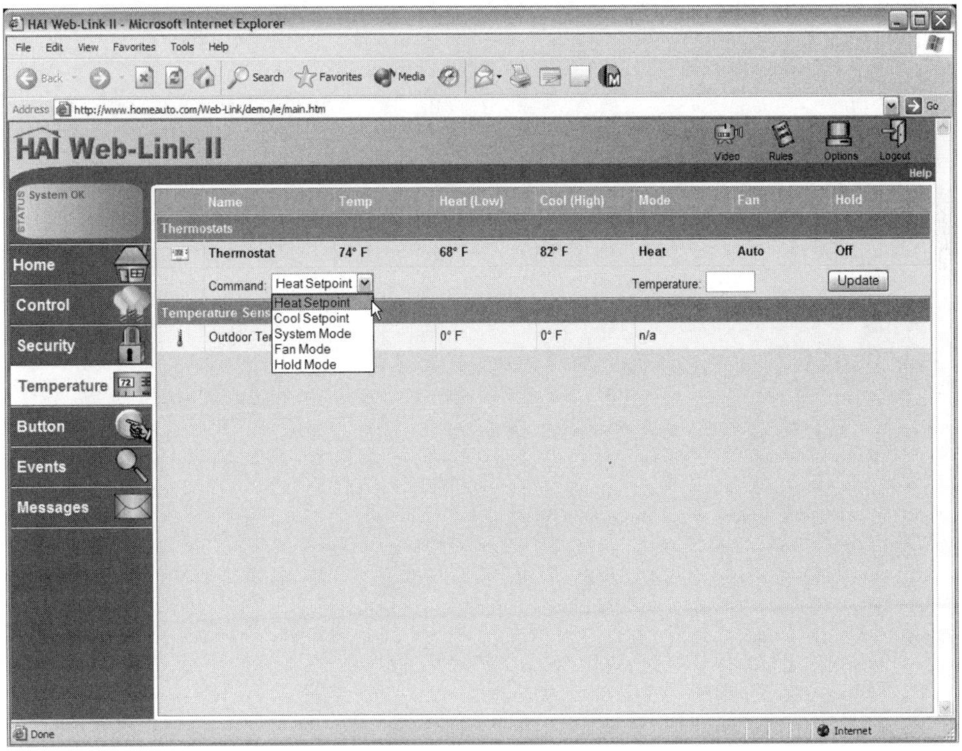

Figure 7-21
Changing thermostat settings

4. Commands requiring additional input (for instance, choosing "Cool Setpoint" from the command list will display a field for inputting a temperature) will generate an edit box for additional input.

5. Click the Update button to send the command to the controller.

Though these two pieces of software are proprietary to HAI's security systems, it should give you a good idea of what is available in terms of PC control of your security system. Also, should you find a security system that interconnects with X10 modules, you'll have a good, well-integrated Smart Home system.

❏ Is the web server installed and properly configured?

❏ Is an appropriate web browser installed?

❏ Have security stamps and passwords been safely stored?

Chapter 8

The Smart Home Garage and Lawn

Tools of the Trade

Level
Sheet metal screws
Wall anchors
Screws
Drill
Tapcon drill bit
Tapcon concrete anchors

The "smart" in your Smart Home doesn't end at its four walls. Even though most of your Smart Home functionality will likely take place inside your home, there is still a fair amount of stuff you can do outside.

In this chapter, we take a look at specific areas of your Smart Home's exterior. First, we'll talk about some things you can do in your garage, including garage door and temperature sensors. Then, we'll step outside to consider some projects you can do on the exterior of your Smart Home. Noticeably absent from this talk about your Smart Home's exterior is any discussion about lighting. We didn't forget about it—we're going to cover all forms of Smart Home lighting in the next chapter.

Garage

You might not think that there is too much going on in your garage as far as Smart Home functionality is concerned, but there are a number of things you can do to smarten up your garage. For instance, you might want to set up your system so that when the garage door is opened, a series of events occurs. When you open the door, your system might be programmed to turn on the lights in the mudroom.

In the first section of this chapter, we'll talk about some of the sensors that you might want to place in your garage, along with some placement considerations. Next, we'll walk through the process of installing the more specialized sensors (specifically, the garage door sensor).

Sensors

The sensors utilized in the garage are largely the same as those that would be used inside the Smart Home. To monitor service doors on the garage, simply use the open door/window sensors that you'd use for access points. Installation is identical to the steps we covered in Chapter 6. However, depending on the state of your garage, the process might be a little easier.

Garages tend to be a bit more "rustic" than the rest of the home. That's a nice way to say that most garages tend to be unfinished (although some garage aficionados out there might argue with my generalized assessment of the American garage, at least as it pertains to their own homes away from home). That unfinished nature makes it easier to pull cabling, anchor to wall studs, drill holes, and mount sensor hardware.

The sensors can be installed on doors and windows to monitor access, and motion sensors and temperature sensors can also be installed. Though most sensors can be used interchangeably between the interior and the garage, there are specialized sensors that are unique to garage use. Garage door sensors are steroid-pumped versions of the window and open door/window sensors. After discussing this sensor, we'll talk about temperature sensors.

Garage Door

One of the first points of entry into a home is the garage (assuming, of course, the home has an attached garage). To be sure, there are easier ways for a burglar to get into your home than prying open a garage door. However, this is a good place to locate a sensor, because we can ensure that the garage door hasn't been left open or—for the really technically proficient bad guys out there—someone hasn't been able to rig up his or her own covert garage door opener to gain entry to our house.

The first sensor we'll install is the garage door open/close sensor. The garage door contact switch is placed on garage doors, roll-up doors, or gates where it might be tough to mount regular magnetic contacts. Smaller contacts (like the ones we'll use on doors and windows in the house) have a small operating gap and must be within a half-inch to be used. While that's fine for a window, or the front door, it's not feasible for large doors. These contacts can be up to two inches apart and still operate.

The sensor mounts to the concrete floor and is made of a heavy-duty polished aluminum die-cast housing. The contact switch is completely sealed within this housing. The magnet is mounted on the door or gate to complete the system. It is mounted on an adjustable L-bracket for horizontal and vertical adjustment. The sensor housing is rounded so vehicles can roll over it without damage to either the sensor or the vehicle. A flexible 24-inch stainless armored cable protects the wires as they run along the ground. Figure 8-1 shows a garage door sensor.

Figure 8-1
Garage door sensor

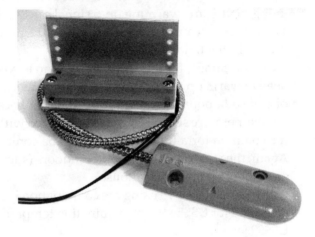

We're using a normally closed sensor that retails for US$14.99. A sensor that can operate in both the normally open or normally closed state runs US$21.99.

Temperature

To monitor the temperature of an area, temperature sensors are used, like the one shown in Figure 8-2.

Figure 8-2
Temperature sensor

Temperature sensors differ from thermostats because the sensors do exactly as their name suggests—they sense temperature, whereas a thermostat is able to react to the given temperature (for instance, turn on the air conditioning when the temperature climbs above a setpoint). But don't let the distinction fool you—even though temperature sensors don't natively start or stop a heater or air conditioner, when coupled with a Smart Home, you can do so much more.

For example, let's say there is a living room in a Smart Home with a temperature sensor and automatic drape pullers installed. Rather than allowing the thermostat to fight against Mother Nature to keep the living room cool when the sun beats in the window, a temperature sensor can be employed to take a specific action when the temperature rises above a certain level. In this case, when the living room starts warming up, a signal can be sent to the Smart Home computer. The computer can then send a signal to the automatic drape pullers to shut the drapes in the living room.

In the garage, temperature sensors can let you know if it is so cold that you'll need to warm up your car before going to work in the morning, or if your stockpile of soda pop is in danger of exploding because of low temperatures.

Temperature sensors can also be merged with other sensors into a single unit. It's common for a humidity sensor to be combined with a temperature sensor. Again, these can be located either indoors (such as in your walk-in humidor) or outdoors (for your greenhouse).

The sensors we're using are combination indoor/outdoor sensors from HAI that retail for US$54.99. A combination temperature/humidity sensor retails for US$99.99.

Installation

Installing these sensors follows similar steps to those of other components we've already installed. The process is essentially the same: run the wiring, connect the sensor, screw the sensor to the wall or door. However, connecting the garage door sensor is a little more involved than saying "simply connect the sensor to the door." Since the sensor is connected to both the garage door and the concrete floor, the steps are a little more involved. Once we talk about the garage door sensor, we'll discuss the installation of temperature sensors and the issues unique to them.

20 MINUTES

Garage Door

Follow these steps to connect your garage door sensor:

1. Once the wires are strung to the location of the sensor, the next step is to place the sensor on your garage floor and mark the mounting holes with a pen or a pencil. This will aid when drilling the pilot holes.

HEADS UP!

Find the Best Location for Your Sensor

When locating the sensor, make sure it is as out of the way as possible, and don't forget to include the magnet to ensure that both pieces of the sensor package will be able to fit where you need them.

2. Remove the sensor and, using a drill fitted with a concrete Tapcon bit, drill pilot holes into the concrete, as Figure 8-3 shows. The size of the drill bit will depend on the concrete anchor that you use for your sensor.

Figure 8-3
Drilling pilot holes using a Tapcon drill bit

TIPS OF THE TRADE

Concrete Anchors and Installation

Concrete anchors are special screws that are capable of being used in concrete. When selecting a concrete anchor, typically you can select between heads that are fitted for a screwdriver or a hex wrench. The best bet for getting the torque you need to screw the anchors into the concrete floor is to use the hex-wrench-headed anchors. Tapcon drill bits can be purchased individually, or they can be purchased in the same package as the anchors.

3. Once the holes have been drilled, take a couple seconds to vacuum out the holes to remove any remaining concrete crumbs.

4. Fasten the sensor to the concrete floor using the concrete anchors. Make sure the sensor is tightened securely to the floor. This step is shown in Figure 8-4.

Figure 8-4
Securing the sensor
with a concrete
anchor

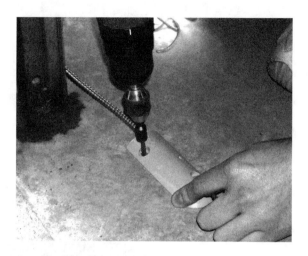

5. Install the door sensors to the frame of your garage door. This is done by lining up the magnet with the installed sensor and using sheet metal screws to secure to the frame. This step is shown in Figure 8-5.

Figure 8-5
Fastening the magnet
to the garage door
using sheet metal
screws

6. Connect the wiring using butt connectors.

Temperature

Temperature sensors can be installed either indoors or outdoors. The most important issue in temperature sensor installation is placement. Because these sensors are reading temperatures and are sensitive to environmental changes, you shouldn't place the sensor too high (it will read hot, as warm air rises), and you shouldn't place the sensor too low (it will read cold, as cold air sinks). Also, you should keep the sensor away from direct sunlight.

Once you've decided where the sensor will be located, installation follows these steps:

1. Run cabling to the location where you want your temperature sensor positioned. You might need to use fish tape if you are running the cabling through a finished wall.

2. Prepare the cabling by stripping insulation from the cable (shown in Figure 8-6) and three of the wires (black, red, and white).

Figure 8-6
Stripping the insulation from the cabling

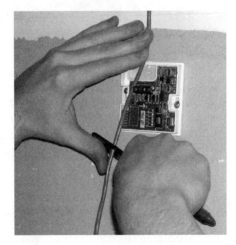

3. Remove the back of the temperature sensor casing. This allows access to the sensor's electronics.

4. Place the sensor on the wall and use a level to ensure it will be mounted squarely, as shown in Figure 8-7.

Figure 8-7
Leveling the temperature sensor and marking its location

5. Mark and drill mounting holes.

6. Install wall anchors if connecting the sensor to sheetrock, as shown in Figure 8-8. This is done by drilling a pilot hole, then tapping the plastic wall anchor into the wall with a hammer.

Figure 8-8
Installing a wall anchor

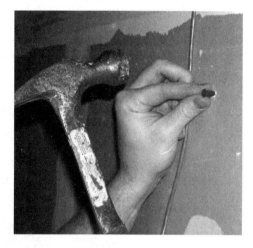

When Are Anchors Necessary?

If you are able to locate the temperature sensor over a wall stud, you don't need anchors. However, if you are placing the sensor on sheetrock, it's a good idea to ensure the sensor doesn't pull out of the wall.

Whether or not you use an anchor (or need the stud) will depend largely on the size of the sensor you're installing. Since temperature sensors are somewhat large, it is a good idea to make sure they won't pull out the sheetrock. In the event a sensor does pull free from the wall, it will be difficult to reinstall it in the existing holes. The next step is to use a larger screw, which might or might not fit the holes in your sensor. Plus, you run the risk of the sensor pulling out of the wall again.

7. Perform any knockouts that are necessary.

8. Fasten the sensor to the wall.

9. Connect the wires to the sensor in the following manner (shown in Figure 8-9):

   ❏ Red to AUX 12V

   ❏ Black to ground

   ❏ White to the (+) side of a zone input

Figure 8-9
Connecting wires to
the temperature
sensor

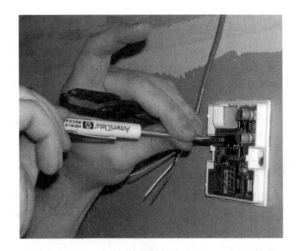

10. Replace the cover on the sensor.

TIPS OF THE TRADE

Connecting Multipurpose Sensors

If you're connecting a combination temperature/humidity sensor, you will use all four wires on the cable. This connection will use not only the power and ground terminals on your control panel, but the other two wires will be connected to the (+) terminals on two separate zone inputs.

This connection on zone inputs is necessary because the sensor will read two items—temperature and humidity. However, because they are combined into a single package, power need only be drawn from a single source.

On the exterior of the garage we placed a second temperature sensor. This sensor was placed on the underside of the soffit. This keeps the sensor out of the elements and direct sunlight. This sensor is shown in Figure 8-10.

Figure 8-10
Exterior temperature
sensor placement

Connection to Smart Home System

Not every Smart Home will be connected the same way. We're using the Omni II, in conjunction with X10 devices, to provide the functionality we want. Depending on the size and complexity of your project, you might not be using an Omni system. You might be using a Stargate home control system, or you can simply connect these devices to an X10 system. How you connect these sensors will depend on the system you're using.

Security System

Connecting the sensors to your security system follows the steps we outlined in Chapter 6. Since the garage door sensor has only two leads, each wire is connected to a terminal of a zone input. When connecting to a security system or a home automation system (like the Stargate), this sensor can be set up to signal the control panel to take whatever action you deem necessary if it is tripped. With security systems that offer the level of X10 functionality that the Omni series provides, a series of events can be triggered when the garage door is opened.

X10

We've been banging the Omni system's gong pretty loudly for the last few chapters. But even though we're enjoying the added benefits of connecting to the Omni system, we don't want you to think that you need to buy a US$1,200 security system to get whole house automation. You can add a Powerflash module to generate a signal for your X10 devices.

HEADS UP!

Other Ways to Use a Powerflash Module

The Powerflash module isn't only meant to work with a garage door sensor. The Powerflash module works with any sensor that detects a contact closure (like a door sensor) or the presence of a low-voltage signal (between 6 to 18V AV, DC, and audio).

The Powerflash module differs from other X10 devices in that it doesn't receive commands; rather, it sends X10 commands from its own inputs. This device plugs into a wall receptacle and when a contact closure is made or a low-voltage signal is applied to the terminals, different behavior can be programmed. For example, the Powerflash can be connected to the garage door sensor that we just installed. Then, when the garage door opens, an X10-capable light can be turned on automatically.

The Powerflash module provides three different modes:

❏ **Mode 1**   All lights are turned on and one appliance is sent either an on or off signal.

❏ **Mode 2**   All lights are sent a flashing on or off signal.

❏ **Mode 3**   An on or off signal is sent for a single unit code.

Setup   The Powerflash, pictured in Figure 8-11, connects to leads from your sensor, then plugs into a power outlet. When the sensor detects a break in the contact (that is, when the garage door opens), the Powerflash module will send a signal to its preprogrammed X10 companion device (or devices) to turn on. In this case, let's set up a lamp in the mudroom to turn on when the garage door opens.

Figure 8-11
The Powerflash module is used to add X10 capability to sensors (Photo courtesy of Smarthome.com)

10 MINUTES

Installation requires a little mechanical ability, but it is very simple:

1. Make sure your sensor is located near an AC receptacle. The leads from the sensor must be able to reach the receptacle. If it cannot reach one, you will have to splice additional wiring to the leads.

2. Strip the insulation from the sensor's wires.

3. Attach the contacts from your garage door sensor to the Powerflash device.

4. Plug the Powerflash into a wall receptacle.

5. Set the Powerflash to Mode 3, Input B (this configures the module so that a single device is turned on).

6. In the mudroom, plug a lamp into an X10 module. These modules sell for US$12.99 An example of a plug-in X10 module is shown in Figure 8-12.

Figure 8-12
An X10 module

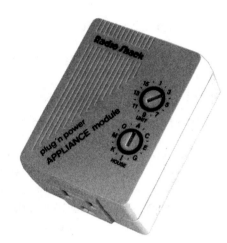

7. Plug the X10 module into the wall.

Using Other Devices with a Powerflash Module

We simply use an X10 lamp module for the sake of explaining this project more simply. Since this project utilizes X10, you could program any X10 device to activate when the garage door is opened. For instance, another way to illuminate the mudroom in our example is to replace the light switch on the wall with an X10-compatible switch.

By the same token, you could connect an X10 appliance module to your stereo. When your garage door opens, the X10 module could automatically turn on the stereo so you are greeted with music upon your return home.

Configuration   Once everything has been installed, configuration is simple enough. Locate the two dials on each of your X10 devices. Again, these dials control the House code (A-P) and Unit code (1-16). In order for the garage door's action to be interpreted by other X10 devices in your home, set the House and Unit code on the Powerflash to the same code used on the X10 lamp module.

Remember, with X10 you are not limited to controlling just one device. If you want more than one device to operate when the garage door opens, set the Powerflash module and all the devices you wish to activate to the same House and Unit code.

Lawn/Exterior

The next stop on our tour of the Smart Home is its exterior, including the lawn. This section examines setting up a sensor on your fence's gate, along with water sensors that can help prevent overwatering your lawn.

Gate Sensor

Open door/window sensors aren't just limited to indoor use. You need not use them simply to monitor your front door, windows, and so forth. Rather, they can be installed outside your Smart Home to extend Smart Home functions into your yard.

For example, we've installed an open/close sensor on the outside gate. When connected to the rest of our Smart Home system, this can be set up to do something as intense as sounding an alarm if someone comes through the gate, simply logging the event, or going the courteous route and turning on an exterior light.

Outside the home, installation still follows the basics of what we've done inside the house (flip back to Chapter 6 for a reminder). However, there are some issues that should be considered.

First, there is a larger danger of tampering than for sensors installed indoors. Consider a gate connected to a chain-link fence. It's easy enough for someone to reach through the fence and tamper with the sensor. That doesn't mean you should forget installing contact sensors on the exterior of your home, but don't let your security system rely too heavily on these sensors. You certainly can connect them to an alarm, but make sure other points of entry are also covered.

Since these sensors will be located outside, they are more susceptible to the elements. As such, you can ameliorate any damage from water, snow, squirrels, or other acts of God by ensuring the butt connectors are seated securely before crimping. There are also waterproof splice kits you can buy that are specifically designed for outdoor use. Splices and connections can also be waterproofed by wrapping the butt connector in electrical tape, or by using some heat shrink tubing. This tubing is cut to a specific length, placed over the connection, and then a hair dryer-like device called a heat gun is used to heat up the tubing, causing it to shrink and encase the connection.

HEADS UP!

Keeping Your Wiring out of Sight

If you connect a sensor to a fence gate, you can keep the wires out of sight and out of the elements by running the wire through a hollow fence post or support.

Water Sensors and Systems

The Mini-Clik Water Sensor (shown in Figure 8-13) connects to an existing lawn watering system. Retailing for US$28.95, when it senses rain the sensor will turn off your sprinkler controller so you don't waste water on your lawn. The Mini-Clik utilizes *hygroscopic* disks to sense the presence of water. When it rains, these disks absorb water and simulate your lawn's drying characteristics.

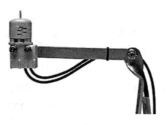

Figure 8-13
The Mini-Clik
water sensor
(Photo courtesy of
Smarthome.com)

The sensor is adjustable from 1/8 to 1 inch of water. The reset rate (this is the rate at which the sensor dries out) is also adjustable. There are two models of this particular product:

❑ **Normally Closed**   With this model, the contacts are closed when the sensor is dry, and then opens when rain is sensed. When the hygroscopic disks dry, the sensors close again. This model is used to turn off the sprinkler system when it starts to rain.

❑ **Normally Open**   With this model, the contacts are open when the sensor is dry, then close when rain is detected. This model would be used to activate a behavior (such as turning on lighting) when rain is detected.

This water sensor can be connected to any home automation controller, like a Stargate or our Omni II system. Like the garage door sensor, this sensor can also be connected to a Powerflash module for X10 operation.

For example, a Mini-Clik (normally open) can be connected to the Powerflash and then plugged into an AC receptacle. When the sensor detects rain, a signal can be sent to turn on interior lighting. For more information on the Mini-Clik, visit the Hunter Products web site at www.hunterindustries.com.

But the sensor need not only be connected to your sprinkler system. Automated sprinkler systems (like those made by Hunter Products, for example) can be connected to the zone inputs of your home automation controller. For example, when connecting our automated sprinkler system to the Omni II system, the solenoid of the sprinkler system is connected to the zone inputs on the Omni. This allows the watering system to become an integrated part of our overall Smart Home system. If the Mini-Clik sensor detects rain, a signal can be sent to the control panel, which in turn can turn off the sprinklers and turn on lighting. Also, the sprinkler system can be set on a schedule, which will allow you to set up a preprogrammed watering plan. For instance, you can set up the watering schedule so it occurs for an hour before the sun comes up.

Other Exterior Smart Home Projects

Some other cool…er…I mean…*useful* projects you can do to smarten up the exterior of your home can help your overall home security, not only from neighborhood thugs trying to make off with your Christmas decorations, but also the critters who nibble at the carrots in your vegetable garden. You can also free up your Saturday afternoons by deploying a robot to tend to the lawn.

In this section, we'll take a closer look at some of these projects. Even though we won't go into the step-by-steps of installing these projects, we'll talk about them so you can decide for yourself if they are something you want to set up. Some don't integrate with the rest of the Smart Home per se, but they do perform smart functions that are unique and interesting all on their own.

Water Repeller

If you've got a garden, you know how much trouble rabbits and other cute little critters can create. Sure, they look all cute and cuddly in Disney movies, but in real life they can be furry little nuisances kicking over your garbage can or digging up your garden. Your hard work raking, hoeing, watering, and weeding can be usurped in one evening by these hungry little beasts. If you want to keep animals out of your yard (whether for the protection of your vegetable garden or for another reason), a water repeller can be installed to scare them away.

The Scarecrow Water Repeller (shown in Figure 8-14) sells for US$69.99. It is anchored to your lawn using a spike and connected to a garden hose. It utilizes a passive infrared sensor to detect motion. When it senses something crawling around your yard, it emits a noise, and then follows it up with a three- to four-second blast of water.

Figure 8-14
The Scarecrow
Water Repeller
(Photo courtesy
Smarthome.com)

The repeller has a 35-foot range and can be adjusted to spray water between a 10-degree and a full 360-degree area.

Scaring Animals with Water and Sound

The sound emitted by the Scarecrow is reminiscent of Pavlov's famous experiment with dogs. When the critters hear the Scarecrow make noise, those who have already been treated to a blast of water will scamper off even before the water hits them. Also, to keep the animals from getting too smart, it's a good idea to rotate the water repeller to different locations in your yard.

Robotic Lawn Mower

You work all week so you can feed and shelter your family. Why should your weekends be absorbed with yard work? Thankfully, 21st century technology has made it possible for you to deploy a robot to perform the menial task of mowing the lawn.

Robotic lawn mowers (like the RoboMower shown in Figure 8-15) look like giant computer mice. They are battery powered (no gas tank to fill or oil level to check), so they don't belch out exhaust. Using a combination of robotic programming and invisible fencing, these robots can mow up to 6,000 square feet of yard on a single battery charge.

Figure 8-15
Friendly Robotics'
RoboMower robotic
lawn mower
(Photo courtesy of
Smarthome.com)

The mower knows to stay in its own yard because the lawn is bounded by a "fence" created by a wire that is placed flush to the surface of the lawn. Installation takes time to place the wire, but there is no digging involved as the wire is kept in place by small plastic stakes. This wire can also be placed around flowerbeds and other areas where you don't want your robotic lawnmower to venture.

With the RoboMower, a series of sensors allows the mower to navigate around trees, and tilt sensors turn off the mower within one second if the ground angle exceeds 20 degrees, preventing runaway mowers.

With your robotic mower making short work of the lawn while you sit in your hammock sipping lemonade, you're sure to be the envy of everyone in the neighborhood. But what happens if that envy takes a more diabolical turn? How do you prevent your Saturday saver from being swiped by an unscrupulous neighbor? The RoboMower has a built-in theft deterrent system. The mower requires a four-digit code to be entered. Without it, the mower won't work.

Friendly Robotics sells its RoboMower RL800 for US$699.99. Toro offers its 30050 iMow robotic lawnmower for US$499.99. For more information on these mowers, visit Friendly Robotics at www.friendlyrobotics.com or Toro at www.toro.com.

Protect Your Belongings

If you've spent the time, energy, and resources to spruce up your yard for Halloween, Christmas, or any other holiday, you know how frustrating it can be when neighborhood thugs come by and either vandalize or outright steal your decorations. There is a good way to protect your stuff utilizing Smart Home technology.

Using a wireless motion sensor (like the Motion Alert wireless sensor shown in Figure 8-16) your decorations or other property can be monitored. The Motion Alert (which sells for US$59.99) consists of two parts: a motion sensor/transmitter and a receiver. This device can also be used to monitor cars parked in the driveway or on the street, sheds, or anything else you need to keep an eye on.

Figure 8-16
Motion Alert wireless
motion sensor
(Photo courtesy of
Smarthome.com)

The motion sensor/transmitter is attached to the item you wish to protect. Use double-sided tape or screws to attach it. Next, place the receiver within 300 feet of the sensor/transmitter. Plug the receiver into an AC receptacle and whenever the sensor is tripped, a loud chime will be emitted.

If you have more than one item you wish to monitor, simply buy additional sensors (individually, they retail for US$24.99). If you want to extend the reach of the device, add an antenna that extends the unit's range up to 500 feet. The antenna sells for US$34.99. For more information on this sensor, visit www.designtech-intl.com.

Don't limit yourself to just taking care of the inside of your Smart Home. There's a lot of stuff going on outside that you can streamline with some technology. In the next chapter, we'll continue our discussion of exterior matters with a project installing a motion-detecting X10 light that is connected to our home's X10 system. From there, we'll step back inside to talk more about lighting the Smart Home.

TESTING 1-2-3

❏   Did you drill pilot holes for the garage sensors?

❏   Are the House and Unit Codes on the Powerflash module the same as the device you wish to activate?

❏   Are your sensors so large they require wall anchors?

❏   Are sensor wires attached to outdoor gates tucked away or otherwise hidden to prevent tampering?

Part III

Smart Home Utility Systems

Chapter 9

Lighting the Smart Home

Tools of the Trade

Assorted screwdrivers
Wire connectors
Exterior X10 floodlight
X10 dimmer switch
X10 motion sensor
Floodlight bulbs
Rotozip tool
Voltmeter or voltage sensor

The cornerstone of most Smart Home projects is the ability to automatically turn on and turn off lights. Naturally, these lights can be located on your home's interior or exterior. This chapter will discuss not only interior and exterior lighting, but also the Smart Home devices you should consider for your own individual projects.

X10 Components

The primary method we're going to use to add functionality to our Smart Home is through the addition of X10 devices. This is a good choice for us because X10 uses existing home wiring to make things happen. This section covers the various types of X10 devices you're likely to use in a Smart Home illumination solution.

Dimmers

Lest you think: "Yeah, sure. Smart Homes are cool and all, but why would I just want to turn lights on and off?" Remember, these are Smart Homes and you can do so much more than simply turn a light on or turn it off. You can add the power of brightening and dimming to your project!

In this context, we're talking about hardwired lighting fixtures—like the one in your entryway, or the one in your bedroom. We'll talk about plug-in units (which can manage not only lights but other appliances as well) in the next section.

Wall Switches

X10 wall switches replace the switches that are already in your home. Once you've turned off the circuit breaker to the switch, these install into the existing switch boxes, connect to the same wiring, and oftentimes are able to use the same mounting hardware.

HEADS UP!

Switches Can Be on/off, Too

Wall switches don't have to be dimmers. A simple on/off X10 switch retails for US$12.99 and can provide X10 functionality for places where you don't want to add a dimmer.

Before the switch is installed, rotate the House and Unit Codes (those two little dials on the device) to the desired code. Once all the connections are made, you're set and ready to go. We'll walk you through the process of installation later in this chapter.

TIPS OF THE TRADE

Develop Your Own X10 Code

When selecting your X10 codes, it's a good idea to stay away from codes A1 through B16. That's because they are popular codes and it's more likely that, if your neighbor has X10 gear, he or she is using codes in that range. Instead, stick to House Codes in the middle range, like D, E, F, and G.

In-line Modules

In some locations, you might not want to change your light switch, but still want X10 functionality. Inline dimmers can be added to a light switch (mounted inside the lighting fixture using double-sided tape) and ameliorate the need to install a special switch. An inline module by HomePro is shown in Figure 9-1.

Figure 9-1
An inline X10 module
(Photo courtesy
Smarthome.com)

For example, these modules (HomePro has both dimming and non-dimming modules that sell for US$27.99 and US$25.99, respectively) can be used when controlling fluorescent lighting without providing dimming capabilities. Also, inline modules are good for applications that control motor loads, like ceiling fans.

Plug-in Units

The previous X10 units we've discussed necessitated turning off power at the circuit breaker, unscrewing an outlet or a switch, removing the old device, then installing the X10 unit. The modules you install are great if you want something that's hidden and integrated with the house itself. However, if the thought of messing with replacing outlets and light switches with X10 modules is more than you care to deal with, there is an easy—a *very* easy—alternative: plug-in modules.

Plug-in modules are used to bring X10 functionality to individual devices. It's rather straightforward to set the House and Unit codes to the desired setting, plug the appliance into the X10 module, then plug that into the wall receptacle.

There are a number of plug-in units that can be used for X10 functionality.

Lamp

Lamp modules, like the one shown in Figure 9-2, are devices into which a standard lamp is plugged. These modules are reasonably inexpensive, costing US$11.99. Once plugged in, the device can be turned on, turned off, dimmed, or brightened.

HEADS UP!

Lamp Modules

Lamp modules look a lot like appliance modules (which we'll talk about next); however, lamp modules should never be used for appliances.

Figure 9-2
A lamp plug-in
module
(Photo courtesy
Smarthome.com)

Appliance

Appliance modules, like the one shown in Figure 9-3, differ from lamp modules in that they accommodate appliances that operate up to 300 watts. Appliance modules are good for fans, stereos, televisions, and so forth. They come in two- and three-pin configurations, for appliances that must be grounded (like stereos, for instance). Three-pin configurations are rated for 15 amps and 1/3 horse-power. Both two-pin and three-pin modules can be purchased for US$12.99.

Figure 9-3
An appliance
plug-in module
(Photo courtesy
Smarthome.com)

Appliance Modules Click when Operating

One consideration when purchasing and using appliance modules is that they make a loud clicking noise when they activate and deactivate.

Two-Way

Two-way modules look just like any other X10 device and provide the same functionality as other X10 devices. However, they offer the ability to check on the status of a device. Assuming you have the requisite controller (stand-alone or computer-based) that can work with two-way X10 modules, you can check to see if a device is on or off. For example, while seated at your computer in your home office, you could use a two-way module to see if you left the lights on in the living room.

Screw-in

The previous modules have all been used to plug into the wall, then plug a lamp or appliance into it. However, what if you want to add X10 functionality to a ceiling mounted light, but you don't feel like installing an X10 wall switch or an inline dimmer? Simple. Use a screw-in X10 module, like the one shown in Figure 9-4.

Figure 9-4
A screw-in X10 module
(Photo courtesy Smarthome.com)

Selling for US$16.99, these modules are as easy to install as screwing in a light bulb. These units are capable of handling incandescent lights up to 150 watts.

HEADS UP!

Screw-in Modules Add Extra Size to an Outlet
Be sure to check the size of your screw-in module and compare it to the area in which it will be used. These modules add some extra size to your light bulb, so if the bulb is already a little low, make sure you won't smack your head against it when the module is installed.

Heavy Duty

Want your spa warmed up and ready when you come home from work? Simply plug a heavy-duty X10 module into the AC receptacle, and you'll be in business. Heavy-duty units, like the one shown in Figure 9-5, are used to control 220V devices—such as the aforementioned spa, water heaters, washers, dryers, hot water heaters, and so forth.

Figure 9-5
Heavy duty plug-in
X10 module
(Photo courtesy
Smarthome.com)

20 AMP   15 AMP

Heavy-duty modules can be purchased in 15 amp and 20 amp varieties (retailing for US$20.99). Make sure to check the prongs on your appliance to make sure you purchase the correct module. Twenty amp modules utilize a t-shaped plug for the leftmost pin and a horizontal plug for the rightmost pin. Fifteen amp modules use two horizontal plugs for both pins.

Wall Receptacles

Wall receptacles, like the one shown in Figure 9-6, allow you to provide X10 functionality to a specific outlet.

Figure 9-6
X10 wall receptacle
(Photo courtesy
Smarthome.com)

Wall receptacles come in a variety of flavors, including standard designs (both outlets are X10 controlled), split (only one of the outlets is X10 enabled, the other outlet is always on), or heavy duty (which can accommodate large appliances). Heavy-duty receptacles (like the one shown in Figure 9-7) sell for US$45.99, while standard 110V units run anywhere between US$18 and US$30.

Figure 9-7
Heavy-duty X10
wall receptacle
(Photo courtesy
Smarthome.com)

There's a certain amount of paradigm shift that must accompany the use of X10 outlets. Whereas plug-in modules are useful to go with a lamp or an appliance to any outlet in the house, once you install a wall receptacle, that receptacle will control whatever is plugged into it. As such, if you decide to reorganize the living room and move the stereo to the other side of the room, you must bring the receptacle (or install a new one) if you expect to continue with your X10 functions.

Lighting Modules

To bring integrated control of our Smart Home—specifically the X10 devices—we're advocating the use of a computer with X10 controller software. However, you need not utilize a computer to provide complex lighting scenes. A lighting module (like the PCS In-Line Scene Lighting Module, shown in Figure 9-8) is used to control multiple lights with different preset dim levels. Lighting modules come in inline or plug-in varieties.

Figure 9-8
PCS In-Line Scene
Lighting Module
(Photo courtesy
Smarthome.com)

For example, the PCS In-Line Scene Lighting Module offers one or four lighting circuits that can remember 16 preset dim levels (they retail for US$266.99 or US$199.99, respectively; a two-channel plug-in version sells for US$129.95.) The lighting modules can be activated using an X10 remote (more on X10 remote controls in Chapter 16) and are programmed using an X10 Maxi Controller (US$21.99).

You can establish various scenes that will deliver specific lighting features. For instance, you can set up specific lights to come on at a certain level when you come home from work; or, when you want to watch a movie in the family room, the lights can fade to a preset level.

These modules also offer a fade-up capability, which prevents the light from coming on at full brightness, ripping the eyes out of your sockets. This is especially useful when using the lights to wake up in the morning (note to my old Army drill sergeant: a gradual wakeup would have been a lot nicer than the full-on fluorescent lights and the garbage can chucked down between the bunks!).

Exterior Project

On the exterior of our Smart Home, we're connecting a motion-sensing light. This type of light isn't uncommon or unheard of—in fact, they are quite popular.

These motion-sensing lights turn on when movement is detected. The light stays on for a preset amount of time, then turns off automatically.

Our project is a little different in that when the sensor detects motion, not only will the dual floodlights turn on, it will also transmit X10 signals so it can turn on lights inside the house.

Installation

For this project, we are connecting a Leviton Decora Electronic Controls Motion Detector Photo Sensor Control. This unit attaches to an existing exterior wall box, replacing an old exterior light.

This floodlight is X10 capable and can activate (or be activated by) up to four X10 addresses. For example, when the detector senses motion, it can turn on its floodlights, and it can also turn on a lamp inside the house. Or, we can configure it so that when we turn on our bedside lamp, it triggers the floodlight to turn on as well.

TIPS OF THE TRADE

Using the Same Code

Remember, the number of devices that turn on will be determined by what their code settings are. For example, every X10 device in the house could turn on simultaneously if they are all set to the same address.

Installing the light requires three separate phases: preparing the light fixture, removing the existing light, and connecting the new light. The following explains the steps necessary for each phase.

5 MINUTES

Preparing the Light Fixture

When you open the motion-sensing floodlight box, the unit is disassembled in four pieces: the detector, two lampholders, and a mounting plate. This is not unique to our X10-enabled floodlight. In fact, this is a common design for motion-sensing floodlights. Before connecting the floodlight to the house, it is first necessary to put these four pieces together:

1. Remove the floodlight components from any packaging and plastic outer wrap.

2. Screw the base of each floodlight holder into the outer holes of the mounting plate (shown in Figure 9-9).

Figure 9-9
Screwing the
floodlight holders
into the mounting
plate

3. Rotate the locking ring on each lampholder toward the plate until it is secure against the plate (shown in Figure 9-10).

Figure 9-10
Rotating the locking
ring on each lamp
holder

4. Screw the motion detector into the center hole on the mounting plate (shown in Figure 9-11).

Figure 9-11
Attaching the motion
detector to the
mounting plate

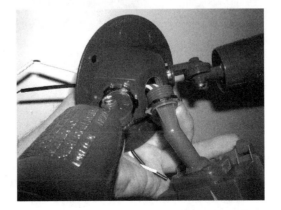

5. Lock the motion detector into place using the locking ring.

6. Find the white (neutral) wire from each lamp holder and the white wire from the motion detector (shown in Figure 9-12).

Figure 9-12
Locating the
white wires

7. Connect all three white wires with a wire connector. Simply hold the three bare wires together and screw the connector onto the wires. Keep twisting until the wires are firmly connected. This is shown in Figure 9-13.

Figure 9-13
Connecting the white
wires using a wire
connector

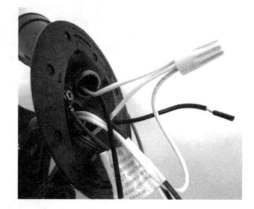

8. Find the black (line) wires from each lampholder and, using a wire connector, connect them to the blue wire from the motion detector.

Once the fixture has been assembled and the connections made, it is time to go outside and hook it to your existing light fixture.

10 MINUTES   ## Removing the Existing Fixture

Installing the light fixture to your home requires an existing wall box that has power supplied all the time, or a wall box that utilizes a wall switch. If you use a wall box that has a connected light switch, turning off the wall switch will deactivate the motion-sensing controls of the floodlight.

Most likely, you will be installing this fixture on a wall box with an existing fixture (as we are). As such, it is necessary to remove the existing fixture, following these steps:

1. The most important step is to turn off power to the fixture at your home's circuit breaker box (as shown in Figure 9-14). Failure to do this can result in a shock or death.

Figure 9-14
Turning off power
at the circuit breaker

2. Once the power has been deactivated, unscrew the two mounting screws holding the light fixture to the home. These screws might be regular standard or Phillips head screws, or the fixture might be held to the home using decorative nuts.

3. Pull the fixture off the house (shown in Figure 9-15).

Figure 9-15
Removing the
old light fixture

4. Unscrew the wire connectors from the white, black, and ground wires.

5. Set the old fixture aside.

Check Color-coded Wiring

When your house is being built, the home is painted with the fixtures not installed, but the wiring having already been pulled. As a result, the wires might be coated in paint, so it will be difficult to tell which wire is which. As such, *before* disconnecting wire connectors, scrape back some paint or mark the wire so you can tell which wire is which.

15 MINUTES

Connecting the New Fixture

Finally, we connect the new, X10 motion-sensing floodlight.

1. Slide the weatherproof gasket over the junction box and route all house wiring through it before making any connections.

2. Connect the green (ground) wire from the light fixture to the bare copper wire in the junction box with a wire connector.

3. Connect the black (line) wire from the house wiring to the black wire from the motion detector using a wire connector.

4. Connect the white (neutral) wire from the house wiring to the white wire from the motion detector using a wire connector. When all the proper connections are made, it will look like the unit shown in Figure 9-16.

Figure 9-16
Completed wiring

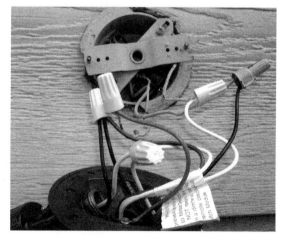

5. Attach the mounting plate to the wall box using the supplied screws.

HEADS UP!

Ensuring a New Fixture Fits

Depending on the size of your junction box and the size of the new light fixture, you might find that the two are not the same size. If your light fixture and junction box do not match up, it will be necessary to buy a mounting bracket that will allow the two to fit together.

6. Turn power back on at the breaker box. When finished, the floodlight will look like the one in Figure 9-17.

Figure 9-17
A connected exterior, motion-sensing X10 floodlight

Configuration

With the particular model of exterior motion-sensing floodlight that we're installing, there are several settings that must also be made: setting up the range, the time the light will remain on, and Smart Home settings.

The following steps are used to configure the Leviton X10-Controlled Motion-Activated Security Lights that we previously installed. We include them here to provide an understanding of what's involved with setting up these lights. However, the steps will be similar for other manufacturers' motion-sensor lights. As always, refer to the manufacturers' instructions when installing and configuring a Smart Home device.

0–? MINUTES

Amount of time required depends on the complexity of your system.

Motion Detector

During daylight hours, it will be difficult to set up your motion-sensing light to identify motion. As such, the detector must be put into the correct mode to allow this behavior. On the Leviton X10-Controlled Motion-Activated Security Light, the control panel is located on the bottom of the motion detector unit, beneath a protective plate. Once the plate is removed, you have access to the motion and

X10 controls, as shown in Figure 9-18. Here's how to configure the lights so they activate when you want them to:

Figure 9-18
The control panel on the exterior motion-detecting floodlight

1. Using a small screwdriver, rotate the DUSK control clockwise to LIGHT. This setting allows the motion detector to think that it is dark, even though it is daylight.

2. Rotate the RANGE control clockwise to MAX.

3. Rotate the TIME DELAY control to the minimum delay (.1 minutes).

4. Loosen the locking nut from the motion detector shaft.

5. Position the motion detector so that it is level, then aim downward, pointing to the area you wish to monitor.

HEADS UP!

Sensor Aiming Considerations

Do not point a motion detector control sensor above the horizon. Direct sunlight will damage the photocell.

6. Walk around the perimeter of the area you wish to monitor. Watch to see if the light comes on when your presence is detected.

7. Reposition the motion detector as needed and continue testing its range.

8. Once you are satisfied with its coverage, tighten the locking nut.

9. As we noted earlier, there are three settings that govern the motion detector's settings. The following explains how they are used:

❏ **Dusk Control** This control is used to tell the sensor how much light needs to be present for it to respond to motion. It is this control that is adjusted to tell at what time the motion-sensing light should be active and inactive. For instance, keep an eye on the lighting. Around dusk, if the lighting comes on earlier than you want, use this adjustment (rotating toward DARK) to cause the lights to activate later. If they come on too late, rotate the dial toward LIGHT.

❏ **Range** This control can also be thought of as the motion detector's sensitivity. When the control is rotated fully to MAX, then the lights will come on for the slightest movement. However, to reduce sensitivity, turn the dial toward MIN. This adjustment is helpful if you want to prevent the light from being activated by small animals, but don't want it so insensitive that burglars are tripping over the TV's power cord as they leave your home.

❏ **Time Delay** This control establishes the length of time you want your lights (or appliances) to stay on once movement has stopped. This setting can range from .1 minute, .5 minutes, 2 minutes, 5 minutes, 15 minutes, or 30 minutes.

Smart Home Settings

The other set of controls manage the exterior light's X10 settings. There are two sets of controls:

❏ **House Code and Start Code** This is where the code is established so that X10 functionality can be included. "Start Code" differs somewhat from the "Unit Code" in that it is a code that will be used in conjunction with your X10 devices' Unit Codes. We'll talk about that in more depth later.

❏ **Sensor** This is a series of four small switches marked IN and OUT. These switches are used to manage behaviors for your other X10 devices. For example, by setting the appropriate House and Start Codes, then selecting the sensor switch, a light in the home can be turned on when the motion detector is activated. The sensor switch can also be set so that if some action inside is taken (a lamp plugged into an X10 unit), the exterior light will come on.

To set these controls, follow these steps:

1. Set the House Code dial on the motion detector to the same letter as all the X10 devices you wish to control. If you want to control the floodlights from other X10 modules, set the House Code to the same letter as the other X10 modules.

2. Set the Start Code to a number between 1 and 16.

3. The Start Code setting is also used to determine the Unit Code for X10 devices that will be controlled by the motion detector. The code for an individual X10 module will be the Start Code, plus the number of the adjacent SENSOR switch. For example, if you want to turn on a lamp inside with the code of D-9, then the code on the motion detector should be set to D-8, with sensor +1 set to the IN position.

4. Set the Unit Code dial on the devices based on the Start Code and Sensor switch selected on the motion detector. For example, if you are using the sensor +2 switch and your code on the motion detector is E-12, then the code on the inside module should be E-14.

Interior Project

Inside the Smart Home, we're installing a number of lighting projects, lights that will turn on given certain behaviors and conditions. One of the projects is to activate a hallway light (at a dimmed level) when a motion sensor detects movement.

This project will require two components. First, we'll need to install a motion detector, then we'll install an X10 light switch that will activate a ceiling-mounted light when the sensor detects motion.

Motion Sensor

For this project, we are using a flush-mounted motion sensor; however, any motion sensor would be acceptable. We chose the Sentrol 6255F Flush Mount SureShot PIR motion detector because it could be mounted inconspicuously. Installation closely follows the steps used for the motion detector in Chapter 6.

In essence, locate your sensor, run the security cabling appropriately, wire the sensor in accordance with the manufacturer's directions, and you're all set. The sensor can be installed either as part of a security system or a home automation system, or it can be a stand-alone unit, connected with an X10 interface. We'll explain how to set up the project both ways.

Hardwired

The major difference between this sensor and the one previously installed is that, because it is flush mounted, we had to find a location for the sensor, then use the Rotozip tool to create an opening into which a gang box was inserted and nailed to a stud. Next, the security cabling was pulled to the gang box and the sensor installed.

TIPS OF THE TRADE

Motion Detector Placement

If you are running security cabling through your attic or ceiling, you can always locate a motion detector on the ceiling. The Motion Detector Police won't come and take you away if you locate the sensor somewhere other than on a wall.

X10

If you choose not to install a security system, it is still possible to enjoy the benefits of this project by only using X10 gear. The Version II Wireless X10 Motion Sensor (shown in Figure 9-19) retails for US$20.99 and requires a US$24.99 wireless receiver (shown in Figure 9-20, the receiver can be used for up to 16 wireless X10 devices). When the motion sensor detects activity, it sends a signal to the wireless receiver, which in turn sends an ON signal to the associated X10 address. In this case, the signal would be sent to the X10 dimmer switch attached to the hallway light.

Figure 9-19
Version II Wireless X10 Motion Sensor (Photo courtesy Smarthome.com)

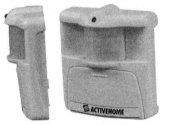

Figure 9-20
Wireless X10 receiver
(Photo courtesy
Smarthome.com)

X10 Dimmer

When the motion detector senses activity, it will send an X10 signal either via our Omni II security system, or via an X10 device. This signal will be programmed for reception by our X10 dimmer switch.

TIPS OF THE TRADE

Different X10 Outlet Options

Remember, there are a number of options for installing an X10-capable light fixture, not just the switch we're installing. You can opt for a screw-in module, an inline module, or a dimmer with different functions, including two-way capabilities. If you'd rather pursue one of the other options, feel free to do so. With the exception of the screw-in module (which is fairly self explanatory), the process for installing other X10 switches and inline modules will be somewhat similar. As always, be sure to read your manufacturer's instructions before beginning.

Before starting, set the X10 code on your switch to whatever you choose. To help remember the code later (and so you don't have to pull the switch out of the wall to check), it's a good idea to jot down the code on a master list somewhere.

To install the X10 dimmer switch, follow these steps:

1. Turn off the power at the circuit breaker.

2. Remove the switch plate of the existing switch.

3. Unscrew the mounting screws holding the switch to the gang box.

4. Once the switch is out, unscrew the terminals holding the wires into the switch, as shown in Figure 9-21. Depending on the switch that is installed, it might be easier to simply use a wire cutter to detach the switch from the wiring. If you have to do this, you'll also need a wire stripper to get at the copper wire beneath the insulation.

Figure 9-21
Remove the old
light switch

Three-way Lighting Wiring

When you remove the switch, you should have two wires coming out of the gang box (and possibly a ground wire). If there are three, then one is likely a traveler wire for a three-way switch. Most often, this third wire is yellow. If you've purchased a switch that is capable of handling three-way lighting, you'll use a wire connector to connect the traveler wire to the appropriate wire on the switch (but not yet!). If you are not using a three-way switch, cap this wire with a wire connector. If your switch is wired for three-way application but there is no traveler wire, be sure to cap the lead on your switch.

5. Next, you must determine which lead is the line wire. Make sure no exposed wires are touching anything else and that no one is near the switch. Go back to the circuit breaker and turn the breaker back on.

6. Being careful not to touch any bare wire, use a voltmeter or a voltage sensor to test each wire. With one wire of the voltage tester on the ground, test each remaining wire. When the voltmeter or the voltage sensor detects 120V, then you've found the line (or hot) wire. Most often, this wire is black. Ensure no one is near the wires, then turn the circuit breaker off again.

HEADS UP!

When to Contact a Professional

If you don't feel comfortable testing wiring to determine which is hot and which is not, don't mess around—call a professional electrician.

7. Once you've turned the power off at the circuit breaker again, connect the line wire to the line connection on the switch using a wire connector, shown in Figure 9-22.

Figure 9-22
Connect the house line wire to the line wire of the switch.

8. With some switches, there will be a bare copper wire. This should be connected to the ground wire in the gang box.

9. If your switch requires a neutral wire to be connected, make this connection with a wire connector. Typically, the neutral wire will be white.

10. Connect the load wire of the house to the load wire on the switch. Secure it with a wire connector. Most often, this wire is red. The final installation will look similar to the picture in Figure 9-23. Note that the shown switch does not utilize a neutral wire and the traveler wire has been capped off.

Figure 9-23
A wired X10 dimmer switch

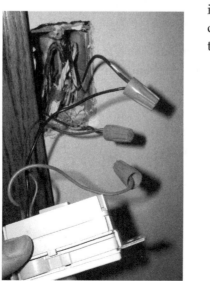

11. Once all the connections are made, turn on the power and test the light. Don't screw the switch into the wall until you've tested it to ensure that it is properly connected; that way, you won't have to unscrew the switch and make changes.

12. When you're happy that the switch is connected properly, reinstall the switch and wall plate.

Now that your switch and motion detector have been installed, it's necessary to program the X10 system to create the dimming scheme we want. If you're using a wireless X10 motion detector, it is easy enough to set the codes on each device (the wireless base and the light) to turn on the light. However, if you are building this project as part of a larger home automation project, it is a good idea to control the light's behavior through an X10 controller. After we cover some more X10 and Smart Home projects, we'll talk about how you can program your sundry X10 devices to work together. If you can't wait to see how this project ends, flip ahead to Chapter 15.

❑ Did you turn off the power at the circuit breaker before installing any switches or light fixtures?

❑ Did you turn the power back on after installing the switches or light fixtures?

❑ Did you test the coverage area of your motion detector to ensure that it is set properly?

❑ Are the X10 codes set up appropriately for all your devices?

❑ Are you trying to run an appliance off a plug in X10 lamp module, rather than an appliance module?

Chapter 10

The Smart Home Kitchen and Bathroom

Tools of the Trade

Thread sealing tape
Adjustable wrenches
Screwdriver
Level
Drill
Pencil
Two-conductor wire
Screws

In most of the Smart Home, we've identified several projects that can enhance a normally hum-drum room. Lights can be programmed to turn on at a specific time, an open garage door can trigger a series of events in the house, and security systems can be monitored via the Internet. True enough, Smart Home functionality can be implemented throughout your home, even the kitchen, bathroom, and laundry room, all of which are the focus of this chapter.

Many of the projects in this chapter won't be integrated to your larger Smart Home project (although some can be). For the most part, these projects are stand-alone by nature. There is, to some degree, a lack of integration when it comes to your Smart Home's kitchen, bathroom, and laundry room. However, don't forget that you can always add X10 AC receptacles, plug-in adapters, and light fixtures to control specific appliances.

Lights need not only be installed in bedrooms and hallways. For example, if you decide you want your bathroom lighting to activate when your alarm clock rings in the morning (or more appropriate to the Smart Home, when your lights slowly brighten at wake up time), you can certainly install and program an X10 light fixture in your bathroom.

However, there are other devices and gadgets that can add security and comfort to these rooms. Let's take a closer look at these various rooms and talk about some of the projects you can connect to provide a smarter living environment.

Kitchen

When considering smartening up your kitchen, there are a number of ways you can add functionality. Again, there isn't a whole lot out there in terms of home automation. After all, why would you want to make your garbage disposal or blender X10-compatible (although you could with the plug-in X10 modules we described in Chapter 9)?

There are two different devices we'll talk about for the Smart Home's kitchen, beyond lights and outlets. The first is somewhat of a pie-in-the-sky device, but if you have the money for it, you might want to buy an Internet Refrigerator. The other, the Stove Guard, is a little more sensibly priced and will help prevent kitchen fires.

Internet Refrigerator

Can't bring yourself to leave the kitchen to check your e-mail or watch some TV? Thanks to a convergence of kitchen appliances, technology, and engineers with way too much time on their hands, LG Electronics has developed its LRSPC2661T Internet Refrigerator. The refrigerator can be used for watching television, surfing the Internet, looking at pictures, or sending and receiving e-mail.

The side-by-side unit has a 16.9 cubic foot refrigerator and an 8.7 cubic foot freezer. In addition to an ice maker, water dispenser, an electronic temperature control with six sensors, and a fingerprint-proof titanium finish, it offers the following features:

❑ A tilting 15.1-inch digital LCD monitor with remote control

❑ Four Hi-Fi speakers from which you can listen to Internet radio or MP3s

❑ A full Internet connection, over which you could control your Smart Home, if you are so connected

❑ A built-in digital camera that allows you to take pictures then save them in a photo album or e-mail them to friends and family

❏ Capability of leaving video or audio messages for family members. You can also leave text messages using a keyboard or electronic pen

❏ Ability to organize favorite recipes or find new ones on the Internet

❏ Capability of monitoring expiration dates on food

❏ Self-diagnostics, which tell you if components are failing

TIPS OF THE TRADE

Installing the Requisite Connections

If you decide to buy an Internet Refrigerator, it is a good idea to install your Ethernet connection and your cable connection to the refrigerator's site before the refrigerator is delivered. Otherwise, the most your new Internet Refrigerator will be able to do is keep food cold. That's so 20th century.

The refrigerator has a Windows-based operating system and a 20GB hard drive (don't worry about junior filling the hard drive up with games; they can't be installed and played on the fridge). The refrigerator has two Universal Serial Bus (USB) connectors and two serial ports to import and export data.

The Internet Refrigerator retails for only US$7,999. For more information on the Internet Refrigerator, go to www.lgappliances.com.

Stove Guard

Probably a more realistic purchase, as compared to the Internet Refrigerator, is the Stove Guard. The Stove Guard is a device that automatically shuts off your stove when you forget to shut it off. The Stove Guard, pictured in Figure 10-1, retails for US$159.99.

The Stove Guard utilizes a combination of a motion sensor and an internal timer. When the Stove Guard no longer senses your presence, the internal timer starts running. If the stove is on, and you leave the kitchen, the Stove Guard will turn off the stove after a predetermined amount of time (you can set the timer between 1 and 99 minutes). If you return to the kitchen before the timer runs down, the Stove Guard will sense your return and stop its countdown.

Figure 10-1
The Stove Guard
(Photo courtesy
Smarthome.com)

HEADS UP!

The Stove Guard is only compatible with electric stoves. If you have a gas stove, the Stove Guard won't work.

5 MINUTES

Installation of the Stove Guard is rather straightforward:

1. Turn off power to the stove at the circuit breaker.
2. Pull out the stove.
3. Attach the Stove Guard power box between the 240V stove plug and the wall outlet.
4. Mount the control and sensor unit in an easy-to-reach location near the stove.

Bathroom

Just because it's usually the littlest room in the house doesn't mean it has to be the dumbest room as well. There are plenty of ways you can add smart functionality to your bathroom. Like the Smart Home kitchen, the bathroom doesn't lend itself to a lot of integrated systems; however, there are a number of gadgets that serve useful, utilitarian purposes.

Toilet FlowManager

The theme song from the movie *Jaws* is synonymous with danger in the water, and anyone who has ever watched the water rise and rise in their toilet bowl may hear the strings in the John Williams classic crescendoing until, finally, the water overflows and spills onto the floor. Now, thanks to the FlowManager, we need never hear that familiar theme, except in a movie theater or while watching the video.

The FlowManager, shown in Figure 10-2, retails for US$89.99 and is used to detect and prevent toilet overflows and leaks.

Toilet overflows may not only be messy and inconvenient, they can also cause damage to floors, baseboards, drywall, and the ceiling below the offending toilet. Additionally, overflows can cause mold growth that lead to allergic reactions and even asthma.

The FlowManager prevents these problems by utilizing a sensor, clipped to the inside of the toilet bowl rim. When the bowl sensor detects rising water, it

sends a signal to a sensor on the main controller to turn off the flow of water, and then emits an audible alarm, alerting you to problems.

Leaky toilets do not pose the same damage dangers that overflows do; however, a leaky flapper—caused by mineral build-up—can waste gallons and gallons of water. This, naturally, jacks up your utility bill. To ameliorate this problem, the FlowManager utilizes a sensor, placed inside the tank, that sends a signal to the main controller when a leak is detected.

Once a trouble signal is sent to the main controller, the FlowManager shuts off water only to the problem toilet; other plumbing in the rest of the house is un-affected. When the situation has been resolved, normal water flow to the toilet is restored with the press of a single button. If the alarm is annoying to you and you are working on fixing the problem, the alarm can be silenced by pressing a single button. The FlowManager operates using four AA batteries.

Motion-activated Soap Dispenser

There's somewhat of a chicken-and-the-egg issue that comes when you wash your hands. When you try to get liquid soap from the dispenser, your filthy hands leave some grunge on the dispenser. Sure, your hands are clean, but now the dispenser is in rough shape.

One solution to the problem is the use of a hands-free, motion-activated soap dispenser, like the one shown in Figure 10-3, which retails for US$34.99.

This particular model is battery operated and is useful not only in your Smart Home's bathroom, but would be well placed in your mudroom, garage, utility room, or anywhere else you want to be able to dole out soap or lotion without touching the dispenser.

Figure 10-3
A hands-free
soap dispenser
(Photo courtesy
Smarthome.com)

Its features include these:

❏ Ability to dispense liquid soap or lotion

❏ Low battery indicator

❏ Window to view the level of soap or lotion

❏ Infrared sensor

❏ Dispenser adjustable between one to four drops of liquid

Installation is rather straightforward—simply mount it to the wall, install batteries, and fill with either liquid soap or lotion.

Heated Towel Racks

You don't have to spend your day in a loin cloth, chasing down animals for meat; you don't have to bang two rocks together to make fire; and thanks to modern science, you don't have to worry much about scurvy, polio, and cholera. With all these advances, why should you have to dry off with a cold towel?

Heated towel racks, like the one shown in Figure 10-4, have been used in swanky hotels and spas for years, but they can also be installed in your own home. They retail for between US$49.99 and US$209.00, depending on the size of the rack.

Towel warmers are not just good for the sake of convenience, but also for improving hygiene by reducing germs and mildew. Electrically heated towel racks utilize a heating element that runs the length of the rack that allows for an even heat that comes up to temperature quickly, unlike liquid filled heating racks.

To make this even more Smart Home–friendly, you can connect the towel warmer with an X10 module so that the towel warmer activates at a preset time or a given condition. For example, you can program the X10 module to start warming up the towel rack when the bathroom light is turned on.

These towel racks aren't just good for your Smart Home bathroom, but they are also useful in exercise rooms and rooms next to spas, hot tubs, and pools.

Figure 10-4
Heated towel rack
(Photo courtesy
Smarthome.com)

They can also be used for warming clothes, blankets, robes, or for drying clothes that are too delicate for the household dryer.

Installation is accomplished one of two ways: either as a wall-mounted unit or as a freestanding device. Once constructed, according to the manufacturer's directions, simply plug the unit into the wall and it should almost instantly come up to 130 degrees.

Light and Fan Timer

Leaving the light and the exhaust fan on in the bathroom need not be a bother anymore. By installing a timer switch, you don't have to fret about electricity bills going through the roof because of family members forgetting to turn off the lights or the fan.

Leviton sells a switch that allows you to select the amount of time a light or fan (or any other appliance connected to the switch) will run. This switch is shown in Figure 10-5. Depending on whether it will drive a motor (like an exhaust or

Figure 10-5
Timer switch
(Photo courtesy
Smarthome.com)

ceiling fan) and what ranges of time you choose, the switch will cost between US$22.95 and US$27.95.

Pressing the button next to a selected time (for example, the switch shown in Figure 10-5 shows timer settings from 15 minutes down to 2 minutes) activates an LED by that button, showing how long the light or fan will remain activated. When the timer reaches two minutes to shut off, the LED will begin to flash.

15 MINUTES

Installation of this particular device is similar to the steps taken when installing an X10-compatible switch, as explained in Chapter 9.

Laundry Room

Smart Homes don't just have to be about stuff that's cool. There's also a fair amount of utility involved. We've already lauded the merits of security and lighting systems; however, there are other dangers—nonhuman dangers—that can cause messes at best, or serious damage at worst.

The laundry room is home to two of the vilest perpetrators of water damage: your washing machine and water heater. When these appliances overflow, you'll get out lucky if a little water simply spills on the floor. At the other end of the spectrum, the water can destroy sheetrock, spill into carpeted areas, and cause untold thousands of dollars in damage.

This section examines two types of sensors. The first are stand-alone units that automatically shut off the overflowing appliance when it senses water leaking onto the floor. The second is used in conjunction with your whole home automation system (be it a smart security system, a home automation system, or X10 devices) to let you know when there's trouble.

Obviously, each solution has its pros and cons. It's great, and likely to prevent messes and damage, if a sensor can automatically turn off the offending source of water. However, the other solution allows you to be notified as part of a larger Smart Home solution, sending messages to pagers, tripping an alarm, and so forth.

Washing Machine Leak Detector

The damage caused by overflowing washing machines can easily be mitigated by installing an automatic shutoff valve for the machine. These sensors detect leaking water, then automatically turn off water at the valves to the offending unit.

The FloodStop System I, shown in Figure 10-6, sells for US$89.99 and installs in about five minutes, using only a screwdriver.

Figure 10-6
FloodStop System I
washing machine
shutoff valve
(Photo courtesy
Smarthome.com)

10 MINUTES

To install a washing machine shutoff unit (like the FloodStop System I), follow these steps:

1. Turn off both hot and cold water supply lines to the washing machine. These are normally two faucets located near the rear of your washing machine.

2. If you are retrofitting an existing installation, disconnect the washing machine's hoses from existing shutoff valves.

3. Connect one valve to the cold-water manual valve.

4. Connect the other valve to the hot-water manual valve.

5. Connect the cold-water hose from the washing machine to the automatic shutoff valve.

6. Connect the hot-water hose from the washing machine to the automatic shutoff valve.

7. Turn on both cold- and hot-water valves and check for leaks. If leaks are present, retighten the connections.

8. Locate the control unit in a place that is convenient for testing.

9. Plug in the valve and sensor assembly to the control unit.

10. Connect the water sensor using the supplied two-conductor wire.

11. Place the water sensor on the floor, directly underneath the hot and cold water supply hoses.

12. Plug the wall transformer into an 110V wall receptacle.

13. Connect the wall transformer wire to the control unit.

14. Look for an indicator light, showing the unit has power.

Water Heater Shutoff

Water damage from a leaking water heater can be stopped by using a water heater auto shutoff kit. A sensor, located on the floor beneath the water heater, sends a signal to a control unit, which automatically turns off the water to the heater.

In the previous section, we talked about auto shutoff units for washing machines (and in the next section, we'll talk about installing a general purpose water sensor). After washing machines, however, water heaters are the next most prevalent source of water damage.

The FloodStop System II, shown in Figure 10-7, sells for US$79.99 and installs in five minutes.

The following steps illustrate how to install the Water Heater Auto Shutoff Kit:

1. Turn off water supply line to the water heater—normally, a faucet or handle on the cold water supply coming into your water heater.

Turning Off the Water Supply

Like dealing with your home's electrical system, be sure to turn off the water supply before messing about with any plumbing. Happily, if you forget this step, you don't run the risk of electrocution, but it may be a messy affair. Another plus when dealing with your home's appliances that use water, the turnoff valve is normally located right next to the appliance, so you know exactly which appliance is having its water supply disconnected.

Figure 10-7
FloodStop System II automatic shutoff unit (Photo courtesy Smarthome.com)

2. If you're retrofitting an existing installation, disconnect the flexible supply hose from the existing shutoff valve.

3. Connect the new, automatic shutoff valve to the cold-water manual valve.

4. Connect the proper flexible hose to the appropriate automatic shutoff valve outlet.

5. Mount the automatic shutoff valve's control unit to the wall. It should be located somewhere easily accessible for testing.

6. Plug the wall transformer into a standard 110V AC receptacle.

7. Turn the cold water supply line to the water heater back on and check the automatic shutoff valve for leaks.

8. If there are leaks, check your connections and ensure they are tight enough.

TIPS OF THE TRADE

Check for Leaks

If there are persistent leaks, turn the water off, unscrew the new valve, and wrap all the threaded portions with thread sealing tape, then reconnect. Thread sealing tape provides a watertight seal when connecting pipes.

9. Where you are satisfied there are no leaks, plug the valve and sensor assembly into the control unit.

10. Using two-connector wire, connect the water sensor to the control unit.

11. Locate the water sensor directly beneath the water heater.

12. Plug the transformer wire into the control unit and look for a green light.

High-water Detector

In the preceding sections, we talked about some specific sensors—and their installation—that help prevent water damage caused by overflowing toilets, washing machines, and water heaters. These are very useful devices that alert you to a problem (via an audible alarm). However, if you want a sensor that is more integrated into your entire Smart Home, you'll need to connect a water sensor that is either powered via X10 or connected to your Smart Home security system.

The WaterBug sensor, shown in Figure 10-8, sells for US$59.95 and comes with one sensor. However, up to five additional sensors can be added to the unit. Additional sensors sell for US$17.99. WaterBug also sells a sensor that can be located under carpeting and retails for US$25.99.

The sensor activates when a thin film of water bridges the two contacts, closing the circuit. However, if the sensor is operating in the normally open/closed mode, the absence of water will trigger an alarm.

Water Sensor Placement

If you have a distilled water cooler that you're worried may leak, water sensors won't be much help. Since distilled water lacks minerals and ions, which are what carries an electrical current in water, the sensors won't be able to detect rising levels of distilled water.

With this project, we are setting up a water sensor near a water heater. However, unlike the previous projects that allowed the device to deactivate the water source to the water heater, this solution will send a signal to our security system. The feather in this system's cap is its flexibility. It allows you to monitor water in different ways (the presence of water, the absence of water, specific water levels, and so forth). Certainly, this project could be assembled in conjunction with one of the above solutions that turn off the water source.

Installation

Installing the WaterBug water sensor comes in two phases. First, one must connect the various water sensors to the WaterBug console. Second, the console must be connected to your security or home automation system.

TIPS OF THE TRADE

Mounting Options

The WaterBug can also be mounted on vertical surfaces, for the sake of monitoring rising water levels (for instance, when monitoring the water levels in a sump). To mount the sensor to a wall or other vertical surface (or to anchor it to a horizontal surface), the sensor must only be drilled and screwed to the wall through its center. This is because the sensor utilizes four contacts, located on the bottom. When water is sensed by these contacts, a message is sent to the control unit. As such, it is necessary to mount the sensor using the hole in the center. Drilling any other part of the sensor runs the risk of damaging the internal wiring.

15 MINUTES

The following steps illustrate how to install the WaterBug console and sensors, and how to connect them to a security or home automation system:

1. Locate where you want to place the WaterBug console, using a level to ensure a square installation (this is more for aesthetics than anything else).

2. Mark the location of the screw hole on the wall.

3. Drive the mounting screw into the wall, leaving 3/16" between the screw head and the wall.

4. Fasten the WaterBug to the screw head and press down.

5. Connect the two-connector wires from the water sensor to terminals 3 and 4.

HEADS UP!

Connecting Multiple Water Sensors

With the WaterBug water sensor, up to six sensors can be connected to the WaterBug console. To connect multiple sensors, connect them all to terminals 3 and 4.

6. Locate the sensor(s) where you wish to monitor for moisture problems. As Figure 10-9 shows, we've placed a sensor near a sump in our Smart Home's basement. To show the contacts on the bottom of the unit, we've flipped it over. Before the project is completed, we'll flip it back over so the contacts are properly placed.

Figure 10-9
Placing a water sensor
near a sump

7. Determine how you want your water sensor to operate, either in normally open (to detect the presence of water) or normally closed (to detect the absence of water) mode. There are seven contacts on the WaterBug console. The first two are used for power, the second two are used to connect sensors, and the last three are used to connect to your security or home automation system.

   ❏ Relay five is common

   ❏ Relay six is normally open

   ❏ Relay seven is normally closed

8. How you connect to your security or home automation system will depend on whether you want a normally open system or a normally closed system. If you want your sensors configured in the normally open position, connect wires from your cabling to relays five (common) and six (normally open). If you want your sensors to be configured for normally closed operation, connect the cabling to your security or home automation system to relays five (common) and seven (normally closed).

9. The WaterBug can be operated either by connecting to a transformer plugged into a wall receptacle or by using 12V DC power.

10. To use AC power, connect the transformer wires to contacts 1 and 2 (they are interchangeable, so it doesn't matter which wire is connected to which contact).

11. To use DC power, connect the positive (+) wire to contact 1 and the negative (-) to contact 2.

HEADS UP!

Check Your Wiring

When connecting the WaterBug to DC power, make sure to mind the polarity.

Test the sensor by using a moistened finger or cloth and touching the sensors on the unit. If the sensor is not registering the presence of water, check the polarity of your power supply connection.

Variations in X10

You need not install a security system to make the water sensor jibe with the rest of your Smart Home gadgetry. You can simply purchase a WaterBug high-water sensor and connect it to an X10 Powerflash module (which we explained in Chapter 8). This will allow an X10 device to send a signal to your Smart Home computer or to any other X10-enabled device. For example, if the water sensor detects the presence of water, you could configure the Powerflash module to turn on a light elsewhere in the house.

Making your kitchen, bathroom, and laundry room "smart" is more difficult than the rest of the house, mainly because the integrated appliances just aren't there, yet. There are a few devices that will work in conjunction with the rest of your Smart Home (like the high-water sensor or the plug-in devices you manage with X10 Powerflash modules). However, there are a number of stand-alone gadgets that can make your kitchen, bathroom, and laundry room more utilitarian.

TESTING 1-2-3

❏ Did you turn off the water before installation?

❏ Were there any leaks?

❏ Did you turn the water back on?

❏ Did you configure the connections properly for normally open or normally closed sensors?

Chapter 11

Smart Home Utilities

Tools of the Trade

Various screwdrivers
Wire strippers
Wall anchors
Screws
Butt splice connectors
Fish Tape
Four-wire cabling
Automated thermostat
Scrap insulation

" Heating, ventilation, and air conditioning (HVAC)" systems is the term applied to your air conditioner, furnace, and fan system. Not only important for your comfort, an integrated HVAC system can be central to a Smart Home in that it can respond to given conditions (like turning on the air conditioning at a certain time), or it can cause certain actions to occur (like automatically shutting the living room curtains when the temperature rises above a certain level).

This chapter examines HVAC systems and how you can integrate them with the rest of your Smart Home. We'll first examine a conventional X10 thermostat, and then we'll take a closer look at the thermostat that works in conjunction with the rest of our Omni II security system and home automation system.

HVAC Systems

There are a number of devices that can be added to your home to make it more comfortable. Humidifiers can be added to your HVAC system (and connected with X10 modules to add functionality); filters can be installed to purify the home's air; and HVAC zone controllers can be installed, which can help provide specific temperatures to specific parts of the home.

In this section, we'll examine the more popular and prevalent device you are more likely to install: a thermostat. First, we'll talk about some HVAC wiring conventions that will assist you when installing your own thermostat, and then we'll talk about some thermostats and monitoring devices that will make your Smart Home more comfortable and safe.

Wiring

You can purchase cabling specifically for thermostat use. Using this cabling is useful because it contains the color-coded wires standard for home HVAC systems. This wiring comes in two-, five-, or seven-wire cables at either 18- or 20-gauge. For heating-only systems, two-conductor wires are fine to use. Systems including both heat and air conditioning require cable with four or five wires. Multistage systems need cable with seven wires. The different gauges are selected based on how far the cabling will be run. Eighteen-gauge is used for runs exceeding 200 feet, while 20-gauge cabling is used for runs up to 250 feet.

Multistage systems mean that the HVAC system operates at different levels. For instance, if the furnace has come on, but the amount of heat being put out simply isn't enough, a second unit (or stage) will activate and more heat will be generated. It works the same way with air conditioners, except a second condenser will turn on if it isn't cooling down adequately.

Thermostat wiring has a color scheme associated with it. That is, when connecting your thermostat, certain colored wires should always be connected to certain devices and for certain functions. Table 11-1 lists the different colored wires, markings, and for which purpose they are used.

Wire Color Code	Marking	Description
Red	R	Power, 24 VAC transformer
Red	Rc	Power from cooling system, 24 VAC transformer
Red	Rh	Power from heat system, 24 VAC transformer

Table 11-1
Standardized Color Scheme for HVAC Wiring

Wire Color Code	Marking	Description
Black/blue	C	Common of 24 VAC transformer
White	W	Primary heat call relay
Brown	E	Emergency heat relay
Yellow	Y	Primary cool call relay
Yellow	Y2	Secondary cool call relay
Green	G	Fan relay
Orange	O	Changeover relay to cool relay
Blue	B	Changeover relay to heat relay
Blue, brown, gray, or tan	L	Service indicator lamp

Table 11-1
Standardized Color Scheme for HVAC Wiring *(continued)*

X10 Thermostat

We've already seen how X10 devices can be used in your Smart Home to add functionality to lights and appliances. However, X10 can also be used as a means of controlling your home's environment. An X10 thermostat, like the TX15 shown in Figure 11-1, retails for US$229.99 and can be used with any X10 controller to manage temperatures or establish temperature schedules.

Figure 11-1
TX15 X10 thermostat
(Photo courtesy
Smarthome.com)

Further, the use of an X10 remote control (we'll talk about them in more detail in Chapter 16) allows you to manage temperatures from anywhere in the house. With this particular model, temperatures can be set anywhere between 60 and 90 degrees, with a low temperature setting of 40 degrees.

Since these thermostats utilize X10 technology, it is necessary use the overall X10 operation in a somewhat different way to allow the fine controls necessary to run a thermostat. Because X10 devices operate by sending "on" and "off" commands to a specific address (G-14, for example), there needs to be a way for more information to be sent to a thermostat. In this case, X10 thermostats utilize a single House Code, and as individual on/off commands are sent to the Unit Codes, those are translated into a specific action by the thermostat.

To receive X10 commands, the thermostat uses an "X10 decode table." These are commands sent via your home electrical system to the thermostat to manage temperatures. For your reference, Table 11-2 shows how temperatures and settings are changed based on X10 commands.

XIO	Temp	XIO	Temp	XIO	Temp	XIO	Temp
1 OFF	OFF	9 OFF	64	1 ON	72	9 ON	80
2 OFF	HEAT	10 OFF	65	2 ON	73	10 ON	81
3 OFF	COOL	11 OFF	66	3 ON	74	11 ON	82
4 OFF	AUTO	12 OFF	67	4 ON	75	12 ON	83
5 OFF	40	13 OFF	68	5 ON	76	13 ON	84
6 OFF	60	14 OFF	69	6 ON	77	14 ON	86
7 OFF	62	15 OFF	70	7 ON	78	15 ON	88
8 OFF	63	16 OFF	71	8 ON	79	16 ON	90

Table II-2
Decode Table for X10 Thermostat

The codes shown in Table 11-2 are used in conjunction with the X10 House Code. No other devices should use that particular House Code, because all the Unit Codes will be used for X10 commands to the thermostat. That is, the X10 thermostat is assigned its own House Code, unique to the thermostat. When commands are sent to the thermostat, the X10 code in Table 11-2 is attached to the House Code. As such, if you wanted to set your thermostat (with a House Code of "J") to 78 degrees, a command from your X10 controller would send an "on" signal to address J-7. To turn off the system, an "off" command would be sent to address J-1.

TIPS OF THE TRADE

Keep Stray X10 Signals out of Your House

We've talked about how a stray signal from your X10-savvy neighbor could start affecting your home's X10 devices. It's one thing when a lamp mysteriously goes on and off, it's another thing entirely when your home's HVAC system is at the neighbor's mercy. To prevent stray X10 signals from coming into your home, a whole house blocking coupler (which sells for US$74.99) can be installed. The coupler fits on the neutral wire feed entering the house and senses the presence of X10 signals. When it detects an X10 signal, it neutralizes the incoming signal. As a bonus, it serves as a passive signal coupler to allow X10 signals to travel between phases within the home.

In Chapter 15, we'll talk about how you can get all your X10 devices to work together, either using a computer interface or a stand-alone X10 controller.

Products

The X10 thermostat can also be linked with a few add-ons to improve its overall usability:

❑ **Indoor temperature sensor**   This module overrides the thermostat's internal temperature sensor and is useful if you want your home's temperature to be based on that of a specific room or area. This is also a useful device if your thermostat is located in an area that doesn't truly reflect the temperature of the house, like in a cold part of the house or somewhere sunlight beats down on it. This sensor retails for US$74.99.

❑ **External temperature sensor**   If you want to base the temperature of your home on the external temperature, this sensor can be added. This sensor retails for US$128.99.

❑ **Pool/Spa remote sensor**   This sensor detects the temperature of your pool or spa and, when used in conjunction with other X10 devices, allows you to manage the temperature of the spa or pool. This sensor sells for US$49.99.

HEADS UP!

Pool/Spa Sensors Require Plumbing Work
If you intend to install the pool/spa remote sensor, you'll wind up having to perform some plumbing work when you have to install a "T" junction in the spa's plumbing.

All the sensors can be located up to 500 feet away from the thermostat, but are hardwired using 22-gauge wire.

Installation

Thermostats that are used in conjunction with home automation systems vary depending on the functions they offer. For instance, some thermostats simply replace your existing thermostat, while others require a connection to a telephone controller or a home computer. The particular thermostat we are focusing on for this discussion is the TX15 X10 thermostat, which is similar in design and function to other X10 thermostats and is comprised of two components:

❏ **Wall display unit (WDU)**   This is the unit that mounts to the wall and will be the physical interface between the homeowner and the thermostat. It contains pushbuttons and an internal temperature sensor. The WDU connects to the control unit with four-wire cable. This unit also connects to the X10 interface and a 12 VDC power supply input so that X10 signals can be sent and received.

❏ **Control unit**   This device works in tandem with the WDU and responds to commands from the WDU, as well as X10 instructions. Where the WDU provides a user interface, the control unit is the device that actually performs the thermostatic functions, sending commands to the HVAC system.

To provide X10 functionality, an X10 interface is plugged into a 110 VAC wall receptacle. Not only does the X10 interface receive commands to facilitate the remote change of temperatures, it can also transmit information via X10 commands.

TIPS OF THE TRADE

How the Thermostat Uses X10

Unlike other X10 devices, the TX15 does not use small dials to establish House and Unit Codes. Rather, it uses four DIP switches which, when set in the 16 possible combinations, represent X10 House Codes. The unit utilizes a total of eight DIP switches (switches 1–4 are used to manage such settings as Fahrenheit or Celsius display and other system variables). Switches 5–8 are used to manage the X10 House Codes. Using a binary code (the switch is "on" or it is "off"), the different combinations of switches correlate to various House Codes. For example, the following switches correspond to the House Code "A":

Switch 5 On	Switch 6 Off
Switch 7 Off	Switch 8 On

If the switches are all off, then the corresponding House Code is "J"; all on is used to specify House Code M.

15 MINUTES **WDU Installation**

To install the TX15 X10 thermostat, follow these steps:

1. Choose a location that will represent the ideal temperature of your home. For example, stay away from locations that are prone to drafts, near doors, near windows, or where direct sunlight will hit the WDU.

TIPS OF THE TRADE

Selecting the Best Location for Your Thermostat

When considering placement, it's most likely you'll replace an existing thermostat with the X10 device, as the wiring is already in place and you don't want a hole in the wall where the old device used to connect. That's not to suggest you shouldn't select a new location—if you prefer the new X10 thermostat to be placed elsewhere, go for it. The only problem is that you'll have to pull wire to the new location and patch up the hole in the wall from the old thermostat.

2. Feed the wires to the WDU through the access hole in the back of the case.

3. Mount the WDU to the wall with screws or wall anchors.

HEADS UP!

Fill the Old Hole to Prevent Drafts

If the hole in the wall from the previous thermostat is too large, it's a good idea to patch the wall as much as possible (using sealer or insulation) to prevent drafts behind the wall and registering false results.

4. Wiring the WDU can be done in a couple ways. For optimal operation, new two twisted-pair 22-gauge cabling should be fed through the wall. However, it is much simpler to use the existing HVAC wiring. The only hitch is that nontwisted wires might be affected by interference from noise coming from nearby wiring.

5. For the following connections, we're using cabling containing red, black, white, and green wires. If you use existing HVAC wiring or

cabling containing a different color scheme, jot down your own color choices so the appropriate connections are made:

❏ The GND terminal is connected to the black wire.

❏ The +12 VDC terminal is connected to the red wire.

❏ The CLOCK terminal is connected to the white wire.

❏ The DATA terminal is connected to the green wire.

6. Once the control unit is installed (as explained in the next section), the same connections will be made on that device.

Control Unit Installation

To connect the TX15 control unit, follow these steps:

1. Install the control unit in an indoor location that is easy to access. It should be placed near the HVAC system and attached to a wall or stud in a vertical position.

HEADS UP!

Placement Considerations

If you prefer, you can connect the control unit directly to the HVAC system, but avoid hot spots near the burner or areas subject to high vibrations.

2. The control unit connects to the HVAC system like a standard thermostat. The following wiring connections are made between the control unit and the HVAC system, assuming the home is utilizing a standard gas/electric HVAC system:

❏ At the control unit, Rc and Rh are jumpered together (using the supplied jumper), then connected with a red wire to the 24 VAC return terminal of the HVAC system (R).

❏ White is used to connect the heat terminals on the control unit (W) and the HVAC system (W).

❏ Green is used to connect the fan terminals on the control unit (G) and the HVAC system (G).

❏ Yellow is used to connect the compressor on the control unit (Y1) and the HVAC system (Y).

HEADS UP!

Installing a Thermostat with a Heat Pump System

If your HVAC system is a heat pump system, check your manufacturer's instructions for details on properly configuring the thermostat and connecting it to the HVAC system's wiring.

3. The X10 interface on the control unit is an RJ11 jack that is connected to an X10 powerline interface module using a four-wire modular phone cable. Simply plug the cable into the control unit, then to the power transformer before plugging it into the AC power receptacle.

Testing

Once the thermostat is installed, you should test it to make sure it works properly. There are two different ways in which you should test this installation.

First, manually turn up the temperature to see if the heat engages. Then, turn down the thermostat to see if the air conditioning comes on. Finally, turn on the fan to ensure that is connected properly. Next, repeat these tests from your X10 controller.

If the heat, air conditioning, or fan fail to operate as they should, go back and check to ensure that the wiring has been connected to the appropriate terminals (you did remember to mark the wires before they came off the old thermostat, didn't you?) or that none of the wires have come loose.

If you are able to control the thermostat manually, but not using your X10 controller, it is possible that your thermostat is connected to a different phase than your X10 controller. Try moving your controller to an outlet closer to the one connected to the thermostat. If it works, you know you'll need to buy a phase coupler.

When the unit is properly installed and tested, it can be made part of your larger X10 home automation system by connecting it as part of a series of events that occur. For example, you could use an X10 telephone responder and, on your way back from a weekend away, turn on your home's air conditioning system from your cellular telephone. You could also connect the thermostat with an X10-capable drape closing system to shut out the sun before turning on the air conditioner.

Remote Monitoring

Thermostats exist so that the furnace or air conditioner knows to kick in when a certain temperature level has been breached. Thanks to thermostats, you don't have to worry about manually turning on the air conditioner or turning off the heating system. It's great to be able to set up your desired temperatures and know that, automatically, the temperature will be taken care of. However, there are times when the house gets too hot or too cold and it's necessary to let you know.

Remote monitoring devices are useful for keeping an eye on vacation properties, or when connected to various sensors and placed around your home. For instance, the Sensaphone (shown in Figure 11-2) can be connected to a temperature sensor. Once a certain temperature has been crossed, the Sensaphone will automatically call you to advise that there is a problem.

Figure 11-2
Sensaphone remote monitoring system (Photo courtesy Smarthome.com)

The Sensaphone is connected to your telephone, a power source (it can also hold six D cell batteries for backup power), and any of the following sensors:

❏ Water sensor

❏ Temperature sensor

❏ Humidity sensor

❏ Any other normally open or normally closed sensor (like magnetic contact switches)

Depending on the model, the Sensaphone can accommodate up to eight of these sensors (connected to terminals on the back of the unit). If a sensor is tripped, the Sensaphone will call up to eight telephone numbers (depending on the model) with its preprogrammed message. The model that accepts four inputs and will call four numbers in the event of trouble retails for US$369.99, and the model accepting eight inputs and will call eight telephone numbers in the event of trouble retails for US$549.99.

Omni II Thermostat

As we've noted earlier, a key component in our Smart Home is the Omni II security system by Home Automation, Inc. (HAI). Not only does this device control security functions for the house, but it also manages home automation functions in that it can control X10 devices. What's germane about the Omni II in this discussion is its ability to control the home's heating and cooling functions. Additionally, because it is part of a larger security and automation control, the rise and fall of temperatures can cause other behaviors to occur. For example, we can program the Omni II so that if the temperature in the house rises above 78 degrees, the living room drapes will be closed. This prevents the air conditioner from working against the midday sun, by simply eliminating the sun from the equation.

In this section, we'll talk more about how the thermostat for the Omni II is installed. There are components to this project that are unique to the Omni II, but the section also covers the sorts of steps that would be necessary if you were to connect a smart thermostat to a home automation system like a Stargate Home Controller.

Physical Install

Installing the thermostat is somewhat more complicated than simply substituting the thermostat with a programmable thermostat. Because this device will be connected both to your home's HVAC system and the Omni II, installation is more involved.

HAI's Omni II supports up to four HAI RC-Series Communicating Thermostats (also known as *Omnistats*). For this example, however, we will be replacing an existing thermostat with a single, RC-80 Communicating Thermostat, as shown in Figure 11-3.

Figure 11-3
RC-80
Communicating
Thermostat

TIPS OF THE TRADE

An Easy Way to Route Cabling

Because thermostats tend to be located at eye level, it is almost always necessary to use fish tape to pull the four-wire cabling through the wall. The new cabling will most likely be pulled through the same hole that the existing HVAC wiring comes through. However, just because the wiring is going to pop out of the same hole doesn't mean it has to start in the same location.

The HVAC wiring in our own Smart Home was difficult to get at, simply by virtue of its placement. As such, it would have been more difficult to feed the new cabling through the existing hole. To ameliorate this problem, we simply drilled another hole *next* to the HVAC wiring. This allowed us to be able to send the fish tape through and connect the cabling, then pull it up to the living room. Naturally, your own home probably won't fit this particular solution; however, the point is to try and make your work as easy on yourself as possible.

The following steps should be followed to install the Omni II's thermostat:

1. Remove your existing thermostat (shown in Figure 11-4).

HEADS UP!

Don't Throw Away Your Thermostat

Don't throw away that old thermostat! It might contain a mercury switch, which is not something you want to just toss in the trash can. Check with your local waste management company to find out how to dispose of old thermostats.

Figure 11-4
Removing the old thermostat

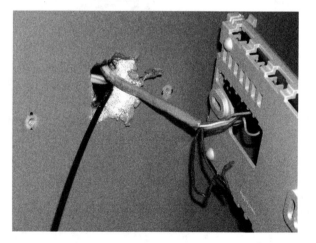

2. Remove existing wiring by unscrewing contacts on the back of the thermostat.

Don't Let the Wires Fall back into the Wall

Tape the existing HVAC wiring to the wall with masking tape, or clamp it off some other way so that the wires don't fall back into the wall.

3. Place the new thermostat on the wall where the old thermostat was located. If necessary, drill new holes in the wall to accommodate the thermostat's new mounting hardware. It might also be necessary to install new wall anchors if the thermostat is being attached directly to the drywall. This is shown in Figure 11-5.

Figure 11-5
Attaching the new thermostat to the wall

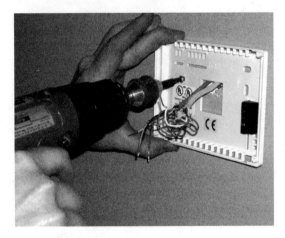

Mark Your Wires for Later Reference

Use small pieces of masking tape as tags to remember which terminals were connected to which wires. Simply attach the tape to the wires and write the corresponding terminal letter on the wire. This can prevent problems later if the wiring was not attached according to the color scheme that we outlined earlier. Don't automatically assume that the correct colors have been attached to the correct terminals. Double-check where they've been attached to make sure they are appropriately reconnected to your new system.

4. Thread the four-wire cable through the wall. It might be necessary to utilize fish tape to pull the cable to its destination (as shown in Figure 11-6).

Figure 11-6
Using fish tape to
bring cabling up
through a wall void

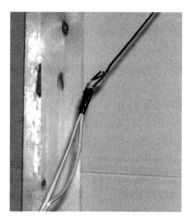

5. Connect the HVAC wiring to the appropriate terminals on the back of
    the new thermostat. The same connections that existed on your old
    thermostat will apply for reconnection to the new thermostat. This is
    shown in Figure 11-7.

Figure 11-7
Connecting HVAC
wiring to the
thermostat

6. Connect three of the wires from your cabling (as shown in Figure 11-8)
    to the cable bundle and plug accompanying the thermostat, following
    these connections (and using butt splice connectors):

    ❏   Black from the cabling is connected to both the red and black
        wires of the thermostat.

    ❏   Green from the cabling is connected to green from the thermostat.

    ❏   White from the cabling is connected to yellow from the thermostat.

Figure II-8
Making connections
on the Omnistat

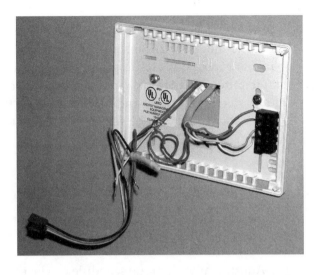

7. At the control panel, the wires are connected to the following terminals:

   ❏ The black and green wires are connected to Output 8 on the upper row of terminals—black is connected to GND, green is connected to 8.

   ❏ The white wire is connected to the Z16 terminal.

HEADS UP!

Connecting More than One Thermostat

If more than one thermostat is to be connected, the thermostats are connected in parallel (that is, the wires from all thermostats will be connected to the same terminals on the control panel).

8. Attach the bundle of wires with the white plug (which is connected to your control panel) into the back of the thermostat.

9. Push the wiring as deeply into the wall as possible so it won't interfere with the mounting of the thermostat.

10. Ensure the wires within the thermostat are out of the way so the faceplate can be reattached.

HEADS UP!

Powering the Thermostat

The thermostat gets its power from the existing HVAC wiring. Do not connect power from the Omni II to the thermostat.

Setup

Once the thermostat is installed and connected to your Smart Home's control panel, it is necessary to program your thermostat. Programming your thermostat requires you to think about what your needs and demands are of the system at various times of day and various days of the week.

The thermostat can be set up to manage temperatures at four times during the day:

- ❏ MORN (morning)
- ❏ DAY (daytime)
- ❏ EVE (evening)
- ❏ NITE (nighttime)

Additionally, a unique schedule can be established for weekdays, as well as Saturdays and Sundays. This allows you to establish individualized heating and cooling rules for specific times of day during the week, while also accommodating a somewhat different schedule on the weekends.

Again, these steps are meant to be performed on an HAI RC-80 thermostat. However, similar (but not identical) steps will be followed for the thermostats of other manufacturers.

To program the RC-80 thermostat, the following keys are used to change various settings:

1. Enter the programming mode by pressing the Prog (or programming) key four times.

2. The item that is being programmed will flash.

3. The up arrow key is used to increase the value.

4. The down arrow key is used to decrease the value.

5. The Prog key is used to advance to the next item.

6. The Hold key is used to return to the previous item.

7. To exit programming mode, press the Mode key.

HEADS UP!

Programming Will Cease After Inactivity

The thermostat will automatically exit programming mode after 20 seconds of no key activity.

When setting up your environmental schedule, the first one to be set is the weekday schedule, followed by Saturday's schedule, and rounding out with Sunday's schedule.

To view or change the programming time schedules of your thermostat, follow these steps:

1. Press the Prog key four times. The weekday MORN time will flash.

2. Use the arrow keys to change the scheduled time for the displayed period (MORN, DAY, EVE, or NITE).

3. Press the Prog key to advance to the next item.

4. Use the arrow keys to change the desired cool setting.

5. Press the Prog key to advance to the next item.

6. Use the arrow keys to change the desired heat setting.

7. Press the Prog key to advance to the next period.

Repeat the aforementioned steps for the DAY, EVE, and NITE settings. Then, repeat those same steps to establish your temperature settings for Saturday and Sunday.

In order to better visualize how your heating and cooling settings can be established, we've provided a table that shows the times of day and days of the week. We've also established at which points the system should kick in to either heat or cool the Smart Home. This table (shown in Table 11-3) is helpful to organize your various heating and cooling settings. We've provided a blank table (Table 11-4) that you can use to sketch out your own HVAC settings.

	Weekdays	Saturdays	Sundays
Morn	6 a.m.	8 a.m.	8 a.m.
Cool	78	78	78
Heat	70	70	70
Day	8 a.m.		
Cool	85	85	85
Heat	62	62	62
Eve	6 p.m.		
Cool	78	78	78
Heat	70	70	70

Table 11-3
A Sample Heating and Air Conditioning Schedule

	Weekdays	Saturdays	Sundays
Nite	10 p.m.	12 a.m.	10 p.m.
Cool	82	82	82
Heat	62	62	62

Table 11-3
A Sample Heating and Air Conditioning Schedule *(continued)*

	Weekdays	Saturdays	Sundays
Morn			
Cool			
Heat			
Day			
Cool			
Heat			
Eve			
Cool			
Heat			
Nite			
Cool			
Heat			

Table 11-4
A Blank Schedule

Testing

Once the thermostat is installed, you should test it to make sure it works properly. There are two different ways in which you should test this installation.

First, manually turn up the temperature to see if the heat engages. Then, turn down the thermostat to see if the air conditioning comes on. Finally, turn on the fan to ensure that it is connected properly.

Next, repeat these tests from your Omni system (both the computer interface and any consoles).

If the heat, air conditioning, or fan fail to operate as they should, go back and check to ensure that the wiring has been connected to the appropriate terminals (you did remember to mark the wires before they came off the old thermostat, didn't you?) or that none of the wires have come loose.

Additional Features

Additional features on the Omnistat make the thermostat even smarter and easier to use. Such features as anticipation and a filter replacement reminder not only help you keep your home comfortable, but they also save you money.

Anticipation

The thermostat has a control system that is meant to keep you comfortable, while saving you money. *Anticipation* is a feature that anticipates the need to turn the system on or off before it actually reaches the desired temperature. This is accomplished by sensing the temperature both in the air and as it is radiated from your home's walls.

For instance, when heating a room, the air heats up more quickly than the wall. As such, the thermostat will briefly turn off giving the wall temperature a chance to catch up. This is a good tool, because it prevents the room from overheating and saves you money in heating costs.

Anticipation also works for cooling. During the summer, the thermostat will turn on from time to time to circulate the air and remove humidity when the temperature nears the cool setting.

Filter Reminder

The RC-80 thermostat keeps track of how long your heating and cooling system has been running and gives a subtle reminder when it is time to replace the filter. When it is time to replace the filter, "FILT" will be displayed in place of the time every four seconds. To clear this reminder, press the Prog key. Make sure you change the filter.

Programmable Energy Saver (PESM) Mode

The thermostat can also be configured to allow a remote system to override it. The thermostat will send its current temperature sensing to the remote system. Then, the remote system will decide whether to override the thermostat, based on its own readings from PESM modules.

When the remote system has control of the thermostat, "REMOTE" will be displayed on the screen. When that is displayed, the user will be unable to use the arrow keys to manually raise or lower the temperature. In order to regain manual control of the thermostat, the energy saver feature must be turned off on the remote system.

On their own, thermostats do a fine job of ensuring that the temperature of a home is maintained at a constant, comfortable level. In the past, however, they lacked the intelligence to warm up or cool down the house at given times of day. Modern programmable thermostats do a good job of accommodating that need; however, the next level—Smart Home HVAC systems—not only manage your home's temperature, but they allow you to control your home's environment based on a range of behaviors going on in the Smart Home. Plus, like the screen shot in Figure 11-9 shows, Smart Home HVAC systems can even be managed via the Internet.

Figure 11-9
Managing your
home's thermostat
remotely

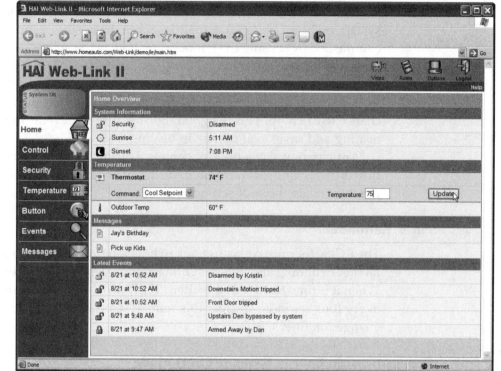

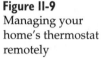

❏ Have you marked the wires coming from your HVAC system for easy reconnection?

❏ Was the thermostat placed in an area free of drafts and direct sunlight?

❏ Is the opening behind the thermostat so large it might cause a draft behind the unit?

❏ Was the X10 thermostat control unit placed near the HVAC system, but not near a heating element or vibrating area?

❏ Are all your settings correct in the thermostat, at the controller, and in the console?

❏ Did you set the House Code on the X10 thermostat to an unused code?

❏ Did you create your own Smart Home temperature schedule?

Chapter 12

Smart Home Communication Systems

Tools of the Trade

Punch-down tool
Four-wire telephone cable
Telephone jack
Cat 5 cabling
Assorted screwdrivers
Drill
One-half inch spade bit
Wire strippers
New phone jack
Tape measure
Drywall saw
Coat hanger

The communications system in a Smart Home can be used for a number of useful things. The first, most obvious use is for conventional, day-to-day telephone use. However, you can do more with your Smart Home than just talk on the telephone. In this chapter, we'll talk about different types of phones you might consider for your Smart Home. We'll start with a discussion and overview of cordless phones and the features you'll encounter when considering a cordless phone purchase.

If you want more than one phone line for your Smart Home, we'll talk about some different options for adding multiline phones to the house. Next, we'll explain how to install phone jacks and discuss some of the issues surrounding telephone wiring. The chapter rounds out with a discussion of connecting your telephone system to a home automation or security system.

Types of Phones

There used to be a time when telephone users were tethered to the phones, as the phones were tethered to the wall. Of course, there also used to be a time when you'd have to ask Mabel to ring up Klondike 227, but no one does that anymore, either. While wired phones are still prevalent (and cheap—you can get one for less than US$10), there have been great strides in the field of wireless telephony.

In this section, we'll examine not only wireless telephones and how to buy one for your Smart Home, but also wireless phone jacks. These devices make it easy to connect a jack in locations that might not normally be conducive for phone jacks. We'll also talk about multiline systems that make it possible for several people to use the phone at the same time—a must if you have teenagers.

Wireless

Wireless technology has made great leaps and bounds in the past two decades. More people have wireless telephones than before, and they work better than ever. This section is a quick primer on wireless technology, so you have a better grip on these appliances and their features when you go shopping for one.

Wireless Phones

Wireless telephones (also widely referred to as *cordless telephones*) are comprised of two parts:

❑ **Base**   This is the unit that attaches to the phone jack. The base receives the incoming call through the telephone line; converts it to an FM radio signal; then broadcasts that signal, which is picked up by the handset.

❑ **Handset**   This is the unit that is mobile and receives signals from the base. It converts the incoming broadcast to an electrical signal, which is sent to the handset's speaker. When you speak into the handset, the sound is converted to an FM radio signal broadcast, then received by the base and converted into an electrical signal, and finally sent back across the telephone line.

The base and handset operate on a frequency pair that allows you to talk and listen at the same time. This is known as a *duplex* frequency. For example, Table 12-1 illustrates how duplex frequency could be used on a given cordless telephone.

Unit	Frequency	Operation
Base	901.38 MHz	Transmitter
	903.22 MHz	Receiver
Handset	903.22 MHz	Transmitter
	901.38 MHz	Receiver

Table 12-1
Duplex Frequency Example

As the table shows, two frequencies are used between both devices—each frequency serves as a transmit frequency on one device and a receive frequency on the other.

Cordless phones have been around since the early 1980s and started with an operating frequency of 27 MHz. As revolutionary as this was, there were still inherent problems, including a limited range, crummy sound quality, and awful security (anyone with another cordless phone could listen to your conversation).

In 1986, the Federal Communications Commission allowed cordless phones to use the frequency range between 47 and 49 MHz. In 1990, the FCC allowed the use of the 900-MHz band. This ameliorated problems of clarity, crowding, and range. In 1998, the FCC opened up the 2.4-GHz range, which increased, again, the range over which cordless phones can operate and also brought it out of the frequency range of most radio scanners—which improves security and stymies that dork with the scanner down the road who holds his glasses together with tape and knows everyone's business. Additionally, as cordless telephones have evolved, they have added improved encoding techniques, which keep prying ears from listening in on a conversation.

Cordless telephones have as many features as a new car. The phone you select will depend largely on the features you want. Table 12-2 lists some of the more common features on modern cordless phones.

Feature	Description
Digital answering machine	Incoming messages are stored on an internal memory chip. The amount of time available depends on the capacity of the chip and the sampling rate at which the message is saved. Your messages can easily be checked from a remote location—some can be deleted and some can easily be saved.
Answering machine	Incoming messages are stored on an audio cassette. They aren't as convenient as digital answering machines. For example, if you want to save a message in the middle of the tape, you'll lose the tape before that message (unless you want to run the risk of erasing the message). On the other hand, replacement tapes can be purchased and they're cheap.
Auto channel scanning	Cordless phones select the best channel (one not in use, or subject to interference) so you get the best connection.
Backup power supply	An additional port on the base allows you to recharge a backup battery. In case the one in the phone dies, you don't have to wait for it to recharge to use your phone again.
Base keypad dialing	Allows you to dial the phone while it is still in the base.
Headsets	Allows you to use the telephone, hands-free.
Built-in Caller ID/Call Waiting Caller ID	Allows you to see who is calling (assuming you've paid the phone company for the service) and to see who is calling when you're already taking a phone call.
Flash	A button used to answer call waiting, or get a new dial tone when the caller hangs up.
Hearing aid compatible	Designed to function with hearing aids.
Hold	Allows you to put the caller on hold.
LCD	Equipped with a screen that shows the number you've dialed, phonebook information, and caller ID information.
Lighted keypad	Allows easier operation in the dark.
Programmable ring	Allows the adjustment of a ringer from louder to softer. Some, like cellular telephones, allow the use of annoying little songs to be played when the phone rings.

Table 12-2
Cordless Telephone Features

Why You Need a Phone with DSS

When looking for a cordless telephone, be sure to find one that utilizes Digital Spread Spectrum (DSS). Not only does DSS allow for maximum range and clarity, but it is also a powerful tool for good security.

Phones using DSS use digital transmissions, which constantly change the duplex frequency during their operation—only the matching base knows which frequency the handset is using. DSS employs millions of scrambling codes that are selected when the phone is lifted from its cradle. As such, radio scanners can't eavesdrop on a cordless DSS telephone transmission.

Like so many other purchases for your home, topping the list of issues is probably the matter of cost. Happily, the price of cordless telephones has come down, drastically. For example, 47–49 MHz cordless phones used to run upwards of US$400. However, you can buy a name brand 2.4-GHz cordless telephone for as little as US$59.99.

This will buy you a fairly low-frills telephone, but it still operates with good quality and utilizes DSS so your conversations are secure. The more money you spend, of course, the more bells and whistles you can add. Some cordless telephones allow you to buy a single base unit and add multiple handsets.

Wireless Jacks

The nice thing about telephones is that they can be installed just about anywhere. Wiring a telephone jack (as we'll talk about later in this chapter) is extremely simple and doesn't cost a whole lot. However, there are simply some places where installing a phone jack isn't possible or it's just too much work. For instance, if you wanted to install a phone jack in the bathroom, but don't want to cut into the tile, you could add a wireless phone jack. Also, wireless jacks would be appropriate for connecting to computer modems, or when connecting your digital satellite dish decoder.

This device, shown in Figure 12-1, is also useful in rooms where you want to rearrange the furniture. With the end table moved to the other side of the room, it isn't necessary to install a new jack or run an extension cord across the floor—simply use a wireless jack. The wireless jack utilizes your home's electrical wiring to turn any outlet into a telephone jack.

Figure 12-1
Wireless telephone
jack (Photo courtesy
Smarthome.com)

HEADS UP!

Compatible with Many Functions

The wireless phone jack is fully compatible with most modems, satellite TV receivers, WebTV, digital video recorder systems like TiVo and UltimateTV, and all online service providers. It is also compatible with Caller ID and Call Waiting and won't interfere with X10 devices.

The wireless phone jack comes with two components:

1. **Base unit** This unit plugs into an open AC receptacle and the telephone line.

2. **Extension unit** This is the unit that can be moved from location to location.

The wireless jack costs US$69.99 for a base unit and extension. Additional extensions can be purchased and added to the system for US$33.99.

5 MINUTES   Installation is fairly straightforward:

1. Plug the supplied telephone cord into an open telephone jack, then plug it into the base unit. If a phone was already using that jack, it can be plugged into the side of the base unit.

2. Plug the base unit into an AC receptacle.

3. Plug the extension unit into an AC receptacle where you wish the phone jack to be located.

4. Plug the telephone into the extension unit.

HEADS UP!

Don't Plug into a Power Strip

If you intend to use the wireless jack with your computer modem, do not plug it into a surge protector or power strip. This will block the signal and render the wireless jack unusable.

Multiline Systems

Most homes have one line coming in, however there are more and more people opting for a second line to facilitate incoming faxes and online computer use. Luckily, most homes are already wired for two telephone lines (telephone cable contains four wires, but only two are needed). Adding a second line is simple and can, in most cases, utilize existing home phone wiring. However, it is likely that some homeowners desire even more than two lines. There are two ways in which you can add more lines to your home.

First, you can call the telephone company. They will be happy to come out to your home, within the next 12 weeks, sometime between the hours of 7 a.m. and 6 p.m. ("No, we can't tell you when, exactly,...")

Once the requisite lines have been installed into your home, you can install a PBX (short for private branch exchange), like the Panasonic KX-TD1232. This system is really designed for small businesses, but if you want a kicked-up home telephone system, you simply install this PBX in your equipment room, run telephone cabling where you want extensions placed, and connect the phones. Out of the box, it can handle 16 extensions and requires six incoming telephone lines. This—and others like it—is a fine system for small businesses or huge families that don't mind paying US$1,300 for a telephone system.

A less costly, more convenient way to get a multiline system is to buy a telephone system that squeezes as much functionality as possible out of your

TIPS OF THE TRADE

PBX Defined

A private branch exchange (PBX) is a telephone system that switches calls between users on local lines while allowing calls to external phone lines. The main purpose of a PBX is to save the cost of requiring a line for each user to the telephone company's central office.

Depending on how beefy you want your Smart Home phone system, you might consider a PBX. However, as we already noted, PBX systems don't come cheap and they can be difficult to set up and install.

existing system. The Panasonic 4-line, multi-handset, 2.4-GHz telephone (shown in Figure 12-2) utilizes your home's existing, single-line wiring to accommodate four simultaneous telephone calls. It also offers such features as separate voicemail boxes, digital answering machines, conference calling, and a slew of other goodies. It also uses multiple handsets, allowing cordless operation for up to eight total handsets.

This phone sells for US$499.99. A two-line version of the phone sells for US$399.99.

Figure 12-2
Panasonic,
4-line, 2.4-GHz
telephone system
(Photo courtesy
Smarthome.com)

Installing a Jack

You might need telephone jacks in different corners of your Smart Home for various functions. Beyond simply adding another phone to your home, additional jacks make it possible to connect your computer to the Internet or connect your satellite receiver to the service provider.

In this section, we talk about the details surrounding phone jack installation and how you can install your own phone jacks (which is a pretty simple endeavor).

Wiring

Before installing a jack, it's important to consider what type of wiring you'll use. In most cases, you'll probably just go for 4-wire, 22-gauge telephone cabling. It's fairly straightforward and easy to work with—it's similar to what we used when installing our security system's sensors. However, there are variables you might want to consider to optimize your own Smart Home communications system setup, including wire size and the number of wires included in the cabling.

Size

As we noted earlier in this book, wire size is measured in terms of American Wire Gauge (AWG) and is more commonly referred to as *gauge*. This describes the thickness of a strand of wire: the smaller the gauge, the thicker the wire. As you remember, when wiring the security, smoke, and other sensors for our security system, we used 22-gauge wire. Telephone wire tends to be 22-, 24-, or 26-gauge. The thicker the wire, the better the signal will carry over longer distances, due to the decrease in resistance.

Wires

Depending on how many lines you have coming into your Smart Home (or how many you expect in the future), you should consider the size of cabling you wish to pull. That is, will you connect just one phone (and that's all you expect to hook up), or do you want to future-proof a bit and facilitate a possible second line?

Two   In a home with only one telephone line, you really only need a two-wire telephone cable. This is because, believe it or not, your telephone only needs two wires with which to work. Homes with a single telephone connection need only two wire lines, however it is more common to see lines utilizing four wires.

Four   The most common wiring used in home telephone systems utilizes four wires, as shown in Figure 12-3. This might seem somewhat wasteful, given that most of us only have one telephone line. However, wire is cheap and it sets the stage nicely for adding a second telephone line. Once the telephone company works their magic on the outside of the house, it's a simple matter of connecting the new wiring to your existing (and already pulled) wires to facilitate fax machines, computer lines, and so forth. A spool of 100 feet of four-wire telephone cable costs US$12.99, or you can buy it by the foot at electronics and home improvement stores.

Figure 12-3
Four-wire telephone
cabling

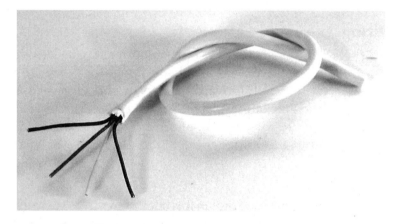

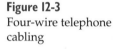

Telephone Line Color Standardization

Looking at a chunk of four-wire telephone cable, you'll notice four colors: red, green, black, and yellow. Even though most homes will only use two wires (and, in fact, any two wires will work just fine), there is a standard for connecting telephone lines:

❑ **Line one**   Utilizes red and green

❑ **Line two**   Utilizes black and yellow

Although there is a standard used for telephone wire colors, you might find that these standards are not adhered to in your own home, especially if you are in an older home. As such, the only way to tell which wire is which is through trial and error—hooking up a wire to one terminal, checking the connection with a telephone, then moving on until you get the right connections. (This is why standards are so important.)

Cat 5   If you have more than two telephone lines, you might consider running Cat 5 cabling. Cat 5 cabling contains four pairs of wires. This is enough to facilitate four separate telephone lines and makes pulling cable much, much easier than having to pull two four-wire runs.

Cat 5 cabling that has no connectors attached to it yet costs around US$10 for 100 feet. Since you'll be using it for telephone networks, anyway, you don't need to worry about the lack of connectors on each end—you'd just snip them off anyway.

Looped System

If you remember a few chapters back, we discussed the merits of home-run versus looped systems. While it is certainly ideal to employ a home-run system for your telephone system, it simply might not be feasible. Home-run systems use punch-down blocks (which we'll talk about in the next section) while loop systems connect the phone jacks in a daisy chain, one to another.

Home punch-down blocks are a reasonably new addition to homes. As such, many homes (possibly even yours) don't employ a punch-down block. Rather, to connect a phone jack, it will be necessary to loop your phone jacks. In this section, we'll talk about two ways you can connect a phone jack to your looped system. First, we'll cover mounting the jack to the wall. This is ideal in rooms that already have a phone jack and you don't mind seeing a little bit of cabling. Second, we'll talk about running the telephone cabling through the wall. Ideally, this would be used in rooms without phone jacks, or those areas where you don't want a phone jack bulging out of the wall.

Wall-Mounted   The following steps are used when connecting another phone jack onto an existing line. If you want to connect a second line to your home, it is necessary to call the telephone company to install the second line and set up service.

HEADS UP!

Disconnect Power to Your Phones

Before starting to wire a new phone jack, to prevent the risk of shock, take one of your home's telephones off the hook. That way, if you happen to be holding or in contact with wiring when a phone call comes in, you won't get a shock. It's a mild shock, but it's still a shock.

20 MINUTES

To install an RJ11 phone jack in a house where the phones are in a loop configuration, follow these steps:

1. Remove the outer insulation from a couple inches of telephone wire using wire strippers.

2. With the sheathing removed, the individual color-coded wires are exposed.

HEADS UP!

Use Caution When Hading Telephone Wires

These exposed telephone wires are fragile, so use caution not to nick or cut them. Also, be careful not to manhandle the wire too much, which might cause the wires to break.

3. Remove the insulation from the end of each individual color-coded wire using smaller wire strippers.

4. Remove the cover from an existing phone jack (shown in Figure 12-4) to expose the wires and contacts. This phone jack should be as close to the location of the new phone jack as possible. Depending on your phone jack, there might be a couple screws that must be removed, or it's a matter of prying open the jack with a standard screwdriver.

Figure 12-4
Remove the cover from an existing phone jack

5. Leaving the existing wires in place, attach each of the new wires to the corresponding contact by wrapping the exposed end around the screw. Curl the wire around the screw in a clockwise direction (shown in Figure 12-5).

Figure 12-5
Attach new telephone
wires to existing
phone jack

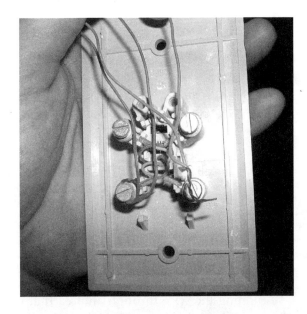

6. Once each wire is wrapped securely, tighten down each of the screws securely until all of the new wires are attached.

7. With all of the connections in place, replace the jack cover, leaving the new wire so that it extends outside the jack.

8. Route the cabling to the site of the new phone jack.

9. On the other end of the new telephone wire, strip and prepare the ends as before, and connect each of the ends to the corresponding contact on the new jack using the color-coding as a guide, as Figure 12-6 shows.

Figure 12-6
Connecting the new
phone jack

HEADS UP!

How Much Do Jacks Cost?

Depending on what type of RJ11 jack you buy (flush-mounted, wall-mounted, single-line, dual-line, and so forth) and the manufacturer, telephone jacks range in price between US$5 and US$10.

10. Install the new jack onto the wall using screws or double-sided tape.

TIPS OF THE TRADE

Placing Telephone Wire

Routing telephone cable follows the same steps we followed when placing security and sensor cabling. Try and make it easy on yourself by running the wire through an area that is unfinished. For example, you could drill a hole in the basement ceiling or attic floor, fish the telephone wire through the wall to the desired location, drill another hole, then finish the job. Especially if you do not have a basement or your basement ceiling is finished, it makes good sense to run the telephone wire through the attic.

Alternately, if you are running wire from one jack to another in the same room, you can hide the wire beneath the baseboard by using a wooden Popsicle stick to press the wire into the crack between the baseboard and the carpeting without damaging the cable.

Flush-Mounted   If you want a phone jack installed that is flush to the wall, it is possible, albeit a little more complicated. The complication doesn't arise in any new sort of wiring scheme. Rather, it has to do with the placement of wire within your home's walls, as opposed to running them along the floors.

Follow these steps to install a flush-mounted phone jack:

1. Go to your attic and locate the top plate over the wall where the existing jack is and the top plate for the wall where you want to install the new jack.

2. Measure to determine where to drill the holes in the top plates to install the new wire. If the existing phone wire is already in the attic, you won't need to drill into the void behind the wall where the existing line is installed, because there should already be a hole there and it'll be easy to locate the top plate.

3. Use a 1/2-inch spade bit to drill into the void behind the wall containing the existing phone jack.

4. On the new telephone cable, tie the end in a knot, and feed plenty of cable into the void behind the wall.

5. From the room housing the existing jack, remove the junction box for the existing phone jack from the wall, or poke a hole into the back of the junction box. You can use a bent coat hanger to retrieve the cable from within the wall, as Figure 12-7 shows, pulling it through the wall or the junction box.

Figure 12-7
Fishing the phone cabling out of the wall

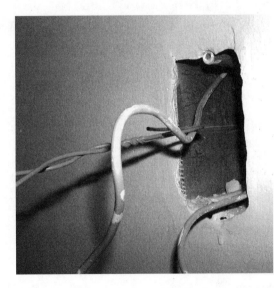

6. For a flush-mounted junction box, use an "old-work" box and hold it against the wall to use as a template to mark cutting lines on the wall for the new phone jack.

7. Using a drywall saw, cut out the hole for the junction box.

HEADS UP!

Don't Worry About a Perfect Cut

Assuming the hole you cut is smaller than the cover plate, the phone jack will overlap the hole, so don't worry about making a perfect cut—the cover plate will cover up any imperfections.

8. Back in the attic, use a 1/2-inch spade drill bit to drill into the void behind the wall where you want the new jack to be installed.

9. Using the same technique as before, thread the telephone wire into the wall void and fish it out with a bent coat hanger through the hole you just cut.

10. Strip the cable and wires as before, then connect them to the new jack.

Home-Run

The other way to install a new telephone jack is if your home happens to have a punch-down block. This facilitates installing your home's telephone system in a home-run topology. If something happens to one of your telephone jacks, the rest of the jacks in the home won't suffer because of it. This allows you to change the configuration at any phone jack in the house without messing with the rest of them.

A punch-down block (also known as a 66 block) is a block that contains 66 connectors in four columns. Columns 1 and 2 are connected together while columns 3 and 4 are connected together. Punch-down blocks are prewired and are used to feed signals to various telephone cables.

Punch-Down Tool   Punch-down blocks allow you to connect to neighboring posts, which allows for a clean connection. The main lines coming into the house will connect to a pair of posts on the punch-down block. Then, each column of posts is connected to these posts. Each telephone extension in the house is connected to the appropriate posts on the punch-down block.

To connect wiring to the punch-down block, a *punch-down tool* is used. The

Figure 12-8
Punch-down tool
(Photo courtesy
Smarthome.com)

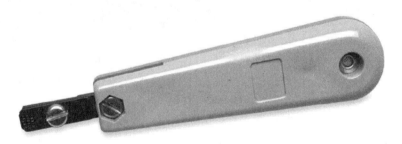

tool, like the one shown in Figure 12-8, is used to jam the telephone wire in between the two sides of the post. The post pierces the insulation and makes contact with the wire without cutting it.

2 MINUTES

Connecting to the Punch-Down Block   Connecting wire to a punch-down block is fairly straightforward, and another benefit of using a punch-down block:

1. Drape the wire in between the two sides of a post (as Figure 12-9 shows).

Figure 12-9
Placing wire on a
punch-down block

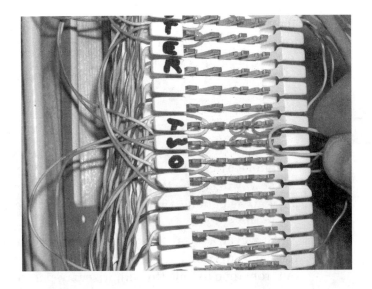

2. Place the slotted end of the tool over the post (as Figure 12-10 shows).

Figure 12-10
Using the punch-
down tool

3. Push the tool in.

Use Some Muscle
You push the tool in with some force—that's why it's called a punch-down tool.

From there, installing the phone jack follows the same steps we talked about before. Run the wire to the location of the jack, connect the wires to the jack, and install the jack, then you're all set.

Combine Topologies

We don't mean to suggest that you can *only* run the cabling for your new telephone extension in a home-run or loop configuration. Certainly, the safest way to ensure the integrity of your telephone system is to connect all your telephones with a punch-down block as the center of your home-run system.

However, let's say that you're installing a new phone jack in the family room next to your satellite dish decoder. Since your decoder needs to call out from time to time (to authorize pay-per-view movie choices or to include you as part of sporting event black outs), it might be wise to install a jack next to the entertainment center. Even if your phone system is home run, it might make sense to connect the new phone jack to a phone jack already in the room in a loop fashion. This will save you the expense and headache of running cable through the walls and so forth for a reasonably simple connection.

Security Systems

Your Smart Home can also use the telephone system to make your security system more functional. We've been using Home Automation, Inc.'s Omni II system for our own Smart Home, and it offers a number of features that rely on the telephone system. Once connected, we'll be able to have the system observed by a monitoring company or dial in to check system status, or the system will call us if a specified event occurs.

This type of functionality is not unique to the Omni II system, and is present on a number of other security and home automation systems, as well. The following section will show you how we set up our Omni II system for use with the telephone. The steps might be somewhat different with other systems, but this should give you a flavor of what's involved with these systems with regard to setup.

Physical

The first step is to connect the security system, physically. We outlined these steps in Chapter 6, but let's cover them again briefly:

1. Install the control panel.

2. Connect a new RJ31X phone jack, either using the punch-down block or looped to another phone jack (these steps are explained previously in this chapter). This jack must be installed between the phone line coming into your home and your punch-down block (or first telephone jack, depending on whether you have a loop or home-run system).

HEADS UP!

Install the Correct Jack

Be sure to install an RJ31X phone jack, not an RJ11 jack. RJ31X jacks are used with security systems, whereas RJ11 jacks are common telephone jacks.

3. Connect the control panel to the newly installed phone jack.

Once the system has been installed and connected to your phone system, it is necessary to set up the software.

Software

For the Omni II system, we're using PC Access (which we talked about in Chapter 7). This software allows us to set up the zones we'll be monitoring and define what the system should do when an alarm is tripped, a temperature exceeded, smoke detected, and so forth.

Two of the things the system can do involve either call a monitoring service or calling one to eight telephone numbers.

10 MINUTES

Calling a Service

If you want your system to contact a monitoring service in the event of trouble, the setup is straightforward:

1. On the PC Access software, select Setup | Installer | Communicator. This will produce the screen shown in Figure 12-11.

Figure 12-11
PC Access'
Communicator

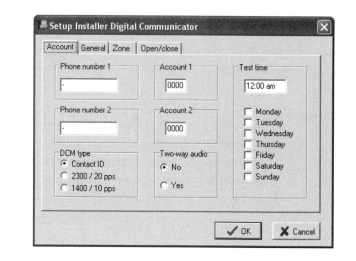

2. This screen allows you to enter the telephone numbers of two monitoring services, along with various setup information that you should discuss with your monitoring service.

3. Other tabs on this tool include General, Zone, and Open/Close. These tabs allow you to specify a code that will be sent to the monitoring service if an alarm is tripped, smoke is detected, or any of the other situations that are being monitored occur.

Calling You

You can set up the system to call your service for any activity that is observed. However, you might not want to have the system call your monitoring service every time the temperature drops below a certain point, or if an outside gate has been opened; however, you still deem it necessary to be advised when the event occurs. To do this, PC Access allows you to establish up to eight telephone numbers that will be dialed in case an alarm is tripped.

To set up this feature, open PC Access and perform the following:

1. Select Setup | Dial. The resulting screen is shown in Figure 12-12.

2. This screen allows you to establish the following settings:

❏ **Telephone access**   Select if you want the system to be managed via telephone.

❏ **Remote commands OK**   Select if you want the system to respond to remote commands.

❏ **Answer outside call**   Select if you want the system to answer phone calls coming into the system.

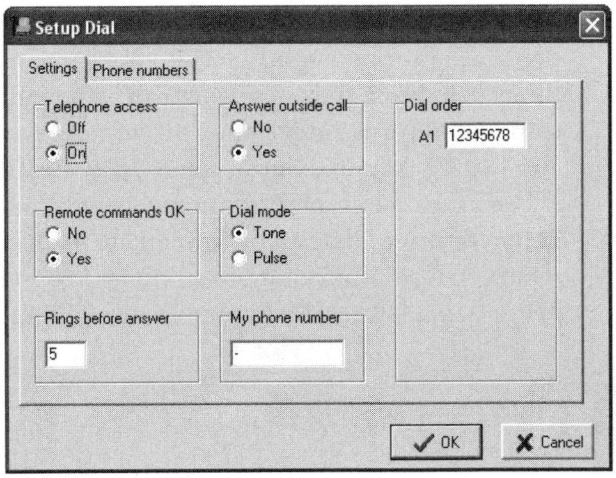

Figure 12-12
PC Access' Dial tool

Figure 12-12
PC Access' Dial tool

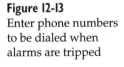

❏ **Dial mode**   Select either tone or pulse.

❏ **Rings before answer**   Select how many times the phone will ring before the system will answer it.

❏ **My phone number**   Enter your home phone number.

❏ **Dial order**   Establishes the order in which the telephone numbers (entered on the Phone Numbers tab) will be called.

3. On the Phone Numbers tab (shown in Figure 12-13), the window shows eight more tabs, each with an entry for a phone number and schedule when those phone numbers can be dialed.

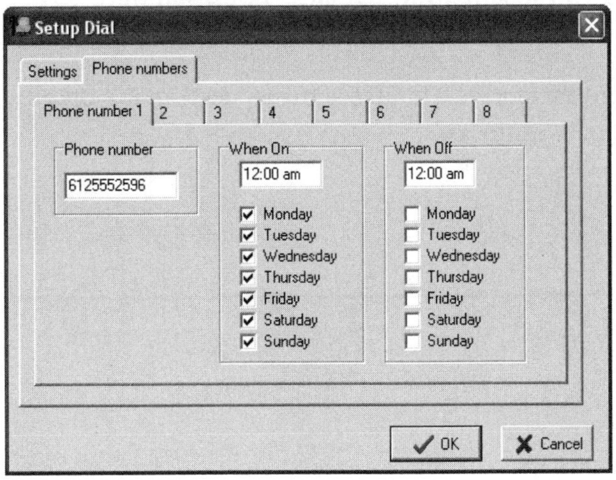

Figure 12-13
Enter phone numbers
to be dialed when
alarms are tripped

4. Enter the telephone numbers (one per tab) and enter the schedule, telling the system when those phone numbers can be dialed.

Once the software has been set up, the system can either call you or a service, depending on your needs and your selections. You also have the ability to call the system (from the home phone or away) and get the status of sensors, change settings, and arm the system. Furthermore, you can pick up any in-house phone and use it as a panic button with the security system.

Smart Home communications systems can do a lot, depending on what gadgetry you buy and how you implement it. Overall, it's a good idea to understand what you want from your Smart Home's communications system and then think about what bells and whistles you're willing to pay for.

TESTING 1-2-3

❏ When connecting a wireless phone jack and there is a poor connection, try moving the base unit to an outlet closer to the expansion unit.

❏ Is your wireless phone jack using the same electrical phase as the base unit?

❏ Did you run enough telephone cabling for future applications?

❏ Are the wires in your new phone jack connected to the correct terminals?

❏ In a loop system, are the wires in your existing RJ11 jack connected to the correct terminals?

❏ Did you install an RJ31X jack (not a standard RJ11 jack) for your security or home automation system?

❏ Have the correct dialing settings been made on any home automation or security systems?

Part IV

Smart Home Entertainment and Integration

Chapter 13

Audio/Video Systems

Tools of the Trade

RG-6 coaxial cable
Four-conductor, 14-gauge speaker wire
Low-voltage gang boxes
Wall-mounted banana jacks
Banana connectors
Wall-mounted RCA jacks
RCA audio cable
Rotozip tool
Various screwdrivers
Mounting screws

Modulator
Lowpass filter
Splitter
Amplified splitter
Crimp tool
Coax cable stripper
Wire stripper
F connector
Attenuator pads

How many times have you and your spouse, your kids, you and your kids, or any combination of the aforementioned rumbled over who was going to get to watch "their" show on television, or listen to "their" CD on the stereo? With a whole-house audio/visual system, you can bring harmony back to your home by letting everyone watch what they want at the same time. True, they'll be in different rooms, but at least there won't be any more fisticuffs!

This chapter discusses the various issues surrounding whole-house A/V systems and we'll explain how to connect your own system.

Components

There are a number of components that can be used in your whole-house A/V system. If you're like most people, you've probably already got a television, VCR, DVD player, cable or satellite decoder, stereo, and all sorts of other goodies. The first section of this chapter covers some of the components you'll need to connect these devices and distribute their signals throughout your Smart Home.

First, we'll talk about speakers and demystify some of the jargon that's thrown around so you can find the best speakers for your whole-home A/V system. Next, we'll cover distribution systems, modulators, splitters, and lowpass filters—all of which are important when distributing video signals through your Smart Home.

Audio Components

For your whole-house A/V system to work optimally, there are a number of specific components you'll need to buy. We've left out discussion of CD players, tape decks, and so forth because that's really outside the scope of our discussion. Here, however, are the bits and pieces you'll need to get your audio signal to various points in your Smart Home.

Speakers

When you're looking at a pair of speakers, it's easy to get overwhelmed by all the specifications. For example, a novice speaker shopper can expect to have his or her brain go numb when they read "3-way, 120 watts, 40 Hz to 22 KHz frequency response, 8 ohms impedance, with a 8" Poly/Carbon with high Temp Voice coil woofer and 1" Soft-Dome ferrofluid cooled tweeter."

These specifications (which we'll demystify in a moment) are a lot to consume, especially when you have to juggle such other variables as the appearance of the speakers, their size, and (topping the list) price.

The good news is that you don't have to get too worried about these specs (but it's still a good idea to keep them in mind). The most important test of a pair of speakers is to actually listen to them in action. Do they sound good to you? If so, press on. That sounds like a quick and dirty way to select speakers, but the specification system depends on each manufacturer. That is, there is no standard among manufacturers, so—when comparing the speakers on paper—it can be an apples-to-tangerines affair.

TIPS OF THE TRADE

Work Backwards with Your Home Entertainment System

One school of thought when developing your home entertainment and whole-house audio solution is to buy your speakers *first*. This might sound backwards, but when you consider that the speakers are the components that receive the boosted signals from the amplifiers, then convert them to sound, you understand the importance of speakers' roles. You could have the most amazing stereo system ever created, but if the signal is being sent to the worst speakers ever created, you'll be very unhappy with your selection.

Speaker load differs greatly depending on which speaker you buy, and will require different amplifier characteristics. Speakers also introduce the most distortion into a system. Most source signals (CD players, amplifiers, cable, and so forth) bring less distortion to the audio party than the speakers.

When you're curled up on the couch, the lights down low, and "Love Rollercoaster" by the Ohio Players is coming through the speakers, you want to make sure you hear every note as crystal clear as possible.

With that having been said, here's a breakdown of the various speaker specifications and what they mean to you:

❏ Speakers are described as 4-way, 3-way, 2-way, or 1-way. *Way* refers to the number of bands into which the frequency is divided. Three-way speakers use three drivers, each handling a different range of frequencies. Woofers handle the low frequencies, midranges handle the middle frequencies, and tweeters handle the high frequencies. A 4-way speaker is not necessarily better than a 2-way speaker, however. Also impacting on the speaker's performance are the speaker drivers, cabinet, and the parts of the crossover.

❏ A speaker's *frequency response* determines how much and how well it can reproduce sound. Most humans can hear sounds within 20 Hz and 20 kHz. So, when a manufacturer advertises that its speaker operates between 40 Hz and 22 kHz +/- 3dB, that means it doesn't handle the lower frequencies as well as the higher frequencies. Also, since it goes about 2 kHz above human hearing range, there's a little bonus in there for the family dog.

❏ The number after the frequency range is called the *tolerance* (in our example, 3dB) and indicates by how much the sound level (in decibels, which is a measure of sound power) at the lowest or highest frequency can be lower or higher than the average midrange frequency. As a rule, look for a wider frequency range with a lower tolerance.

- ❏ Output power (measured in watts) determines how much power the amplifier can provide to the speakers before the speakers are damaged. A larger output power means that you can enjoy louder output from your speakers.

- ❏ *Impedance* is the speaker's resistance to current flow from the amplifier. This measurement is made in *ohms*. This measurement won't determine if you have a "better" or "worse" set of speakers. It's simply a measurement to indicate what level of resistance is present. As such, you want to buy a pair of speakers that are matched in their impedance and to your receiver outputs. Especially with whole-home audio connections, it's important to keep in mind the impedance levels of speakers connected to your amplifier. Connecting loads beyond the amplifier's capabilities will cause the amplifier to overheat, causing damage to the speakers and the amplifier.

- ❏ A speaker's sensitivity indicates how loud the speaker will be per 2.83 volts input. If you have speakers with a low sensitivity, you'll need a more powerful amplifier to drive them. The converse is also true: if you have speakers with a high sensitivity, you don't need as beefy an amplifier.

- ❏ *Signal-to-noise ratio* indicates the ratio of the speaker's pure signal to the static. A higher ratio is better because it gives a cleaner sound with less noise.

HEADS UP!

Physical Placement Is Also Important

Where you place your speakers (that is, in which room they are located) will also have a big impact on sound quality. Rooms with reflective surfaces, like windows or hardwood floors, ultimately decrease the quality of sound.

Distribution Systems

There are a couple ways in which you can send an audio signal (either from your stereo or video system) to points within your home. First, you can buy a component designed solely for use as a distribution system. For example, the NuVo

Simplese, as shown in Figure 13-1, sells for US$999.99. It has two inputs (meaning it can accept the signals from two different sources, like a DVD player, VCR, or cable box), four outputs (meaning it can send signals out to four different television sets), and includes four wall-mounted infrared control panels along with an IR remote control. This allows people at the device's four end stations to control the source without having to be standing in front of it.

Figure 13-1
NuVo Simplese audio
distribution system

The other option is an amplifier with multiple outputs, like the SpeakerCraft 8-channel amplifier, shown in Figure 13-2. The unit sells for US$1,399.95 and has eight separate level controls.

Figure 13-2
SpeakerCraft
amplifier with
eight outputs

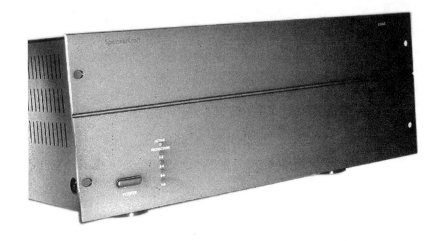

Impedance Matching Volume Controls

Piping audio to a room in your home is one thing. However, it's more than likely you'll want to be able to turn it up or down. In order to make those changes, you'll want to install an impedance-matching volume control. These devices (like the one shown in Figure 13-3) are installed in the wall and control the volume from the speaker and present a constant load to the audio amplifier.

Figure 13-3
Impedance-matching
volume control

This means that when you add impedance-matching volume controls to your receiver, you will not damage the receiver when more than one pair of speakers is added. Most impedance-matching volume controls allow you to add up to 16 pairs of speakers. We'll show you how to install an impedance-matching volume control in Chapter 14.

HEADS UP!

More Speakers Means Less Volume

As you add more speakers to your whole-home audio solution, expect the total volume to decrease. This is because the speakers all have to share the same signal, and with each pair of speakers added, the signal strength drops by half.

Impedance-matching volume controls range in price from US$30 to US$100.

Video Components

Video distribution requires different components than audio distribution. Where audio systems can simply split the signal and then manage it with an impedance-matching volume control, video systems can do so much more. When deciding what to do with your whole-house video solution, there are a number of components to consider.

Distribution Systems

When distributing video signals, the biggest factor to consider is the distance between the video source and the room to which the signal will be piped. For simple signal distribution (that is, everyone watches the same thing on their televisions), a signal splitter or amplified signal splitter can be employed. Alternately, you can connect a modulator to your inputs before the signal is split. A modulator makes it possible to run several signals across the coax cable, then flip the channel on the destination television set to the predetermined channel, and everyone can watch different things in different rooms. We'll explain modulators and splitters in more detail later in this chapter.

Figuring out how all the components fit together for a video distribution system can be somewhat of a head scratcher. If you want a turnkey video distribution system, an all-in-one system that includes modulation of two signals (that is, the ability to select between two video sources) along with outputs to six zones is shown in Figure 13-4. It sells for US$159.99.

Figure 13-4
Video distribution
system with
two-source
modulation

Modulators

Most modulators built into VCRs, satellite receivers, and so forth only output to channel 3 or 4. As such, you cannot place this signal onto a line that already has a signal on channel 3 or 4. Further, the signals that come from these devices are usually "wider" than they should be, and these signals tend to spill over onto neighboring channels. This is why you sometimes are able to see your VCR signal (albeit faded, fuzzy, and distorted) on a neighboring channel.

The cable company and broadcast stations are able to put signals on specific channels because they have devices called *modulators*. In order to distribute multiple video signals across coax cabling, you will need to install an external modulator.

For instance, if a VCR in the bedroom is connected to a modulator that sends the signal to channel 102, then when the VCR is playing, any TV in the house connected to the whole-home A/V system can tune in to channel 102 and watch the video.

External modulators, like the one shown in Figure 13-5, can pipe video onto UHF and cable channels (the exact number of available channels will differ, depending on the modulator you purchase). External modulators aren't cheap, however. The Theater 4202g 4-Input Modulator shown in Figure 13-5 sells for US$699.99. However, less expensive models can be purchased for as little as US$150. Price will also depend on how many channels your modulator serves.

Figure 13-5
External modulator

Modulators offer different options. Some features you're likely to encounter when selecting a modulator include these:

❑ The number of input and output channels (typically, modulators come in three- and four-channel systems, however single- and double-channel systems are available).

❑ The range of channel numbers. The Theater 42045g system, for example, allows you to use UHF channels 14 to 69 and CATV channels 54 to 94, and 100 to 125.

❑ Stereo or mono audio outputs.

❑ Modulators can either be in-wall or freestanding units. In-wall units give a neater look to a room.

TIPS OF THE TRADE

How to Get a Stereo Signal...on a Budget

For a video signal with an accompanying stereo audio signal, a modulator designed for stereo applications must be used. Unfortunately, stereo capable modulators are the pricier models. You can save some of this cost by utilizing your whole-house audio distribution system (assuming, of course, that you have one).

To connect such a system, simply attach the stereo outputs from your source (DVD, VCR, etc.) into open inputs on your whole-home audio amplifier. Then, when you want to watch television in stereo, simply use the source audio from your amplifier.

Lowpass Filter

When modulating a video signal onto a specific channel, you must select a channel that does not already have a signal on it. In the event you cannot find an open channel, don't worry. A lowpass filter (like the one shown in Figure 13-6) can be used to remove channels before adding your own signal.

Lowpass filters eliminate frequencies above a certain level so that your channel can be distributed throughout your video distribution system without interference from the cable company. Channels below the filter's rating will come through without any changes. Lowpass filters cost about US$29.99 and can be purchased for various channel ranges.

Figure 13-6
A lowpass filter is
installed inline from
your video source.

Lowpass Filters Aren't Just for Removing Channels

There can be a lot of junk on your cable—junk that could interfere with
your whole-home video signal. Lowpass filters also remove cable system
noise, test, and monitoring signals from the cable company, and signals
from cable modems.

As a bonus, these filters prevent your modulated signals from traveling back down the cable and into your neighbors' homes, or even
traveling back up the rooftop antenna and being broadcast across the
neighborhood.

Use Two Filters

*In some cases, where the signal strength on existing channels to be blocked is too high, two
filters connected in a series may be necessary to completely block the signal.*

Splitters and Combiners

Signal splitters and combiners are, essentially, the same product (like the one
shown in Figure 13-7). In fact, if you buy one, all you have to do to convert it from
a splitter to a combiner is to flip it over and change the inputs and the outputs.

Figure 13-7
Signal
splitter/combiner

Splitters and combiners make it possible to split a TV antenna or cable signal and send it to multiple end sources, or to combine multiple inputs into a single output. Splitters and combiners came in 2-, 3-,4-,6-, or 8-way configurations and cost between US$5.99 and US$19.99.

Amplified splitters allow a signal to travel further across coax cable. As a rule, if you are sending a signal farther than about 50 feet, an amplified signal splitter should be used.

TIPS OF
THE TRADE

Keeping Your Signal Clean

If you have empty connectors on your splitter (for instance, you buy a 4-way splitter, but only use three of the terminals), use a 75-ohm terminator on the unused signal output. Frequently, unterminated outputs cause a "herringbone" pattern to appear on some channels of the other television sets attached to it.

These terminators cost US$6.99 for a 20 pack and screw on to coaxial outlets.

Zones

In Chapter 5, we talked about zones in relation to security systems. Just to confuse you, the word "zone" is also used in Smart Home entertainment systems. When discussing security systems, "zone" was used to describe various sensors or devices connected to the system. When we talk about whole-home audio and video systems, "zone" is really meant to describe a room or area in your home served by a portion of your whole-home A/V system.

For example, if you want to wire your family room and three bedrooms, your family room might be referred to as zone one, while the bedrooms will be referred to as zones two through four. In this section, we'll talk about the different ways in which you can distribute A/V signals to your various zones.

Single Source Distributed to Multiple Rooms

The easiest and least expensive method is to send the signal from a single receiver to multiple zones. The signals are input to the receiver from its various sources (VCR, DVD, CD player, satellite dish, and so forth). From there, the signal is sent to a signal splitter with built-in impedance-matching capabilities, then split off to the four zones.

HEADS UP!

The Number of Zones Depends on What You Buy
We're only using four zones as an example. The number of zones possible will depend on the impedance-matching system you select and can certainly be more than four.

The downside of this particular design is that, while each zone is connected, they all receive the same signal. It is possible to control the volume on the zone's television set, but not change the channel or source of the audio.

Multiple Zones, Multiple Sources

To facilitate the need for different zones to receive different video or audio inputs, it is necessary to employ multiple amplifiers and receivers. Each amplifier or receiver is used for each zone.

The amplifiers and receivers can be stacked together and the source inputs can be shared. The signals are sorted out and sent to the appropriate zone using a signal distributor. The volume and source for each zone can be controlled via a number of remote control options, which we'll discuss in Chapter 14.

For example, if Jimmy in Zone 1 wants to listen to a CD, he turns on the CD player via an IR remote control. This sends a signal back to the A/V cabinet where the CD is activated and sent to the receiver that feeds Zone 1. Meanwhile, Jane (watching a movie in Zone 2 from the satellite dish) won't be cut off because a different receiver is feeding a signal to her zone.

Purpose-Made Zone Systems

A less costly alternative, assuming you only have two zones to feed, is an amplifier that has built-in capabilities for serving two separate zones. If you have more than two zones, another option is the NuVo Multi-Source/Multi-Zone system. This distribution system has the capacity to handle six sources and six zones. It contains built-in amplifiers and source distribution systems. This system costs US$2,094.95.

Designing Your Distribution System

When designing your audio and video distribution system, the ideal situation is to have a signal that is balanced between all zones.

As a rule, RG-6 coax cable loses between 2 and 6dB per 100 feet. When you add a passive splitter or combiner, expect to lose between 4 and 6dB for each two-way splitter, and between 6 and 9dB at each four-way splitter. Add up the total of your coax cable run along with any splitters and combiners, and add amplifiers inline if needed so that all your zones have the same signal strength.

Additionally, it is a good idea to make sure your incoming signals are all balanced so they enter the amplifier with the same signal strength. This information can be approximated by examining the outputs from each of your devices. For example, if your DVD signal is piping in at 5dB and your cable line is coming in at 15dB, install a 10dB attenuator on your cable line prior to its connection to a modulator.

TIPS OF THE TRADE

Attenuator Pads

Attenuator pads are a lot like resistors in electronics work. That is, they knock down the power of a signal. This helps not only balance your signals, but it prevents so-called "hot" signals from overwhelming your system. Additionally, attenuators cut back the power so that, when modulated with other signals and amplified, they will not create extraneous noise.

Attenuator pads are cheap, so don't wince at buying them. They come in 3dB, 6dB, 10dB, and 20dB specifications for US$1.59 each at Smarthome.com. If you need (or expect to need) more than one, you can find mixed bags containing two of each specification for US$11.99.

Make sure your signals do not exceed the maximum output of your amplifier, or else noise will be introduced into the signal. Your output level can be calculated by adding the amplifier gain (amplifier gain is the amount the device increases the amplitude of the signal relative to itself. That is, if the amplifier gets a 1-volt signal and the output is 5 volts, then the amp has provided a gain of 5 times) to the input signal level.

On long runs of cable, you should use a tilt compensator to bring the higher frequency signals into balance with the lower frequency signals. This shift occurs because high frequencies lose strength faster than low frequencies. Tilt compensators are US$19.99 devices that screw in to your video line and ensure that you're getting good image quality from both the high end of the frequency range and the low end. How do you know which signals reside where? Table 13-1 shows which channels exist within which frequency. Each channel uses about 6 MHz of bandwidth.

TV/Cable Channel	Frequency
FM	88–108 MHz
VHF	54–211 MHz
Low-mid band (CATV channels 95–99)	90–115 MHz
Mid band (CATV channels 14–22)	121–169 MHz
Super band (CATV channels 23–36)	216–295 MHz
Hyperband (CATV channels 37–64)	300–463 MHz
UHF (Broadcast channels 14–69/CATV 65-140)	468–890 MHz

Table 13-1
Which Channels and Signals Use Which Frequencies

Connecting Whole-House A/V

Televisions, DVD players, and digital video recorders certainly make a whole-home A/V system utilitarian (not to mention cool), but the heart of the system isn't what you see—it's what you don't see. Buried in the walls are runs of coaxial cable, feeding the various zones from a distribution system.

In this example, we are connecting a four-zone system. That is, coaxial cable and speaker wire will be run from our A/V cabinet to the family room, the living room, and two bedrooms. We'll talk you through the installation of each component (the audio and the video). However, for best results, it's a good idea to pull the audio and video cabling at the same time. This will reduce the severity of any headaches greatly.

A/V Cabinet

Like the placement of a security system, your home audio and video system should be placed in a central location. Many people have A/V cabinets that contain all of their whole-home gear. This site will contain the stereos, the amplifiers, modulators, DVD players, cable boxes, and so forth.

An A/V cabinet is a good way to keep all your components organized and makes the process of connecting more equipment much easier. Some Smart Home enthusiasts even buy special racks for equipment that pull out of the cabinet and swivel around so that the rear of the equipment can be easily accessed.

HEADS UP!

Keep Your A/V Cabinet Somewhere Cool

When selecting the site of your A/V cabinet, be sure to keep everything well ventilated and cool. All that equipment can get really hot, really quickly.

Wiring

Audio and video infrastructure requires different types of wiring. They also require different types of wiring at various points of installation in your Smart Home. This section explains the types of wiring you can expect to run into and how you can connect it appropriately.

Audio

In your whole-home audio solution, you're likely to use two types of cabling:

❑ **RCA audio cables**   These cables, shown in Figure 13-8, are used to connect components together. They connect to the back of your CD player, then to your amplifier, and so forth. They cost about US$2 for a three-foot length.

Figure 13-8
RCA audio cables

❏ **Speaker cable**   Speaker wire is used to run through the house before terminating at a remote jack in another room. From there, either speaker wire or RCA audio cables (depending on your speaker) are used to connect the speakers to the wall jack. Speaker wire commonly comes in a range of sizes (commonly 10 to 22 gauge) with two- or four-wire configurations.

HEADS UP!

Use Four-wire Speaker Cable

It is highly recommended that you buy four-conductor, in-wall speaker cable when running cable from room to room. This is for the sake of installation simplicity. Four-conductor wire contains enough wire to feed two speakers so you need only pull the cable once. Depending on the manufacturer, the price of the cabling (for the same 500-foot length) can be within US$20 or as much as US$100. However, it's still less expensive and conducive to headaches than placing two runs of two-conductor cabling.

Wiring comes in different thicknesses. Thicker cabling is better for longer runs and provides more fidelity. Table 13-2 tells the ideal run lengths for different wire gauges.

Gauge	Maximum Run Length
16	Up to 50 feet
14	50 to 100 feet
12	100 to 200 feet
10	Over 200 feet

Table 13-2
Wire Thickness and Maximum Length

Audio Jacks

There are three ways of connecting wire you'll encounter when connecting your whole-house audio system. Depending on your speaker types, you might find that one method or the other better suits your needs:

❏ **Banana jacks**   Banana connectors look like tiny bananas (hence the name) and plug into banana jacks. Figure 13-9 shows a banana jack.

Figure 13-9
Banana jacks

❑ **RCA jack**   RCA jacks are the jacks that are used to connect RCA cables.

❑ **Bare wire**   The third option is an even more prevalent way to connect audio equipment (especially on speakers). Bare speaker wire can be inserted into the appropriate jacks on the back of audio equipment. The wire is held in place with clips or nuts.

60 MINUTES

Audio Connection

Follow these steps to connect your whole-home audio system:

1. Measure the distance from your A/V cabinet to the termination site in each room. Add a few extra feet to the cabling to account for obstacles you might encounter.

2. Run the cable to its destination through walls, ceilings, and so forth.

3. If mounting the gang box to a wall that's already been finished, locate where you want the terminal to be located and use the back of a low-voltage gang box as a template. Trace around the low-voltage gang box with a pencil. It's best if this location is next to a wall stud so the gang box can be securely mounted.

4. Using a Rotozip tool, cut out the area you just marked.

5. If you are terminating your audio inputs to an area that hasn't been finished, installation couldn't be easier. Simply locate the low-voltage gang box where you want it to be placed and nail it to a wall stud.

TIPS OF THE TRADE

Low-Voltage Gang Boxes

You can use any type of gang box for your audio and video jacks. However, consider buying low-voltage gang boxes, instead of high-voltage gang boxes. Where the high-voltage variety are usually colored blue and have a solid back, low-voltage gang boxes are a different color like orange and have no back. This is helpful, first, in the pulling of cabling—you don't have to try and thread your cables through a knockout. Second, it tells people looking at the box (like a building inspector, for instance) that the wiring routed to that gang box is low voltage in nature.

HEADS UP!

Hammer Height

You can mount your gang boxes at any level you want, but a standard height for electrical outlets is the length of a hammer handle, as shown in Figure 13-10. If you're mounting audio and video terminals near the floor, keeping them at a hammer's height is a good way to keep everything symmetrical.

Figure 13-10
Using a hammer handle to measure the height of a low-voltage gang box keeps all your outlets symmetrical.

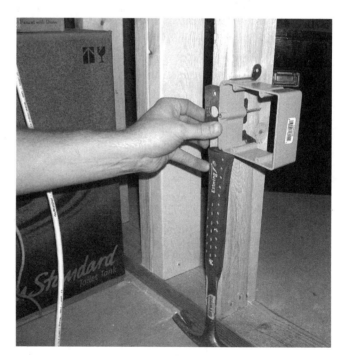

6. Feed the speaker cable through a knockout hole or back of the gang box.

7. Using wire strippers, strip both ends of the cable about three inches, then strip the individual wires back a third of an inch.

8. Connect the end of the speaker cable to the jack you'll be using (either the banana or RCA type). This is shown in Figure 13-11.

Figure 13-11
Connecting speaker
wire to the jack

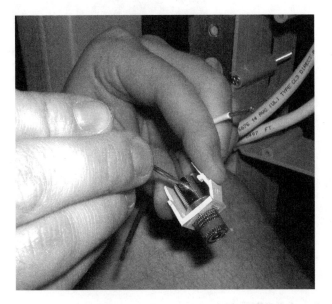

TIPS OF THE TRADE

Customize Your Jacks

You need not worry about filling your room up with all sorts of jacks, each serving a different purpose. Several companies—like Leviton, for example—sell kits that allow you to mix and match different jacks that will be used in a gang box. For instance, in Figure 13-12 we have a unit that allows three different types of jacks. The uppermost jack is a coax cable jack, while the lowermost jack is an RCA jack that we'll use for a subwoofer. In the middle, we're going to place a telephone jack for the satellite decoder's use. These units allow you a great level of customization when setting up your whole-house A/V system.

Figure 13-12
Customizing your
speaker jacks

9. Attach the terminal to the wall and screw on a face plate.

10. At the A/V cabinet, connect the wires to the appropriate outputs on your amplifier. It might be necessary to attach RCA or banana connectors to the wires, depending on the type of amplifier you've purchased.

Video Connection

Pulling coaxial cable should follow, quite similarly, the steps we followed when installing the security cabling. There are some unique steps for this particular project, however. To connect your coaxial cable infrastructure, follow these steps:

1. Measure the distance from your A/V cabinet to the termination site in each room. Add a few extra feet to the cabling to account for obstacles you might encounter.

2. Run the cable to its destination through walls, ceilings, and so forth. Be sure to try not to run these low-voltage wires along runs with high-voltage electrical wires where possible. This will reduce the chance of generating a hum on your line.

3. If mounting the gang box to a wall that's already been finished, locate where you want the terminal to be located and use the back of a low-voltage gang box as a template. Trace around the low-voltage gang box

with a pencil. It's best if this location is next to a wall stud so the gang box can be securely mounted.

4. Using a Rotozip tool, cut out the area you just marked.

5. If you are terminating your audio inputs to an area that hasn't been finished, simply locate the low-voltage gang box where you want it to be placed and nail it to a wall stud.

6. Feed the coaxial cable through a knockout hole or the open back of the gang box.

7. Using a coaxial cable stripper, strip both ends of the cable.

8. Place an F connector on the stripped end of the cable by the A/V cabinet; then, using a crimp tool, crimp the connector to the cabling.

9. Connect the end of the coaxial cable to the wall-mounted F-connector, as shown in Figure 13-13.

Figure 13-13
Connect the coax cable to the rear of the wall jack.

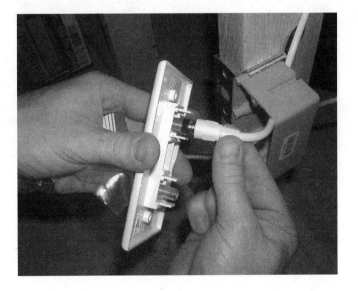

10. Screw the connector to the wall and attach a face plate.

11. Connect the end of the cable in the A/V cabinet to the distribution panel.

TIPS OF THE TRADE

The Cost of a Coaxial Cable System

There are a lot of little bits and pieces that can add up in price when computing how much you'll need to spend developing the infrastructure of your whole-home video system. First is the consideration of the cabling itself.

If you use a single run of RG-6 cabling, 1,000 feet will cost about US$109.99. If you decide to future-proof or add an "outgoing" line from a room, it's a good idea to use dual cable so you needn't run the cabling twice. A spool of dual cable costs US$369.99. Other costs include these:

- ❏ A package of 20 crimp-on connectors costs US$6.99.
- ❏ A crimp tool costs US$19.99.
- ❏ A coax cable stripper costs US$12.99
- ❏ Wall-mounted F-connectors cost US$5.99.

The above steps assumed you would connect your cabling to a wall outlet, which makes for a nicer, neater appearance. However, if you want to save a couple dollars and don't mind the cable poking out of the floor, just drill a hole in the floor, run the cable through the hole, and crimp on a connector.

It is vitally important that you keep good records as to the lengths of various runs of coaxial cable. This is important because how you amplify a source signal will depend on how much cabling has been run. It works the other way, too, however. If most of your destination television sets are 200 feet away and you've installed an amplifier, the one or two televisions that are within 50 feet of the distribution panel are going to be overamplified. As such, it's a good idea to make good measurements of the cabling so you know how much signal needs to be pumped to each television set.

Same Length Runs

If the cable runs in your home are more or less the same distance from the distribution panel, you can use an inexpensive amplified splitter, like the one shown in Figure 13-14.

Figure 13-14
Amplified splitter

The splitter amplifies incoming signals, increasing the gain (in the 4-way model) by 8dB to each of its outputs, as compared to a 7dB loss in most 4-way splitters. The 8-way model provides a 4dB gain as compared to the 11dB loss experienced by most 8-way splitters.

The maximum range on these amplifiers is 200 feet for the 4-way model and 100 feet for the 8-way model. The 4- and 8-way amplified splitters sell for US$99.99 or $114.99, respectively.

Installation of the splitters requires the following steps:

1. Using two screws, mount the amplifier to an easy-to-access location near an AC power receptacle.

2. Connect the source signal (cable, antenna, DVD player, etc.) to CABLE IN.

3. Connect modulator output to MOD IN.

4. Connect OUTPUT jacks to distribute the signal to your zones.

5. Connect power supply using coaxial cable to DC12V INPUT.

Different Length Runs

The previous example explained how to connect a whole-house video system with an amplified splitter. However, it is more likely that your runs will be quite different in length. When connecting your system, expect to lose signal strength when the source is split (the more televisions it is branched off and split to, the more signal you will lose), and expect to lose signal strength as it travels across the coax cable.

TIPS OF THE TRADE

When and Where to Amplify a Signal

Obviously, signals that are to travel on longer runs need more amplification than those traversing shorter runs. The common solution to this problem is to amplify a signal ahead of the splitter to get more strength. There are a couple of problems with this approach:

- ❏ On short runs, the amplification will be too much for the system. You can tell when the signal is overamplified when the TV audio buzzes when white print appears on the screen. To ameliorate this problem, install signal strength attenuator pads on the line to reduce the signal strength.

- ❏ On long runs, the lower channels might look fine, but the higher channels are weak. This occurs when a signal amplifier increases the signal strength across all the channels, but coax cable attenuates the higher frequencies more than the lower channels. This problem can be fixed by installing a tilt compensator.

Depending on how kicked-up you want your whole-home audio and video system to be, you might consider purchasing a distribution panel like the one shown in Figure 13-15. This particular model (with three inputs and eight outputs) sells for US$299.99. A 3-input, 12-output model sells for US$339.99.

Figure 13-15
Preconfigured distribution panel

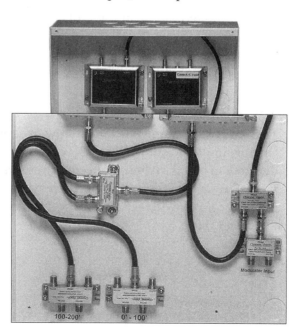

The panels are set up for both short and long runs. The panels have outputs for runs of 100, 200, and 300 feet. This solution is a good turnkey because it has already been set up with amplification and tilt compensation already calculated and installed.

Installation follows these steps:

1. Install the panel surface mounted; or, using a Rotozip tool, cut a hole in the wall the size of the panel and flush mount it. The panel fits between two wall studs.

2. Connect your input cabling to the appropriate inputs (DVD, cable, a modulated source, and so forth).

3. Connect your destination cabling to the appropriate connections, being mindful of the distance between the panel and the destination television.

We covered a lot of ground in this chapter in terms of connecting your Smart Home with whole-house audio and video. The preceding sections talked about the basics of whole-house entertainment systems, but there are still some ways in which you can add more functionality to your system, such as the use of volume controls and remote controls. If you're ready, turn the page to Chapter 14 where we'll cover these topics.

TESTING 1-2-3

❏ Did you add a few extra feet of length to your coax and stereo cable measurements?

❏ Did you amplify weaker signals?

❏ Did you use attenuator pads for stronger signals?

❏ Will you need a lowpass filter to get your modulated signals on a channel you want?

❏ Did you bring a favorite CD to the store when you tested your speakers? Does the music sound the way you want it to?

❏ Are your signal strengths the same in each zone?

Chapter 14

Audio and Video Distribution

Tools of the Trade

Various screwdrivers
Sheet metal screws
Wire stripper
Two-wire plus ground, 22-gauge cabling
Two-wire, 14-gauge speaker cabling
Connecting block
Flush-mounted IR sensor
IR emitters
Impedance-matching volume control

Connecting your whole-home audio and video system is a huge undertaking and if you stopped after pulling all that cabling, connecting all those components, and shelling out all that money, no one would blame you. But once completed, a whole-house audio and video system will add nothing but fun and functionality to your home. Now, you'll be able to watch television in your family room while your spouse listens to the stereo in the den, and while your son watches a DVD in his room.

That's all fine and good, but what happens if your spouse wants to skip ahead a couple songs on the CD? What happens when your son wants to turn off the DVD and watch a little MTV? With the system we installed in Chapter 13, you need to make all control changes at the A/V cabinet. Certainly, we can do better with our Smart Home.

In this chapter, we'll talk about remote control options and how to manage volume controls in your rooms. Additionally, we'll connect a bedroom to our whole-home A/V system, incorporating volume controls and an infrared (IR) remote control system.

Remote Control Options

There are several ways to control your whole-home A/V system remotely. In this section, we'll explain those methods so you can decide which solution is best for your own particular system. Like other Smart Home projects, some are inexpensive (and somewhat limited in functionality) while others can be costly but provide great features.

X10

X10 can be used to manage your remote control needs. "But wait," you say "X10 is a signal run over the power lines. How is it going to help me turn the volume up on the stereo?" Using an X10-to-IR controller, X10 signals can be converted to IR signals. One such product, the X10 to IR Linc (shown in Figure 14-1) sells for US$119.99.

Figure 14-1
X10 to IR Linc

The unit is located in your A/V cabinet and is plugged into an AC receptacle. When a signal is sent by an X10 remote control to your PC or X10 controller, you can change channels, turn up the volume, or accomplish any other feats made possible by remote control.

There is an added bonus, however. What if you want your television to turn on and go to a particular channel the moment your garage door is opened? By using a Powerflash (this is an X10 device that connects to a sensor, causing other X10 devices to activate and deactivate) and connecting to a garage door sensor, simply set the appropriate codes on the X10 to IR Linc and you can have this functionality.

Additional modules can be added to the X10 to IR Linc to make the system even smarter:

❑ **TV detector probe** This unit tells the X10 to IR Linc whether your TV is on or off by sensing the RF signals commonly emitted by TVs. This would be useful if you've forgotten to turn off your television set at night, or if you suspect your son is watching TV after lights out.

❑ **LED light sensor probe** This probe is placed over the LED power indicator and can tell the X10 to IR Linc whether a given component is on or off. This would be useful, again, to indicate whether a component was left on.

❑ **Video detector probe** When plugged into an RCA video output jack, this sensor can detect whether a video signal is present. This can be used to tell your X10 system whether a system is already on or off so that the system need not send a repetitive command.

HEADS UP!

More Equipment Is Necessary

An X10 Maxi-Controller is required for programming the X10 to IR Linc. The X10 Maxi-Controller is a stand-alone X10 control unit used to manage all your X10 devices and—as a bonus—is used to program the X10 to IR Linc. This controller costs US$21.99.

Wireless

The simplest solution to deploy is also the least expensive. This method employs wireless radio frequency (RF) signals. The Powermid, shown in Figure 14-2, is one such product that allows you to control your equipment from remote locations.

Figure 14-2
Powermid wireless remote control system

The Powermid, which retails for US$52.99, consists of two pieces: a transmitter and a receiver. The transmitter is located in your remote location (for instance, a bedroom) and it picks up the signals from your remote control. The transmitter then sends those signals to the receiver (which can be located up to 100 feet away). Finally, the receiver converts that signal back to an IR signal, passing it along to the desired component. The transmitter and receiver work through walls and floors, but you're still limited by a 100-foot range. Additional transmitters and receivers can be purchased if you want to control equipment in more than one location, or if you want to control your home entertainment equipment from more than one zone.

Coax Transmission

The next option uses your coax cabling infrastructure (whether existing cabling or new runs you've just installed for your whole home A/V system) to send signals back to your A/V equipment. This solution requires the purchase of an IR signal coax cable splitter/injector, IR receiver, and IR emitter.

Installation is simple. Plug the IR signal coax cable splitter/injector (shown in Figure 14-3) inline with your coaxial cable, then plug an IR receiver into the IR jack. In the A/V cabinet, connect a second splitter/injector inline before the video distribution system. Finally, plug in the IR emitter to the splitter/injector and point it at the equipment.

Figure 14-3
IR signal coax cable
splitter/injector

HEADS UP!

Affix the Emitter

Some IR emitters can be affixed directly to the component to be managed via remote. This will make your remote control endeavors much more reliable.

This method is more reliable than the RF transmitter solution. A complete package, like the Xtra Link 2, shown in Figure 14-4, costs US$79.99. This includes the requisite equipment for connecting one zone. However, the only requirement is that your coax cabling has been laid out in a home-run fashion. If it is in a looped or daisy-chained configuration, this solution will not work.

Figure 14-4
Xtra Link 2 contains all the components necessary for coax transmission.

Hardwired

The ideal solution is to install a hardwired system. This provides the most reliability, but it is also the most difficult to connect. This requires pulling cables through your walls to connect IR sensors (located in each zone) to a connecting block. This block is located in your A/V cabinet; then, IR emitters are connected between your components and the connecting block. A connecting block is shown in Figure 14-5.

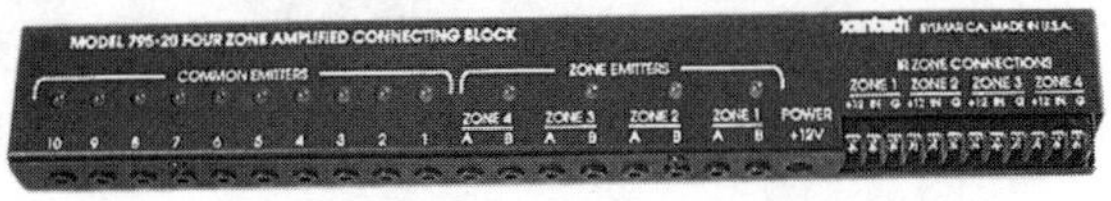

Figure 14-5
A connecting block

Connecting blocks can serve two to six zones and can emit signals for up to 10 devices (100 if 10 units are daisy chained together). The cost for a connecting block varies, depending on its configuration, but a four-zone connecting block sells for US$179.95. This system provides the most flexibility and the best signal reliability.

Connecting a Bedroom to A/V System

Finally, we're going to connect another zone in our Smart Home to the whole-house A/V system. This connection will go beyond simply piping in the video and audio signals—it will also incorporate a volume control for the audio system along with a remote control system to change channels, skip the DVD ahead a chapter, and so forth.

Audio

In Chapter 13, we explained how to connect your home for whole-house audio. It did the trick of connecting the appropriate wiring, but now you need a way to manage the volume of the incoming signal. Impedance-matching volume controls make it possible to control many sets of speakers, if you so decide to set the system up in that way. For example, if you decide to install more than one set of speakers in a room (maybe you want surround sound), you can control all those speakers from a single volume control. Or, maybe you just want one volume control to regulate the volume to the speakers in both the kitchen and the dining room.

Volume Control

For this phase of the project, we're using a low-profile impedance-matching volume control, as shown in Figure 14-6. This unit retails for US$59.99.

Figure 14-6
Impedance-matching
volume control

The first step toward installation is to locate the unit in an accessible location. It's good to locate the control somewhere close to entrances, exits, or light switches.

Place with Other Low-Voltage Devices

The volume control can be collocated in the same low-voltage gang boxes with other low-voltage controls, like keypads or IR remote control devices. However, do not mount volume controls in the same gang boxes as 110-volt devices without a divider between the two parts of a multiple-gang box. This is to comply with electrical codes.

The gang box manufacturer may say it is okay to install other devices alongside 110-volt devices—indeed, it might be partitioned for this very purpose. However, the issue is not one of electrical safety—it is one of sound quality. Neighboring 110-volt devices might cause buzzing or popping sounds to be heard in your speakers.

With this particular model of volume control, the next step is to calculate the proper impedance settings for the system and set the appropriate jumper on the device. The correct setting is determined by knowing the number of speaker pairs, the speakers' impedance, and the output impedance of the amplifier (which is found in your amplifier owner's manual). Once you know these numbers, refer to the instruction sheet that accompanies the volume control unit to determine if the jumper is to be set to either the 2X, 4X, or 8X setting. For example, we're installing a pair of 8-ohm speakers. As such, the correct jumper setting is 2X.

30 MINUTES

Once the unit has been set up for your particular use, the next step is to wire the room and install the volume control. Follow these steps (this process assumes whole-house audio has already been installed and that it is in an already finished home).

1. If installing the volume control in a finished room, determine where you want the gang box to be located (be sure to place it next to a wall stud so it can be securely attached). Use a gang box as a template and trace around the box with a pencil.

2. Using a Rotozip tool, cut out the drywall and mount the gang box to the wall stud.

3. If installing the volume control in an unfinished room, simply locate where you want the controls to be placed and hammer or screw the gang box onto the wall stud.

HEADS UP!

Use Nail Plates

When installing wiring (either high voltage or low voltage) within 1 1/4 inch from a wall stud, and drywall has not yet been hung, it's a good idea to install a nail protector plate, like those shown in Figure 14-7. Nail protector plates prevent damage to wiring if, once the wall has been finished, someone drills or nails into the wall.

Figure 14-7
Nail plates prevent wires from being damaged

4. Pull the speaker wire coming from the amplifier through the back of the gang box. (This assumes you've already wired a room with audio cabling. If not, flip back to Chapter 13 for more information about connecting audio cabling to your zones).

5. Use a piece of masking tape to mark this wiring as "Input." Jot down the color scheme you're using for the left channel and right channel, positive and negative leads.

6. If you are using a home-run wiring scheme, each room's cabling should run back to the A/V cabinet.

HEADS UP!

Check Local Codes

Many building and fire codes require any in-wall cable to be CL-2, CL-3, or FT4 rated. These ratings apply to a cable's sheathing characteristics. Check with your local building inspector before prewiring.

7. Run two lengths of two-conductor speaker cable from the gang box to the corresponding left and right speakers (or speaker jacks).

8. Mark the cable for left or right and for their polarities.

9. Trim the cable, allowing enough to hang outside the gang box so it can connect the volume control.

10. Strip 1/4 inch of insulation from each wire. Tightly twist the end of each wire until there are no loose threads. Before the volume control is connected, the wiring should look like that depicted in Figure 14-8.

Figure 14-8
The impedance-matching volume control connects to a four-wire cable and two two-wire cables.

11. Remove the two four-conductor plugs (connectors) from the volume control. Both plugs are marked L+ L- R- R+. One connector is for the amplifier output connections and the other for speaker connections.

12. Insert the amplifier and speaker wires into each hole. Ensure the wires are connected to the appropriate connectors (left, right, positive, and negative). This is shown in Figure 14-9.

Figure 14-9
Connect the speaker wire to the holes on the connectors.

13. Secure each wire by tightening the connector screws or soldering them in place.

14. Plug the wired connectors into the volume control unit, as Figure 14-10 shows. Ensure that the output from the amplifier is plugged into the amplifier side of the control, and the speakers are plugged into the speaker side of the control.

Figure 14-10
Attaching the connectors to the volume control

15. Tuck excess cable inside the gang box and insert the volume control into the gang box.

16. Secure the volume control with screws.

17. Add a Decora-style face plate over the volume control.

TIPS OF THE TRADE

Dialing Up Your New Volume Control

When you have two volume controls working in tandem (your newly installed volume control as well as the volume control on the amplifier itself) you will undoubtedly run into problems with distortion. This occurs when the second volume control amplifies a signal that is already loud enough (or too loud).

To fix the levels on your two volume controls, play sound or music through the stereo, keeping the volume at the amp turned all the way down. Next, turn the newly installed volume control all the way up. There should still be no sound (as the amp volume is turned all the way down). Slowly add volume at the amp until it is playing at about the loudest level you want. Then turn down volume on the wall. The volume setting on the amp is where you want to leave it. If you turn this up, then you will distort the sound coming out of the speakers.

Video

In this section, we'll talk about connecting a remote control system to your whole-house video endeavors. Although we've included the remote control section along with video applications, this will work for any application that uses IR remote controls. That is, if your stereo system uses an IR remote control, you can set up the system to manage your stereo as well as your DVD player.

Wiring Considerations

Like audio connections, video can also be connected in home-run or loop configurations. Ideally, you should connect your video system in a home-run fashion. This not only ensures system integrity (if one point in the system fails, other points will remain able to access the video signal), but it's also helpful if you decide to connect a coax cable remote control system, since it relies on a home-run configuration for proper operation.

Remote Control

For our Smart Home's bedroom, in addition to the ability to manage the volume of the stereo (we have also connected the outputs from the entertainment system into the amplifier, so when watching a movie, we simply select the entertainment system as the audio source and we're able to watch the movie in stereo), we're also making the system more intelligent by adding a remote control system. As you remember from the beginning of this chapter, there are four ways to control your whole-house A/V system: wireless (the cheapest and easiest), via coax cable (a little more expensive, but more reliable), via X10, or using a hard-wired system.

In our Smart Home bedroom, we've decided to go with a hardwired system. It's more expensive and requires more installation than the other methods, but it is more reliable and flexible.

For this project, there are five components necessary:

❏ **Sensor**   This is located in the bedroom and converts the IR light from the remote control into an electrical signal. For this part of the project, we are using a wall-mounted IR sensor. There are other options for IR sensors, including table top sensors, sensors that fit in the door of a home entertainment cabinet, and some that are built in with volume controls. The model we've chosen (shown in Figure 14-11) sells for US$49.99.

Figure 14-11
IR sensor

❏ **Cabling**   We're using two-conductor plus ground, shielded, 22-gauge cabling (the sensor only needs three wires). This cabling connects the bedroom with the devices in the A/V cabinet and carries the signal from the IR sensor. A 1,000-foot spool of this cabling costs US$79.99.

❑ **Connecting block** This is a device that accepts all incoming signals and sends them to the appropriate IR emitters. When connected to the 12-volt DC power adapter, the connecting block will power the IR sensors throughout our whole-house A/V system. For this project, we are using a four-zone connecting block that sells for US$179.99. This block will accept inputs from four zones and output signals for up to ten devices.

❑ **IR emitter** These devices plug into the connecting block and are either pointed at or affixed to the sensor window of A/V components. The IR emitter takes the electrical signal from the connecting block and converts it back into IR light. Even though they are affixed over the sensor window of your A/V components, you can still use your remote control at the source, as the emitter allows other IR signals to pass through. For this project, we are using a mini stick-on IR emitter that sells for US$5.99.

❑ **Power supply** This provides the 12-volt DC power to run the connecting block. This unit costs US$12.95 and simply plugs into the connecting block, then an open AC wall receptacle.

The hardest part of installing the hardwired IR remote system is placing wires. Again, if the thought of pulling even more wire makes you agitated, you might be better off pursuing another remote control option, like a wireless system or (if your coax cable has been home-run) a coax remote system.

TIPS OF THE TRADE

Pull All Your Cabling at Once

Here's a time when planning ahead will pay off for you in big rewards. If you decide to develop a whole-house A/V system and end up pulling coax cable, speaker cable, and cable for your IR remote control, it only makes sense to pull all your cabling at one time.

Even if you're not planning on installing whole-house audio, video, and hardwired IR remote capabilities, spending the money now on the cabling will make the whole procedure much, much easier in the long run.

45 MINUTES   Follow these steps to connect your hardwired IR remote control system:

1. If installing in a finished room, locate where you want the low-voltage gang box to be located (be sure to place it next to a wall stud so it can be securely attached). Use a gang box as a template and trace around the box with a pencil.

HEADS UP!

Different Mounting for Different Projects

Again, the preceding step assumes the use of a wall-mounted IR sensor. However, if the sensor was a tabletop device, it would be unnecessary to cut into the wall. Also, if you were to buy the all-in-one IR sensor and volume control unit, you could mount both devices into the same gang box. It all depends on what type of sensor you opt to use.

2. Using a Rotozip tool, cut out the drywall and mount the gang box to the wall stud.

3. If installing in an unfinished room, simply locate the low-voltage gang box on a wall stud at the desired location and nail it in place.

4. Mount the connecting block to your A/V cabinet using four sheetmetal screws.

5. Measure the distance between your A/V cabinet and the location in the bedroom where the IR sensor will be mounted. Add a couple feet for good measure.

6. Measure that amount of cabling and, using the techniques we've previously described, pull the cabling through the walls, floor, or ceiling to reach the newly installed gang box.

HEADS UP!

Avoiding Insulation Makes for an Easier Run

If you stick to inside walls, you're not as likely to run into insulation, which will make your cable pulls more difficult to perform.

7. Pull the IR sensor wire coming from the wall into the back of the gang box.

8. Strip a half inch of insulation from each of the wires of the IR cabling.

9. There are three terminals on the back of the IR sensor. Connect your wires to these terminals and be sure to jot down which color wire is connected to which terminal. For our project, we've made the following connections:

V+	Red
GND	Ground wire
SIG	Black

10. Make the same connections on the connecting block in the A/V cabinet. On our connecting block, there are terminals for + 12, GND, and IN. As such, we'll connect the red wire to +12, the ground wire to the GND terminal, and the black wire to the IN terminal.

11. Connect the IR emitters to the connecting block. These units plug into the 3.5mm mini monophone jacks on the connecting block. The particular connecting block we're using allows the connection of ten emitters; however, our whole-house A/V system only has six devices, so there is room for four more components to be added.

12. Point the emitters at the A/V equipment. For best results, use the supplied adhesive tape to affix the emitters to the sensor windows on your components.

When everything is connected, plug the AC adapter into an open wall receptacle and test the system. You should be able to change channels instantly with virtually no delay between your remote control and the desired changes.

HEADS UP!

Reposition Your Gear if It Doesn't Work Properly

IR sensors can be tricked by stray IR light coming from fluorescent light fixtures, sunlight, and plasma-screen televisions and monitors. This problem can be ameliorated by experimenting with the location and placement of your IR sensors.

Connecting a whole-house A/V system can be an inexpensive project, with no wiring beyond plugging a couple wireless devices into the wall. However, you'll garner better results with systems that use more complex wiring connections. In this chapter, we talked about how to connect an IR remote control system using a hardwired configuration. This is by no means the only way to do it. It's best if you examine your own needs, wants, and resources and consider which of the four remote control options is best for you.

❏ Is your wiring connected to the appropriate terminals on the speakers, volume controls, and amplifiers?

❏ Is your wiring connected to the appropriate terminals on your IR sensors and connection blocks?

❏ Did you measure the length of speaker and IR sensor wire, then add a couple feet for your final measurement?

❏ Does your cabling meet local codes for in-wall use?

❏ Are your IR emitters close (or better yet attached) to the components they will control?

Chapter 15

Working and Playing Together: The Smart Home Way

Tools of the Trade

PC
HomeSeer software
Webcam
X10 controller
Web-Link II software

O ver the past several chapters, we've thrown a lot of information at you about how to set up various X10 devices to manage sundry aspects of your Smart Home. These pieces all work fine and dandy on their own, but to get real whole-home integration of our X10 gadgetry, we need some way to get everything to work and play together.

Enter the X10 controller.

We talked about these devices briefly in Chapter 4. Now, however, it's time to roll up our sleeves and see how we can use a home computer to do all the heavy lifting. To demonstrate X10 Smart Home functionality, we'll use HomeSeer, X10 management software from HomeSeer Technologies. We don't have the space to go into all the facets and features of this software, but we'll take a look at how to get started.

Setting Up the Computer

There are two components involved when using a computer to manage X10 devices. First, it is necessary to have the requisite computer and X10 controlling hardware. Second, there needs to be software that will be used for programming your various events. Think of it this way: The software is the interface between yourself and the computer, and the X10 controller is the interface between the computer and your X10 devices.

In this section, we'll talk about what hardware is necessary for using the HomeSeer application, and then we'll talk about how you can use HomeSeer to get set up and use your Smart Home's X10 devices.

HEADS UP!

Smart Home Management for the Macintosh

Like so many other pieces of software, there are several X10 controller applications for the PC, but few for the Macintosh. However, if you are using a Macintosh (or would prefer to use a Macintosh), you aren't totally left out in the cold. Thinking Home for the Macintosh sells for US$38.95 and can be used to manage an X10 controller via your Mac.

Hardware

You'll need a couple pieces of hardware in order to tell your X10 devices what to do: a computer and an X10 controller. The computer is the brains of your Smart Home scheduling, while the X10 controller takes those commands and issues them to your X10 devices.

Computer Requirements

Ensure that whatever X10 control software you purchase will work with your particular computer and operating system. HomeSeer, for example, runs under Windows XP/2000/NT4/ME or 98. HomeSeer does not, however, work on earlier versions like Windows 95, 3.1, or DOS. If you intend to add the voice recognition feature (something we won't be covering in this chapter), you should have at least a 300-MHz system.

To view your devices and events online, it is necessary to have a web browser installed, and you must have TCP/IP installed. To utilize HomeSeer's e-mail features, you need to have installed a MAPI-compliant e-mail application, like Outlook or Outlook Express. You also need Internet access.

USB X10 Controller

An X10 controller, which we talked about in Chapter 4, is the interface between your computer and your X10 devices. The controller plugs into your computer (usually with a serial or universal serial bus (USB) connection), then plugs into an open AC receptacle that is not part of a power strip. When commands are issued by the computer, they are sent to the controller, which translates them into X10 signals. Also, when the X10 controller "hears" X10 signals on your home's wiring system, it translates those commands and sends them back to the computer where requisite action is taken.

TIPS OF
THE TRADE

Use a Separate Module If You Want to Turn Off Your Computer

Even though our X10 control solution utilizes a computer that is left on all the time, if you'd rather not leave your computer on, you can buy the X10 CM11A Activehome Computer Interface. This is an X10 controller that connects to your computer's serial port and wall outlet. Once you've established your overall X10 program, all your X10 commands are downloaded into this module.

This allows you to turn off your computer, yet still maintain a complex schedule of device and event interactions. The downside of this module, however, is that if you want to employ any web functionality (such as control via the Internet), it is not possible using a CM11A unit. This device and its software sell for US$44.99.

It is possible to use HomeSeer to program a CM11A Activehome Computer Interface. However, that functionality does not come bundled with the core HomeSeer software and requires the purchase of an additional add-on module.

Software

Like other titles, HomeSeer allows you to test out its functions before plunking down your US$149.95. HomeSeer allows a 30-day trial period. By all means, whatever X10 management application you choose, make full use of the trial periods to ensure that the application has all the features you want and need.

You can download a 30-day trial of HomeSeer from www.homeseer.com/downloads. The file is about 62MB, so if you're downloading using a modem, expect it to take a little while.

20 MINUTES

Configuration

Once you've downloaded the software from HomeSeer (or purchased the application on CD-ROM), it is next necessary to install it.

1. Double click on the **setuphs_full.exe** application and follow the onscreen commands for installation and setup.

2. When the application is installed, double-click the newly created HomeSeer icon. If you've installed the application using default values, there will be an icon on your desktop.

3. When the application starts, you will be asked to either enter an unlock code (the code came with your software if you purchased it) or click Run As Trial if you are testing the software. If you elect to run the software as a trial, you will have 30 days before it requires an unlock code to work again.

4. Next, a list of wizards appears. This allows you to set up various features of HomeSeer without having to go through the applications menu system. Wizards include the following:

   ❏ Telling HomeSeer what X10 interface you're using

   ❏ Telling HomeSeer what X10 devices you have

   ❏ Setting up a web server

   ❏ Creating schedules

You can use the wizards to manage these and other features. However, we'll explain how to set up devices and events without using the wizards.

X10 Interface   You might have needed to install software when installing your X10 controller, but HomeSeer still needs to know what type of interface you're using.

1 MINUTE

To do so, follow View | Options and then click the Interface tab. This is shown in Figure 15-1.

Since we are using a PowerLinc USB controller, we've selected it from the pull-down menu. Once you've made your selection, click OK.

Sunrise and Sunset   There are times at which you might want to activate and deactivate X10 devices based on sunrise and sunset. For example, you might want exterior lighting to come on at dusk and remain on for a couple hours before turning off. Naturally, your computer will not instinctively know when the sun is rising and setting. As such, you must tell the computer where you live, and it can compute the settings from there.

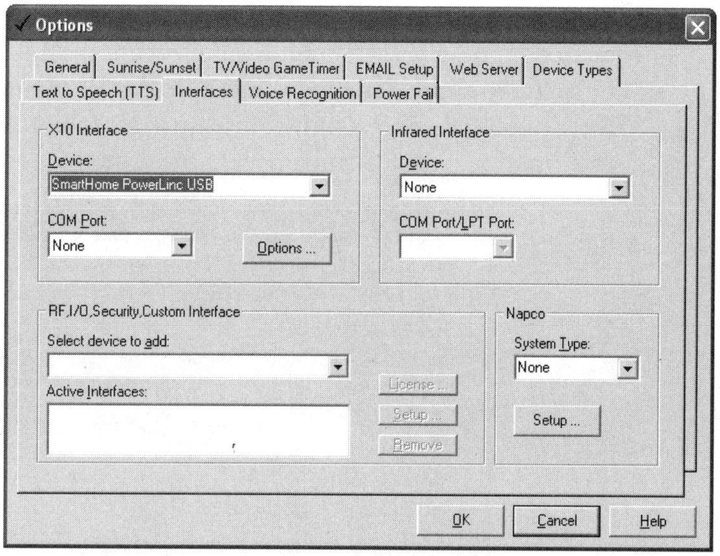

Figure 15-1
Setting up your X10
controller to work
with HomeSeer

With HomeSeer, sunrise and sunset can be calculated by following these steps:

2 MINUTES

1. Follow View | Options and then click the Sunrise/Sunset tab.

2. Select your location from the drop-down list (shown in Figure 15-2) and
   click OK.

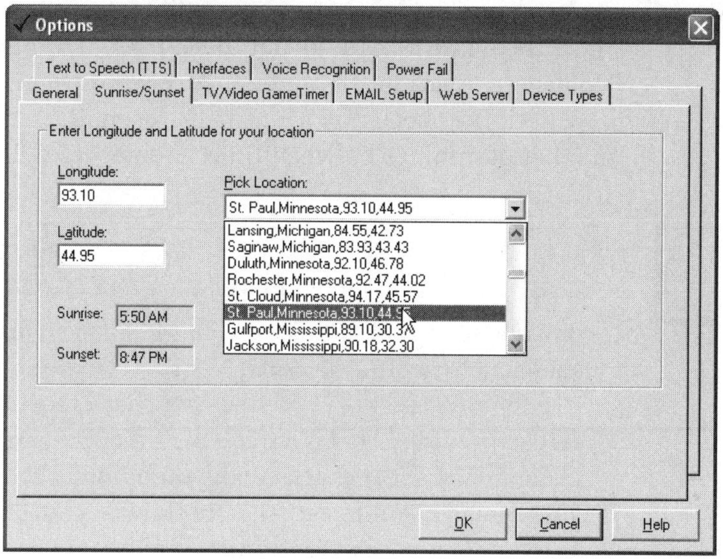

Figure 15-2
Selecting your
geographical location
to establish sunrise
and sunset times

3. If your location is not listed, or you want even finer precision on your
   location, you can enter your longitude and latitude. The values are
   entered as positive values east of longitude 0 and negative west of
   longitude 0.

4. Click the Calculate button if you entered longitude and latitude values.

Setting Up E-mail   Many X10 control applications allow you to manage your devices remotely via e-mail. HomeSeer allows this functionality, but it must first be set up to allow e-mail operation. To enable HomeSeer to use e-mail, first open the e-mail dialog box (shown in Figure 15-3) by following View | Options, click the Email tab, and then complete these steps:

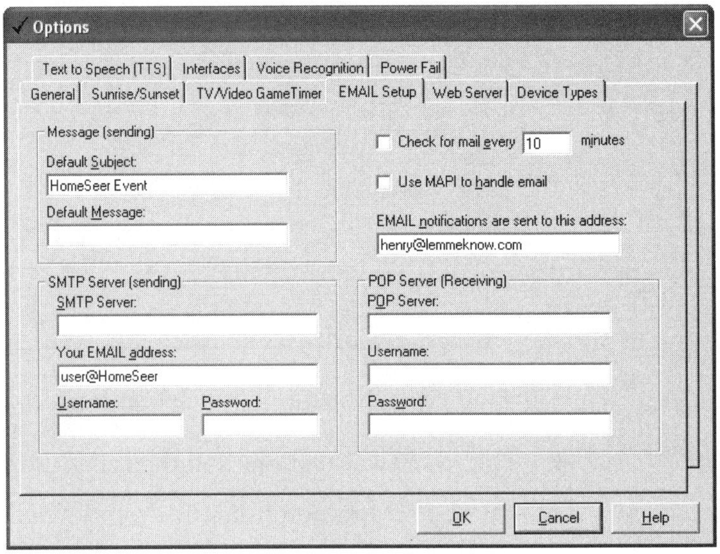

Figure 15-3
The e-mail
configuration
dialog box

If you are using a MAPI-compatible e-mail client (like Outlook), check the check box Use MAPI to handle e-mail. This is necessary because it tells HomeSeer to use incoming e-mail as event triggers.

Check the check box for "Check for mail every # minutes," then enter the number of minutes between times HomeSeer will check for new e-mail.

TIPS OF THE TRADE

Commands Might Not Be Executed Immediately

It would seem that setting up your MAPI client to check for e-mail would be sufficient to get the job done. Not so. HomeSeer only asks the MAPI interface for any new mail and does not check the mail server at your Internet service provider. That is, your e-mail client checks for new e-mail with your ISP and HomeSeer checks with your e-mail client. It is necessary to set up your e-mail client to actually check with your ISP for new e-mail.

Because you have to instruct HomeSeer to check for new messages with your e-mail client at predetermined periods of time (60 minutes, 30 minutes, 15 minutes, 10 minutes, or whatever you choose), when you send an e-mail command, the system might not pick up the e-mail for several more minutes. As such, e-mail control is not ideal for issuing emergency commands.

5 MINUTES   If you want to check and send e-mail using your ISP's POP and SMTP e-mail servers (for instance, if you want an e-mail notification if an event is triggered), it is necessary to enter the information shown in Table 15-1.

Setting	Description
SMTP Server	The name of your ISP's outgoing mail server, usually something like mailout.joesisp.com or smtp.joesisp.com.
Your e-mail address	The e-mail address you want to appear in the From field of your outgoing HomeSeer e-mails.
E-mail notifications are sent to this address	The e-mail address where you want notifications sent. For example, if you want to receive e-mail notices at your work, enter your work e-mail address.
Default subject	The subject line you would like to appear in the subject line of all e-mail notifications.
Default message	HomeSeer can send a standard message with any e-mail notifications that are generated, and this is where you enter it. Be aware, however, that depending on what event is triggered, different text will be included with the e-mail so that the events can be kept separate.
POP server	Your ISP's POP server address.
Username/Profile name	The username you use to access your ISP's POP server.
Password	The password you use to access your ISP's POP server.
Use MAPI to handle mail	HomeSeer can be configured to handle all your e-mail and allow you to read your e-mail remotely.
Check for mail every # minutes	Check this box and enter a value to tell HomeSeer how often it should check your e-mail client for new e-mail.

Table 15-1
Properties for Setting Up E-mail Reception

Figure 15-4 shows a completed e-mail configuration.

The aforementioned procedure was used to set up HomeSeer to interface with your e-mail system. Later in this chapter, we'll show you how to draft e-mail messages for remote control of your X10 system.

Figure 15-4
Completed e-mail
configuration

Options

| Text to Speech (TTS) | Interfaces | Voice Recognition | Power Fail |

General | Sunrise/Sunset | TV/Video GameTimer | EMAIL Setup | Web Server | Device Types |

Message (sending)

Default Subject:
HomeSeer Event

Default Message:
Something happened...

☑ Check for mail every [10] minutes

☐ Use MAPI to handle email

EMAIL notifications are sent to this address:
henry@lemmeknow.com

SMTP Server (sending)

SMTP Server:
smtp.lemmeknow.com

Your EMAIL address:
user@HomeSeer

Username: Password:
Henry   xxxxx

POP Server (Receiving)

POP Server:
pop.lemmeknow.com

Username:
henry

Password:
xxxxx

OK   Cancel   Help

Managing Devices

One of the great things about X10 is its flexibility. The system can easily be added to, and you can move a module from the living room to the bedroom with little hassle. Since it's so easy to manipulate components here and there, it is necessary to have that same flexibility with your X10 management software. HomeSeer allows the addition and management of X10 devices quite simply.

5 MINUTES

Adding Devices

Adding devices to your HomeSeer program is accomplished either from the toolbar or by right-clicking in the Devices pane. The device can be managed or deleted by right-clicking on the device and selecting your choice from the context menu. To create a new X10 device, follow these steps:

1. From the main window, click on Devices located in the Views pane. This will show a list of all your added devices in the top pane.

2. Click on the Light Bulb icon in the toolbar (or right-click in the Devices pane, then select Add Device from the context menu).

3. A new dialog box (shown in Figure 15-5) will appear. Enter a name for this device—for example, a lamp.

4. Type in the location of this device. You can either select a location from a list you've already created, or type in a new one.

Figure 15-5
Adding a new device

5. Select the device type, using the drop-down box to use an already created device type.

HEADS UP!

Managing Device Types

Selecting a device type will automatically set the check boxes appropriate for this type of device: Device can be dimmed, Dim Type, and Device supports status response. If there isn't a device type that matches your device, pick the closest match and then check or uncheck the appropriate boxes. You can create your own device types from the Options dialog box. This can be brought up by following View | Options and then clicking the Device Types tab.

6. Enter the X10 code for the new device. This code is the House and Unit codes that are set by rotating the small dials on your X10 devices.

7. If this device is a SwitchLinc, Compose, or LampLinc device, the default on brightness level and the ramp-up brightness rate can be established by clicking the Options button.

8. You can hide the device from being viewed on your web site by checking the Hide Device From Views check box. This is useful to prevent those logging on to your HomeSeer web site as a guest from seeing a particular device and its status. The device can be hidden from the Windows

application by clearing the Show All Devices check box from the View menu.

9. The Include In Power Fail Recovery Tests selection tells HomeSeer to set this device to its proper state when coming back from a power failure. Note, however, that the power failure recovery feature must be enabled in the Options window.

10. The Voice Command check box should be checked if you want to be able to control this device via voice commands. Check the Confirm check box, as HomeSeer will double-check to make sure.

Views

When using HomeSeer, you're looking mainly at two different things: devices and events. Devices are, as the name suggests, the individual X10 modules and devices scattered throughout your Smart Home. Events are the programs you write to activate when something happens. In HomeSeer, you look at your devices and events using views.

Device

The *Device* view (shown in Figure 15-6) allows you to quickly check the status of your various X10 devices, letting you check their states:

- ❏ On
- ❏ Off
- ❏ Dim

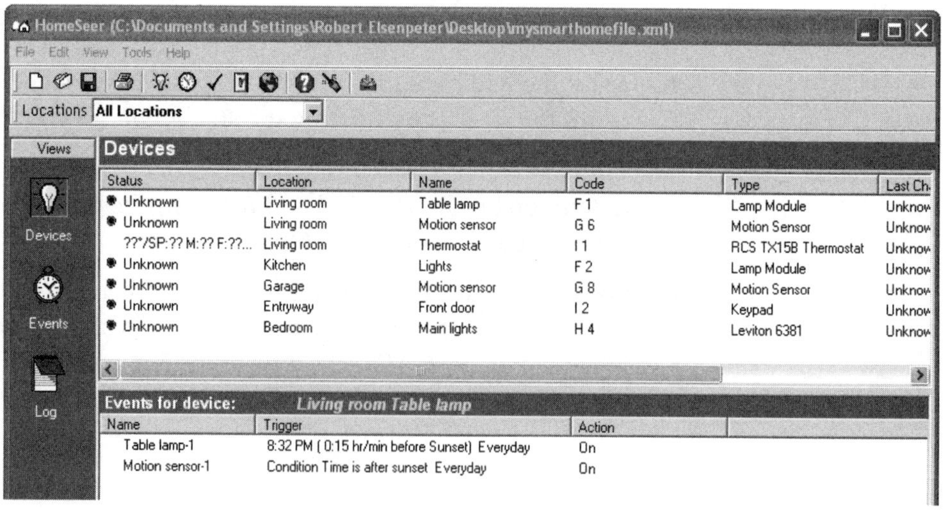

Figure 15-6
The Device view

Status	Location	Name	Code	Type	Last Ch:
● Unknown	Living room	Table lamp	F 1	Lamp Module	Unknow
● Unknown	Living room	Motion sensor	G 6	Motion Sensor	Unknow
??*/SP:?? M:?? F:??...	Living room	Thermostat	I 1	RCS TX15B Thermostat	Unknow
● Unknown	Kitchen	Lights	F 2	Lamp Module	Unknow
● Unknown	Garage	Motion sensor	G 8	Motion Sensor	Unknow
● Unknown	Entryway	Front door	I 2	Keypad	Unknow
● Unknown	Bedroom	Main lights	H 4	Leviton 6381	Unknow

Events for device: **Living room Table lamp**

Name	Trigger	Action
Table lamp-1	8:32 PM (0:15 hr/min before Sunset) Everyday	On
Motion sensor-1	Condition Time is after sunset Everyday	On

Your devices can be sorted by clicking the titles of the columns, and you can also limit the devices shown to a particular area. Beneath the menu bar is a drop-down list of all your Smart Home's locations. Pull down the list, as shown in Figure 15-7, and select a particular room. The display will generate a list of all X10 devices in that room and their status. If you want to view all your X10 devices, simply select All Locations.

Figure 15-7
Viewing devices
by location

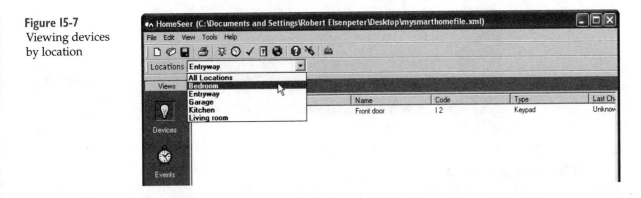

You can check the events associated with a particular device by right-clicking in the Devices pane. This will call up a context menu, on which you select Show Events. Now, the Devices pane will be split into two panes. The top pane shows your devices, while the bottom pane shows all the events associated with that device. This pane can be hidden by right-clicking in the Events pane and selecting Hide Events from the resulting context menu.

HEADS UP!

Columns Can Be Rearranged for Easier Reading

To make the Devices list easier to read, you can customize it by dragging the column headers to locations you choose. Simply click on the header and drag it to the new location.

Event

The other way to view your HomeSeer system is by *event*. This view, shown in Figure 15-8, displays a list of all your configured events. Click on an event and all the devices associated with that event will be listed in the bottom pane. In the bottom pane, you can right-click on a device and, from the resulting context menu, edit its properties, delete it, edit its action, or add another device.

Figure 15-8
The Events view

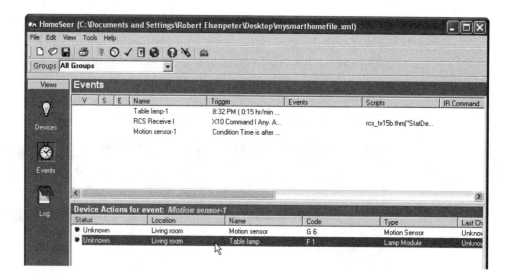

Managing Events

Using X10 control software, there are two ways in which you can manage your X10 devices. You can establish an event to trigger the action of a single device, or you can configure events that trigger multiple devices.

5 MINUTES

Events for Single Devices

To set up an event for a single device in HomeSeer, follow these steps:

1. In the View pane, click the Devices icon.

2. Click the device for which you wish to create an event.

3. If there are any other events for this device, they will be displayed in the lower pane.

4. Click the Add Event icon (it looks like a little clock), or right-click in the Events pane and select Add Event.

5. A new event will appear in the Events pane. Its name will be the same as the device it controls.

6. Right-click the new event and select Event Properties to edit its trigger and global actions. By default, the trigger will be set to manual and the only way to cause the X10 device to activate is by selecting Execute Now after clicking the event name. The Event Properties dialog box is shown in Figure 15-9.

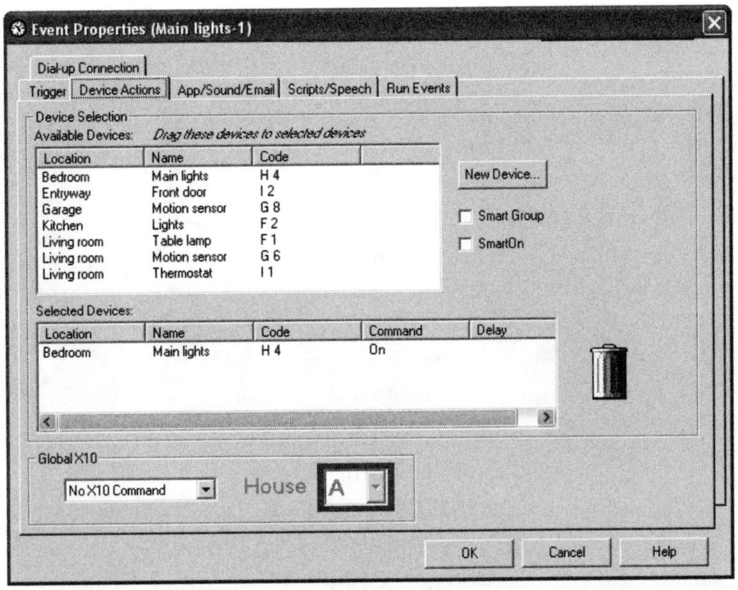

Figure 15-9
Event Properties
dialog box

You can manage all aspects of the event by clicking on these tabs and managing the settings found within. The tabs include the following:

❑ **Trigger**   Establishes what must happen for an event to be triggered.

❑ **Device Actions**   Establishes what your device(s) will do once they are triggered.

❑ **App/Sound/Email**   Allows you to launch an application, play a sound file, or send an e-mail when an event is triggered.

❑ **Scripts/Speech**   When an event is triggered, a script can be run or a message spoken by the computer.

❑ **Dialup Connection**   Tells the system how it connects to the Internet.

10 MINUTES

Events for Multiple Devices

To set up events that use multiple devices, follow these steps:

1. In the View pane, click on Events.

2. Click the Add Event button, or right-click on the Event List pane and select Add Event from the context menu.

3. The Event Properties dialog box appears and the event will be titled as UnNamed. Enter a name for this event.

4. Select the Device Actions tab.

5. From the upper pane, select the device you wish to control and drag it to the lower pane.

HEADS UP!

You Can Still Add a Device

If you want to control a device that is not on the list, click the Add Device button and you will be able to set up and manage the new device. Once the device has been set up, it will be added to the list of devices. Devices can also be managed from this view by double -clicking the device.

6. A delay for the action on your X10 device can be added. Double-click the device in the Selected Devices pane. In the Actions dialog box (shown in Figure 15-10), set the action for the device (On, Off, and so forth) and then select a time delay offset. The offset ranges between 1 second and 24 hours. Each device in the event can have its own unique delay time.

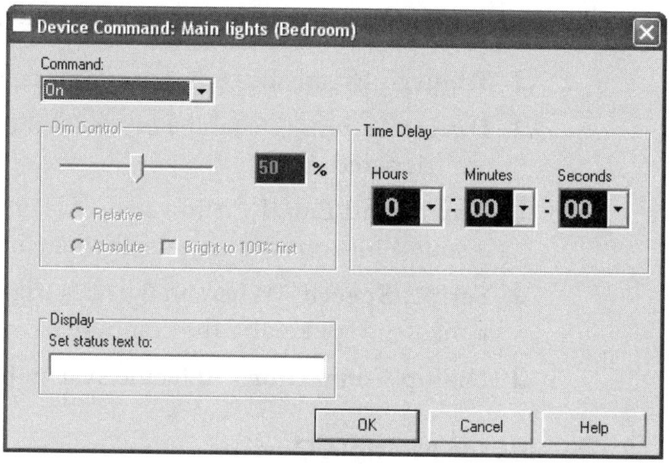

Figure 15-10
Use this dialog box to establish a delay for the activation/ deactivation of X10 devices.

7. Select the Trigger tab to set a trigger for this event.

Triggers

Triggers are what tell the computer to cause an X10 device to perform a particular action. There are a number of triggers in HomeSeer:

An absolute time and/or date	At Sunrise	At Sunset
By X10 command	By condition	By e-mail received

At a specific interval of time (recurring)	By a voice command	By an infrared match
By a change in status of a device	By a change in value of a device	Security panel event
Forced to execute from the web page	Manually	From a plug-in

Triggers are edited by right-clicking an event, then selecting Event Properties. Next, select the type of trigger you want from the drop-down box named Type. The current trigger settings are shown. The following explains some of the different ways triggers can be managed.

Manual   If you elect for an event *not* to have a trigger, select the *manual* trigger. This is a trigger used when devices and events are used as part of a macro. A *macro* is the activation of a series of devices, triggered simultaneously. For instance, if you have several lights and the stereo turn on when a specific event occurs, that series of devices is activated as part of a macro. They can be triggered from other events, or from the Run button on the Events web page.

Event   Events can be triggered at given times or time spans. For example, you could set a trigger for a specific time of day (maybe you want your stereo to turn on every day at 5:26 p.m., right as you pull into the driveway). You can also set events to run at predetermined intervals—five minutes, ten minutes, half hour, hour, and so forth.

X10   Another trigger is based on X10 commands. HomeSeer listens to all the X10 commands that are coursing though your home's wiring system. When a particular command is seen, an event can be triggered. For example, if you have a door sensor connected to a Powerflash (this is that X10 device that connects to a sensor, causing other X10 devices to activate and deactivate) and its code set to G12, when the door opens, the Powerflash would send a signal to G12. However, you need not have any devices set to respond to G12. Rather, you could have HomeSeer set up to monitor for a G12 signal. When it hears that signal (i.e., the door opens), you could automatically set the lights to come on and the stereo to turn on.

Condition   Conditions give you a great deal of flexibility when determining when an event should trigger. You can establish as many conditions as you like on a trigger. The event will only trigger when *all* of the conditions are true.

For instance, continuing the example from the previous section, you might not want the stereo and lights to come on every time the door is opened. As such, the conditions before a specific time and after a specific time can be used to manage when the lights and stereo are to come on. If you get home from work about 5:30 p.m. each day, you can set up the condition so the lights and music only come on when the door is opened and it is after 5:15 p.m., but before 5:45 p.m. (this gives you a little wiggle room if you make it home a littler earlier or a little later.)

The following are some time conditions available in HomeSeer:

- ❏ An absolute time value
- ❏ Before a specific time
- ❏ After a specific time
- ❏ Anytime before sunset
- ❏ Anytime after sunset
- ❏ Anytime before sunrise
- ❏ Anytime after sunrise
- ❏ Minutes before sunset
- ❏ Minutes after sunset
- ❏ Minutes before sunrise
- ❏ Minutes after sunrise
- ❏ Day time (after sunrise but before sunset)
- ❏ Night time (after sunset but before sunrise)

The following are device conditions used in HomeSeer:

- ❏ Whether the device is ON
- ❏ Whether the device is OFF
- ❏ Whether the device has been ON for a specified amount of time
- ❏ Whether the device has been OFF for a specified amount of time
- ❏ Whether a device has just changed its status (supports On, Off, Dim, Bright, or ANY)
- ❏ The device has been ON for at least a particular amount of time (keeps triggering after specified time as elapsed)
- ❏ The device has been OFF for at least a particular amount of time (keeps triggering after specified time as elapsed)

E-mail Reception You can also set events to trigger with the reception of e-mail. In the Trigger dialog box, select E-mail reception, then enter the address of the person for which you want HomeSeer to check. For example, if you only want HomeSeer to respond to requests from you when you're at work, and your work e-mail address is me@mywork.com, enter this address in the box. However, if you don't care who is able to issue commands to your system, you can enable any incoming e-mail (properly formatted, of course) to trigger events. If you want HomeSeer to respond to commands sent by anyone, check the All Addresses check box.

E-mail

In the previous section, we explained how HomeSeer can respond to incoming e-mails to take action. Based on the subject line in an incoming e-mail, an X10 command can be sent by House and Unit Code, by the device name, or to force the trigger of an event.

The command must be listed in the subject line of the e-mail message. To set up HomeSeer to receive e-mail commands, follow these steps:

1. Configure a new event and set its trigger to e-mail reception.

2. On the e-mail from field, set the address to the address authorized to submit commands, shown in Figure 15-11.

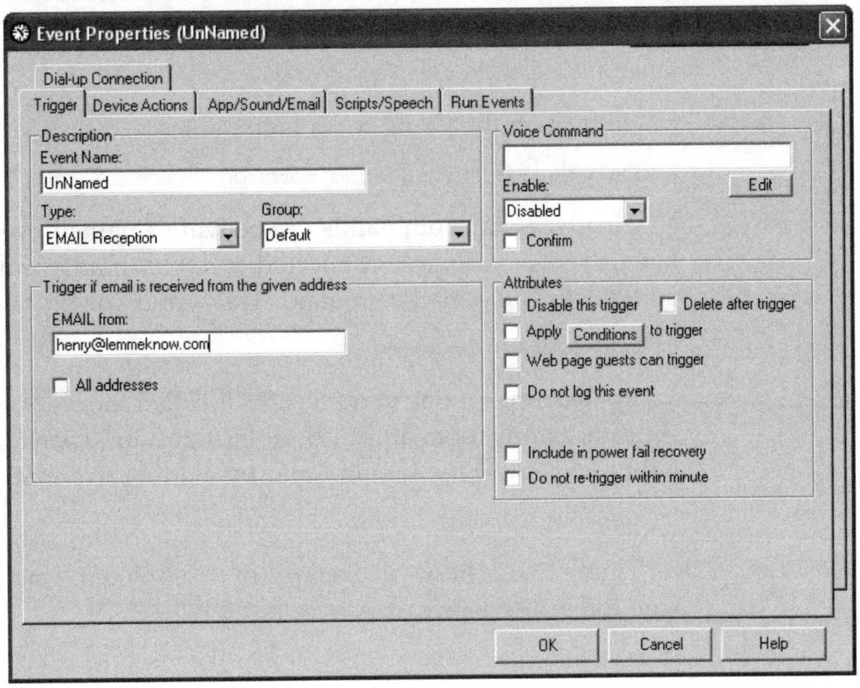

Figure 15-11
Entering the e-mail address that will be honored when commands are sent via e-mail

3. No actions are necessary to be set, as you'll be issuing commands via e-mail.

2 MINUTES

Once HomeSeer is configured to accept e-mail commands, you must draft your e-mail messages properly. Follow these steps:

1. Enter your home e-mail address (assuming, of course, your HomeSeer unit will be monitoring home e-mail accounts).

2. Enter the commands into the subject line of your e-mail. (The commands are not case sensitive, so don't fret about making sure everything is upper- or lowercased.)

To control a device by House Code and Unit Code, the command starts with the command `execx10`. The command is entered using the format:

```
execx10:devices,dimval
```

For example, if you want to send a command to two light modules (with the addresses of H7 and H8), enter

```
exec10:h7+h8,ON
```

To dim device G12 to 50 percent:

```
exec10:G12,DIM,50
```

An event can be triggered by using the device name. To do this, the command follows this convention:

```
execx10byname:devicename,dimval
```

To turn on the living room lamp, enter

```
execx10byname:living room lamp,ON
```

Finally, e-mail commands can activate a named event. For example, if you have a series of devices connected together in an event, the event can be triggered using an e-mail command. The syntax for the trigger command is

```
triggerevent:eventname
```

For example, if one of our events is called Movie Night and it automatically shuts the family room drapes, dims the lights to 30 percent, and shuts off hallway lights, we can trigger this via e-mail by sending an e-mail with the subject line:

```
triggerevent:movie night
```

Figure 15-12 shows an example of a completed e-mail message that will activate three X10 devices.

Figure 15-12
A sample e-mail
message that will turn
on three X10 devices

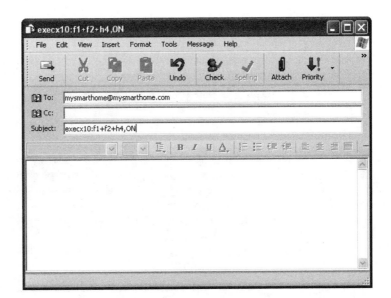

Web Access

You can manage your X10 gadgetry via the Internet by using HomeSeer's web access tool. HomeSeer comes with a built-in web server that generates a web page giving yourself and others access to your X10 devices. All the functionality achieved through the Windows interface is possible through the web interface. This allows you to monitor the status of your devices, plus you can add, delete, and edit all your devices and events.

HEADS UP!

Use Either Windows or the Web Interface

On the local computer, you can use either the web interface or the Windows interface. This is a nice feature, because you can use whichever tool you're more comfortable with.

5 MINUTES

Web Server

To set up the web access, you must first activate HomeSeer's web server. First, you must have TCP/IP installed on your computer. If you aren't sure, an easy way to tell is whether you are able to access the Internet. If you can, then you're all set. If not, refer to your operating system's Help for information on installing it. Once TCP/IP is installed, follow these steps:

1. Follow View | Options.

2. Click the Web Server tab, shown in Figure 15-13.

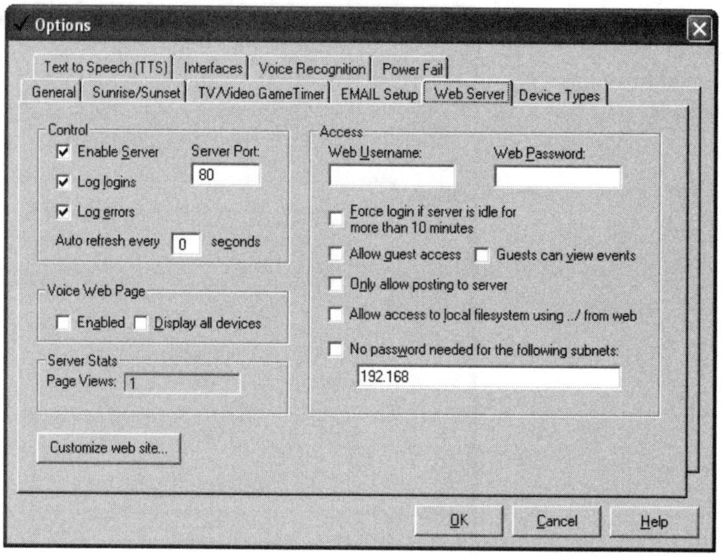

Figure 15-13
The Web Server tab
is used to set up and
manage HomeSeer's
web server.

3. Enter the server port number. If you aren't already running a web
   server on your computer, leave the default port number at 80.
   Otherwise, enter a different number (81 is a good choice). *Port* is a
   commonly misunderstood term. It seems to suggest a port on the back
   of your computer somewhere. In actuality, a port in this context is a
   software device, simply used to keep track of the various functions in
   your computer.

4. To limit access to your HomeSeer web site, enter a username and
   password. When someone tries to access the web site, they will be
   prompted for this information.

HEADS UP!

Why Enable Force Login?

*By checking the Force Login box, if the server is idle for more than ten minutes, a user is forced
to log in again. This prevents some unauthorized person from accessing your X10 system if
someone leaves the web page open, forgetting to log off.*

5. Check the check box Enable Server.

6. Click OK.

HomeSeer's web server is set up and ready to go.

TIPS OF THE TRADE

Web Access with a Router

If you are using a router as part of your home LAN, it might not be possible to access HomeSeer from a remote PC. To ameliorate this problem, set up your router to forward all requests to the HomeSeer server port to the HomeSeer PC IP address. For instance, if the IP address of the PC on which HomeSeer is running is 192.168.0.100, and HomeSeer is using port 81, set up your router so it forwards all requests on port 81 to IP address 192.168.0.100. This information can be found in your router's documentation or by contacting the manufacturer.

Using Web Access

HomeSeer's web interface operates almost exactly like the Windows interface, except it has to be coded so it works with a browser interface. Again, the tool allows you to manage your Smart Home using either devices or events. To start your session, on a remote computer connected to the Internet, enter the IP address of the computer on which your web server is installed (you might have to get this information from your ISP).

If you are using your computer locally, you can simply enter `localhost` into the URL line on your web browser.

Device Status   The start page for your web site shows the status of all your X10 devices and looks like the one in Figure 15-14.

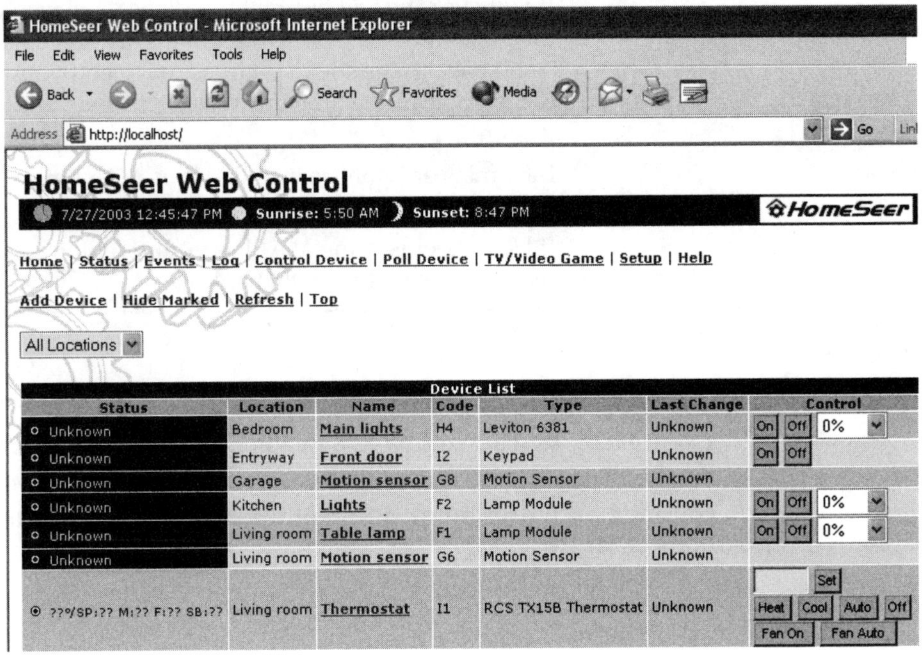

Figure 15-14
HomeSeer's start page, using a web browser

Along the top of the Device Status page (as well as the Event List, explained in the next section) are a number of hyperlinks. Table 15-2 explains the function of these hyperlinks.

Link	Function
Add Device	Allows you to add a new X10 device.
Add Event	Allows you to add a new event.
Event Log	Displays your event log.
Control Panel	Brings up a control panel for accessing a specific X10 device.
Get Device Status	Brings up status information from X10 modules that support the X10 Status Request command.
TV/Video Game Timer	Brings up a form to add or edit users for TV and game timers.
Setup	Brings up a form to allow the configuration of HomeSeer.
Security	If the security panel interface has been enabled, this link calls up an image of the security panel keypad. Not all security panel devices support this feature, and other links might appear for different panel types.
Hide Marked/Show All	Within their Properties dialog box, devices can be marked as hidden. Clicking this link allows you to hide those devices. If the link is shown as Show All, clicking this link will bring them back.
Refresh	Causes all devices to be updated with their current status.
Log Out	This link is available if you've set up a username and password. It allows you to close out your session when you're completed with your web session.
Top	If you click the ON button for a device, the web page will redisplay the page from the point you left it. This prevents you from having to scroll back to the site of your last device. If you want to go to the top of the page and tell the browser to "forget" where you just were, click this link.
Messages	If HomeSeer Phone is installed, this will show all your waiting voice messages.
Mail	If HomeSeer is using MAPI as your e-mail transport system, you can read local e-mail from this link.

Table 15-2
Web Access Functions

Event List   By clicking on the Event List link, a page (like the one shown in Figure 15-15) is called up that displays all your events. The page is divided into columns, each displaying different information about your events. The following describe what each column shows:

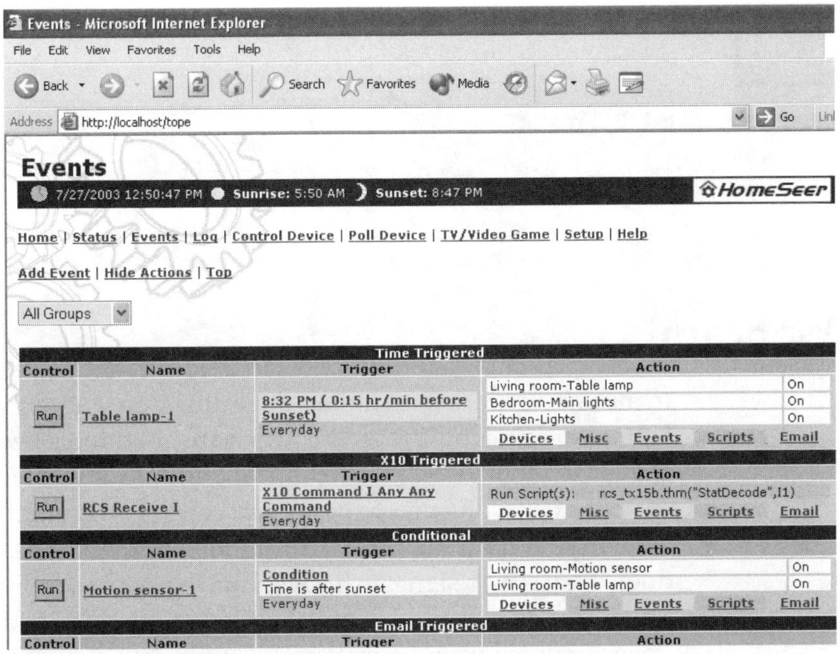

Figure 15-15
Event list using the
web interface

❏ **Name** This column uses the following settings:

❏ The *Run* button forces the event to trigger and execute any actions contained within the event.

❏ The *Event name* link calls up a form allowing you to change the name of an event, as well as disabling it and marking it as a voice command.

❏ **Trigger** Clicking on the trigger calls up a page with a list of trigger types.

❏ **Action** The Action column contains the following settings:

❏ The *Devices* link calls up a page displaying all the X10 devices this event controls.

❏ The *Events* link calls up a page with all the events that are triggered by this event.

❏ The *Scripts* link calls up a page showing all the scripts that will be run when an event is triggered.

❏ The *E-mail* link calls up a form, enabling the generation of an e-mail when the event is triggered.

HEADS UP!

More Links Might Be Present

Though the preceding was a list of the standard links shown in the action column, additional options might be present, depending on any add-ons augmenting the application.

Webcam

In the final section, we'll talk about setting up a webcam to work with your Smart Home computer software. Webcams are good tools because you can set up the camera to monitor a certain area. For example, if you are wondering who comes to your door while you're gone, you can set up a motion detector and webcam outside your front door. When the motion detector senses someone approach the door, it can send a signal to the webcam to snap a picture or start recording video. Then, an e-mail can be dispatched to you at work and you can download the image or video from your system. Or, you can simply review the log when you come home at the end of the day.

Webcams are inexpensive video cameras that plug into an open USB port on your computer. For instance, the Creative Labs WebCam Pro sells for US$39.88. Don't expect a high definition signal. Since the images are going to be traversing the Internet, you don't want to wait forever for a huge image file to be transferred from your home to your remote location. The WebCam Pro offers video resolution at 640 × 480 pixels.

Unfortunately, HomeSeer does not support webcam features (it's a feature that's starting to gain popularity in Smart Home computer applications). However, Web-Link II (which we introduced in Chapter 7) supports webcam functions. In order to bring webcams into our Smart Home (and to demonstrate how they are set up and monitored), we're shifting gears a little and using the Web-Link II software. (There's nothing that says you cannot use two applications [Web-Link II and HomeSeer, for example] for the control of your Smart Home.)

Setup

Setting up a webcam will depend largely on what type you buy. Very simple webcams connect to your computer's USB port, and it's usually a very simple plug-n-play affair. However, the problem with these cameras is that you are limited by the length of USB cable as to where you locate them. Because of the way USB is designed, the maximum length for a USB cable connected to a video camera is only about nine feet. As such, you might need to only monitor areas within nine feet of your computer, or be willing to relocate your Smart Home computer somewhere closer to the area you wish to monitor.

Another option is to buy a wireless camera, like the D-Link Internet camera. This camera uses two components—a camera connected to a transmitter and a base that connects to the computer. The base does not plug into a USB port; rather, it uses an Ethernet connection. The signal is sent from the transmitter to the receiver using the 802.11b specification, allowing the camera can be up to 100 feet away from its receiver. While this is good, there is a downside. The wireless camera costs about ten times more (US$499.99) than a USB camera.

For the sake of this example, we're going to use a USB webcam. Since our Smart Home computer and security system are located in the basement, we can position the camera to point out of a basement window to keep an eye on the backyard. This will allow us to keep an eye on the family dog and also to see if anyone has let themselves into the backyard.

Setting up a USB webcam is a fairly straightforward affair:

1. Make sure Windows is running.

2. Locate the camera where you want it to survey.

3. Ensure there is enough cable to reach the computer. If not, think about repositioning either the camera or the computer—remember, at most you have nine feet of USB cable to play with.

4. Connect the webcam's USB plug to an open USB port.

5. If you are using a version of Windows that recognizes USB devices (Windows 98 and later), you should see a window pop up telling you that the device has been recognized.

6. Depending on your USB camera manufacturer's instructions, you might need to install additional software. In all likelihood, if your camera is plug-n-play compliant, you should be ready to go.

Setting Up the Software

Setting up the software will depend, of course, on which application you are using to monitor your Smart Home and manage your devices. The following steps show how to set up a webcam with the Web-Link II package. For more information about this particular piece of software, flip back to Chapter 7.

Recording

At the top of the Web-Link II home page are four icons—the leftmost is a video camera:

1. Click the Camera icon to start the HAI Video-Link Player. When the player first starts, the Windows Media animation will be shown in the viewer. The viewer will show the status of the video as it is encoded and buffered.

2. Once the video is buffered, you will see the video in the viewer and hear audio if a microphone is connected.

3. To record the video coming though the feed, click the Record icon.

4. When you've finished recording what you want to record, click the Record Stop icon.

5. When you're finished using the webcam, click the Close icon.

Viewing

When you're ready to watch your videos, click the Videos icon to see a list of your recorded videos along with the date and time of the recording.

Recorded videos are listed two ways:

❏ **By user**   These are videos that were manually recorded. That is, while watching the video feed, the user decided it was worthwhile to record.

❏ **By event**   These are videos that were recorded based on a predetermined event. That is, the system was programmed to start recording when an event occurred.

To play or delete a video:

1. Select the video from the list by pointing to it using your mouse pointer.

2. Left-click on the desired video.

3. The size and length of the selected video are displayed.

4. Select the desired remote control button.

5. To play the video, press the Play button.

6. To delete the video, press the Delete button. You will be prompted to confirm your selection to delete the video.

Like many other X10 management software applications, HomeSeer is a great way to manage, activate, and deactivate multiple X10 devices. In this chapter, we gave an overview of this software's use. In Chapter 16, we'll drill down a bit more and show how to make detailed, customized events, along with the setup of remote controls for the Smart Home.

❏ Have you entered e-mail settings appropriately?

❏ Do the X10 codes on your devices match the codes in your program?

❏ Do you have TCP/IP installed on your computer?

❏ Did you establish the X10 interfaces setting to let HomeSeer know which type of X10 controller you're using?

Chapter 16

Smart Home Controls

Tools of the Trade

X10 remote control
X10 control software

In preceding chapters, we talked about the different sorts of devices you can use for your Smart Home. Once you've got all these devices in place, you need some way to manage them all—either singly or as part of larger multiunit activations. This last chapter will focus on ways you can manage your Smart Home devices. We'll start with a continuation of the HomeSeer software that we introduced in Chapter 15. Next, we'll show some other devices that you can use to manage your X10 gear, such as control panels and remote controls.

Event Programming on Your Computer

In Chapter 15, we gave a quick and dirty look at how to use HomeSeer's software to set up and manage your sundry X10 devices and events. However, we didn't have the space to talk about crafting specific events to respond when a condition is met, like a certain time of day or the activation of another device.

Since there is no way we can anticipate all your X10 programming needs, this section will demonstrate how to create two different sorts of events. The idea here is to show you how to set up your own events and program them with your computer-based X10 software. Further, these multidevice actions, also known as *macros* can be used in conjunction with the X10 control panels and remote controls we'll talk about later in this chapter.

Action When a Motion Detector Is Tripped

The first example we'll use is something we demonstrated in Chapter 9 with simple hardware settings. With this project, however, we're using HomeSeer to manage lighting levels so a midnight run to the bathroom isn't dangerous and we're not blinded by full-level lighting.

This project calls for three pieces of hardware: an X10 motion detector (we're using a Version II Wireless Motion Detector, which sells for US$20.99), an X10 RF base (which sells for US$24.99); and two X10 light switches with dimmer capability. Physical installation follows the steps we've covered previously: the switches are installed to control the hallway and bathroom lights. The RF base is plugged into an AC wall receptacle, and the motion detector is located so it covers the hallway. When someone enters the hallway, the lights will turn on to 25-percent brightness.

Once these devices have been programmed into HomeSeer (we're using House Code "G" for these projects) a new event is created. In this event, we use the trigger of a condition (as shown in Figure 16-1). In this case, the condition is if the "Hallway Motion Detector" is "On." That is, if the motion detector has sensed movement, it sends an "on" signal to the RF base.

However, since we don't want the lights to turn on just whenever motion is detected (for instance, at 2 p.m.) we've added two more conditions. Not only does the motion detector have to send an "on" signal, but it must also be after 10:30 p.m. and before 5:30 a.m. To add additional conditions, simply click the Add button.

Next, we click on the Device Actions tab (shown in Figure 16-2). Here, we drag the two sets of lights (the hallway lights and the bathroom lights) down to the lower pane, also shown in Figure 16-2.

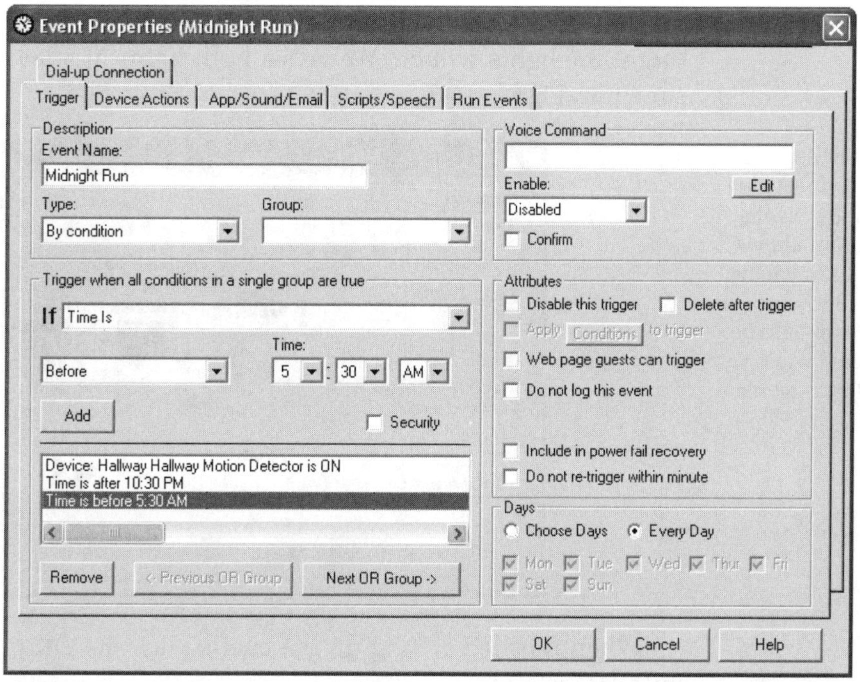

Figure 16-1
An event's Trigger tab allows the definition of what has to happen for an event to start.

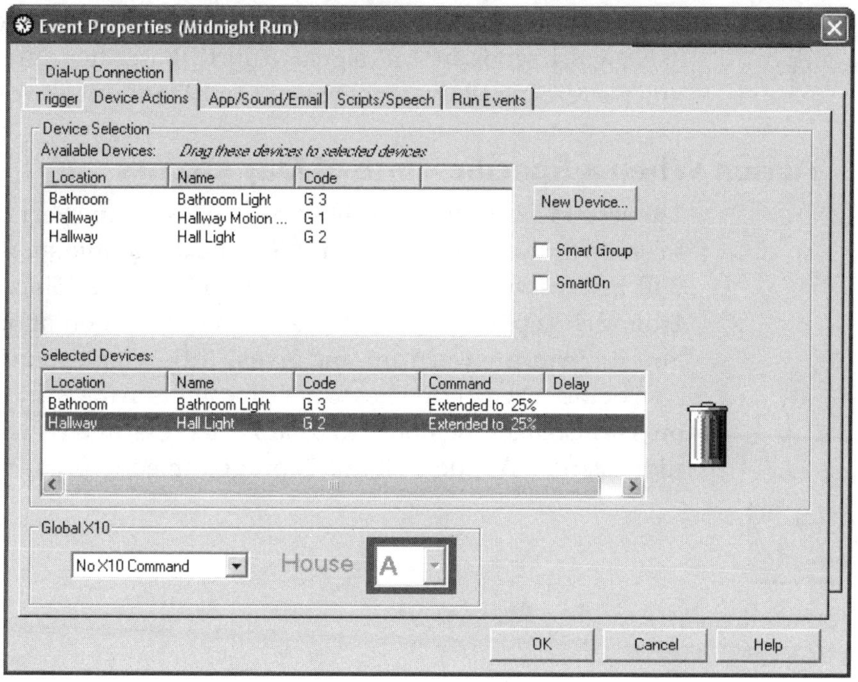

Figure 16-2
Drag the desired devices to the Selected Devices pane.

Double-clicking each device calls up a window, allowing us to establish how bright the lights will be. We've set both lights at a level of 25 percent. This is shown in Figure 16-3.

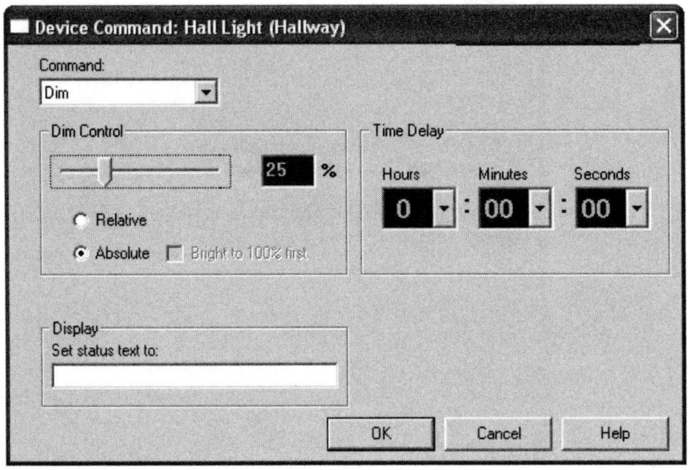

Figure 16-3
The Device Action tab in the event's properties allows the user to tell the computer which devices should be activated when an event is triggered.

When finished setting up the event, click the OK button to save the event with HomeSeer.

Once we've finished in the bathroom and have made it safely back to bed, we don't want the lights on all night—even at 25 percent. As such, we've set up the lights to turn off after 10 minutes. This setting is made on the motion detector itself, which sends an "off" signal to the RF base after a preset amount of time. The unit we're using allows for between 1 and 256 minutes; we set it to 10 minutes.

Action When a Specific Time of Day Occurs

The second example shows how you can use HomeSeer to trigger a macro when a certain time of day rolls around. This next example shows how the Smart Home will behave when Dad comes home from work. Since he walks in the door around 5:30 p.m., we've set everything to turn on at 5:25 p.m. This gives the house a chance to warm up, and gives a little wiggle room in case traffic is light.

For this macro, Dad likes to have the lights in the entryway and the living room on. He also likes the house to be at 72 degrees, and he wants to hear his favorite radio station. As such, all this is programmed to occur at 5:25 p.m. on the dot.

HEADS UP!

Thermostats Get Their Own House Codes

Remember, because of the complexity of sending commands to a thermostat, thermostats require their own dedicated House Code. The appliances, lights, motion detectors, and other devices in our examples have all been using a House Code of "G." However, when we add a thermostat to the mix, it is necessary to give it its own House Code. We've chosen "J."

To set this up, we plug in an X10 appliance module to his stereo (which is preset to his favorite radio station); we install an X10 light switch on the entry-way light; and plug the living room lamp into a lamp module. Then, it's time to set up the HomeSeer software.

We created a new event called "Dad's Home." The trigger for this event (as shown in Figure 16-4) is an "absolute time." That is, we've established the time at 5:25 p.m. on weekdays. (Other times that can be used include sunrise, sunset, or a certain amount of time before sunrise or sunset.)

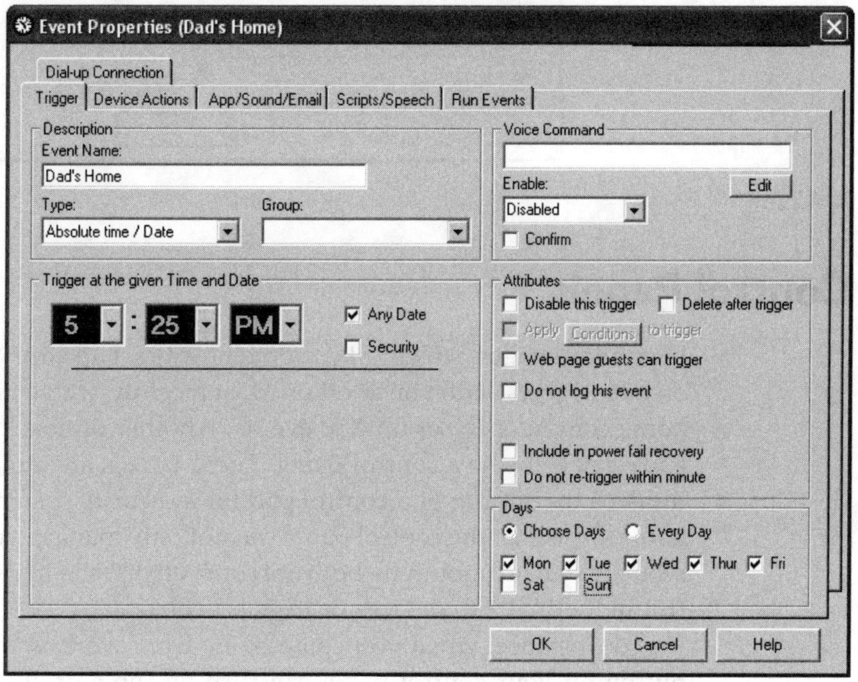

Figure 16-4
In this example, the trigger is a certain time of day.

Next, on the Device Actions tab, we drag the thermostat, stereo, and both lights to the lower pane. There, we simply tell the lights and the stereo to turn on at 5:25 p.m. The thermostat is a little different. As Figure 16-5 shows, once the thermostat is double-clicked, there are several settings that can be managed. First, we set the desired temperature, then tell HomeSeer if we want the fan on, off, or set to automatic. We can also set whether the system should be in heat, cool, or automatic mode. If we wanted the thermostat to come on some time after the event is triggered, we could set up the thermostat on a delay.

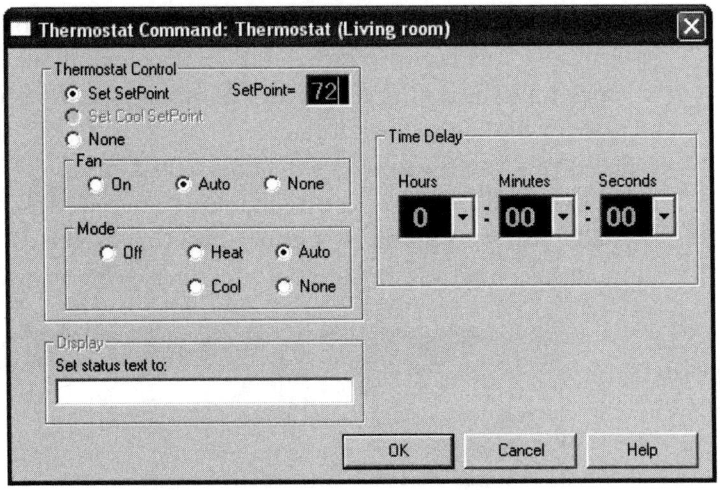

Figure 16-5
Setting a temperature
on the thermostat

Control Panels

In previous pages, we've talked about how to set up your X10 devices so an event on one triggers action on another. Most recently, we've talked about using your home computer to set up X10 events. Another option for managing your X10 gadgetry is to use a control panel. These panels are attached to your wall, not unlike a thermostat or a control pad for a security system. The difference here, naturally, is that the control panel can not only manage your thermostat or your security system (assuming both are connected to the X10 system), but it can control individual X10 devices or trigger events.

For instance, when you come home from work at night, pressing a single button on your control panel can turn on the entryway, living room, dining room, and kitchen lights. Another application might be to have the control panel mounted in your family room. When you want to watch a movie, simply press one of the buttons and the drapes will automatically close, the lights dim, and the television and DVD player turn on. In this section, we'll take a closer look at the types of control panels on the market and talk about what they have to offer you and your Smart Home.

Types

There are two common types of control panels: wall-mounted and tabletop. The only differentiation between the two, really, is that one is stuck on the wall while the other sits on a table top. In fact, some control panels can either be mounted to the wall or used as tabletop devices. That having been said, there's good utility to both types, and you should weigh the pros and cons of each to find out which configuration is best suited to your needs.

Wall-Mounted

These control panels fit inconspicuously onto your wall. This is nice because it gets your controls out of the way. All it takes to control your X10 devices and events is to go to the panel and press a few buttons. There are a number of brands and models of X10 control panels, each offering varying degrees of functionality. Some use small buttons to control your devices and events; others are pretty slick and employ touch screens, which allow you to tailor the menus to your specific needs. An example of a wall-mounted control panel is shown in Figure 16-6.

Figure 16-6
A wall-mounted
control panel

At the top end of the spectrum is a device like the TouchLinc On-Screen Programmable X10 Controller. This touch screen device is highly customizable and allows you to create your own displays, control up to 72 X10 devices, and create 12 macros. The device connects to a nearby AC receptacle, or—if you want a neater appearance—it can connect to your home's electrical system via either a doorbell chime or the HVAC wiring. The TouchLinc sells for US$399.99. However, if you want something a little easier on the wallet, such devices as the KeypadLinc (which sells for US$89.99) allow you to control up to eight X10 devices or macros.

HEADS UP!

A Maxi-Control Console Might Be Needed for Setup

In order to use the advanced features and macros with some controllers, you might also have to invest in a Maxi-Control Console. This device, which sells for US$21.99, allows you to set up House and Unit Codes for your stand-alone controllers. It also serves as its own stand-alone X10 controller. As always, double-check the product literature before you buy anything to determine whether you need to buy a Maxi-Control Console.

Tabletop

If you don't want to mess with cutting a hole or mounting anything to your wall, another option is a tabletop X10 controller. These devices look like really beefy remote controls and are used to manage your X10 devices and events. These devices are useful because, unlike a wall mounted unit, you can move them around the room or even between rooms.

One of the more popular devices in this realm is the X10 Maxi-Control Console, shown in Figure 16-7. It allows one-touch control of X10 16 devices. However, the House Code dial allows the management of up to 256 devices.

Figure 16-7
Tabletop X10
control panel

The devices are similar in function and features to the wall-mounted units. For example, the TouchLinc On-Screen Programmable X10 Controller we mentioned in the previous section need not be mounted to the wall. Rather, it can also be used as a tabletop unit.

A much less expensive option is an eight-device minicontroller that sells for US$11.99. This device can turn on, turn off, dim, or brighten eight devices. Of course, you're not getting the level of functionality that comes with the TouchLinc. This particular unit does not handle macros on its own, but when used in conjunction with two-way X10 controllers, it can be used to trigger macros on other devices.

Setting Up the Control Panel

Setting up these control panels will differ, depending on the model you purchase. Some are ready to go right out of the box. For example, the X10 Maxi-Control Console simply needs to be plugged into an open AC receptacle. Then, rotate the House Code dial to that of your X10 device, press the button corresponding to the Unit Code, and press the "on," "off," "brighten," "dim," "all on," or "all off" button.

Other controllers are more complex to set up, but this goes hand in hand with their utility. For example, programming the TouchLinc On-Screen Programmable X10 Controller will take some time to work though the onscreen menus. However, once you've completed the programming, you'll be able to trigger specific devices and macros with the touch of one button.

Remote Controls

Control panels are great ways to manage your Smart Home, but they aren't mobile solutions. A good way to manage your X10 devices is by way of an X10 remote control. Sure, your coffee table is probably filled with remote controls that say they're universal, but there's always a function on the DVD player that isn't duplicated on the TV's remote control and vice versa. The last thing you need is another remote control.

However, by using an X10 remote control, you can not only set it up to manage all your home's X10 functions, but you can also move over all your home entertainment remotes so the remote is truly universal. In this final section, we'll look at X10 remote controls, the various types out there, and how you can set them up to work with your Smart Home.

X10

X10 remote controls employ two components. The first is a standard-looking remote control (shown on the left side of Figure 16-8). Naturally, this is the device on which you'll be making your control choices. This unit also houses an RF transmitter. This particular model, the Leviton DHC, sells for US$33.99.

Figure 16-8
Leviton DHC X10
remote control and
RF receiver

The second component is an RF receiver. This device (shown on the right side of Figure 16-6) plugs into an AC receptacle, like any other X10 device, and receives signals and commands from the remote control. This model, the Leviton DHC, sells for US$49.99 and can receive up to 16 X10 codes.

Because these devices use RF transmission instead of IR, you need not be standing in front of the receiver to make changes. As long as you're in range (within 100 feet), you can manage any of your X10 devices—even from different floors and through walls.

Not only will the remote control work throughout your home, but you can also add additional remote controls for each RF receiver. Each remote will wind up controlling the same devices, but it is much easier to locate a remote in strategic locations in your home than to have to lug it around. Sure, they make holsters for remote controls, but that's just dorky.

TIPS OF THE TRADE

Keychain Remotes

If you want something a little smaller to run just a couple X10 devices or events, consider a keychain remote control. Like other X10 remote controls, this employs two components: the remote transmitter and the receiver.

For example, when you're coming in the front door after a walk, press one of the buttons on the remote (two are "on" buttons, the other two manage dimming) and you can have your whole system set up to turn on a few lights, turn up the air conditioning, and turn on the television set. If you're using the keychain remote when you are coming in the house, position the receiver in the garage or on an outlet near the front door—this will give you the best range.

TIPS OF THE TRADE

Keychain remotes have their pros and their cons. On one hand, they can be used to manage your X10 gear. On the other hand, you can't use them to change the channel on your television set or change CDs in your stereo. However, a bit of ingenuity can add to these devices' functionality. By sending a signal over the RF to X10 receiver, you can have your computer's X10 control module "listen" for the X10 command. When that command is heard, your computer system can trigger a macro that causes a number of X10 devices to activate. For example, maybe when you come home, you want to be greeted with music and the lights turned on in the entryway. By setting up a macro on your computer to activate these devices, when you press a button on your keychain remote, these devices can be automatically activated.

If you decide to buy both a "regular" remote control as well as a keychain remote, you need not buy two receiver units. If you have enough codes left (most receivers allow the use of 16 codes), then you can use the same receiver with both your remote and your keychain remote. However, if you need more than 16 codes, you'll need another receiver, or you can buy a 32-code receiver like the X10 Mega-36 Remote (although this will not work with other X10 remotes, but can be used in conjunction with other remotes).

Repeaters

You might discover, however, that your X10 remotes (or other wireless X10 devices) aren't picking up signals. To ameliorate this, you might want to consider purchasing a repeater. Repeaters, like the one shown in Figure 16-9, retransmit signals to an X10 device.

Figure 16-9
X10 signal repeaters improve the range of wireless X10 devices.

Repeaters have a 150-foot range and four repeaters can be used together for ranges up to 600 feet. These devices sell for US$49.99. These devices also have re-chargeable batteries, which makes it possible to use them if the power fails—ideal for wireless security systems.

Programming

There are two modes in which you will likely program your whole-home remote control. First, you need to program it so you can manage your home entertainment system—that is, turn on the television set, change the volume on the stereo, and so forth. Second, you'll want to program it so it handles your X10 devices. This section explains how to set up your remote control for both activities.

For this exercise, we'll be programming a PUR09 5-in-1 Learning Remote, like the one shown in Figure 16-10. This remote transmits signals in both IR (to control your home entertainment equipment) and RF (to control X10 devices). This remote sells for US$34.99—and just a reminder, in order to control X10 devices, you must buy a separate X10 plug-in RF base. First, we'll set it up to control our Smart Home's home entertainment system, and then we'll configure it to manage our X10 devices.

Figure 16-10
PUR09 5-in-1
Learning Remote

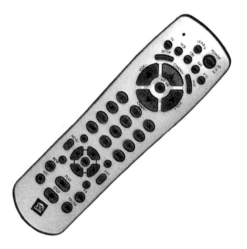

Setting Up for Home Entertainment

The 5-in-1 remote allows you to set up the remote control like most universal remote controls. That is, you can look up your component on a sheet provided by the manufacturer, and then enter that code into the remote; or, you can scan through the remote's stored codes; or, you can have the new remote "learn" the code from the existing remote.

The steps here will likely be different for other makes and models of all-in-one remote controls. However, it should give you an idea of what is neces-sary to set up remote control for universal control.

2 MINUTES

Manual Setup

1. Turn on the component you want to control (television, DVD player, satellite dish decoder, and so forth).

2. Press and hold the Setup button until the LED indictor lights constantly.

3. Release the Setup button.

4. Press and release the Mode button for the device you wish to control. The LED will blink once.

5. Locate the three-digit code for the device you wish to control on the Library Code Table (for instance, an RCA VCR might have the code 342).

6. Enter that code into the remote control. The LED should turn off after the last digit is entered.

7. Point the remote at the device you wish to control and press the Power button. The device should turn off.

8. Turn the device on again using the remote control and press the Channel + button.

HEADS UP!

Try a Code for Another Model

If the code does not work, you might discover that codes for other models of your particular device will work. For example, if you have a SuprPlayr SUX5000 VCR, but the only SuprPlayr model listed is the SUX6000 model, give that number a try—it might work.

Another method is to try searching for the correct code.

10 MINUTES

Searching for the Code

1. Turn on the component you want to control (television, DVD player, satellite dish decoder, and so forth).

2. Press and hold the Setup button until the LED indictor lights constantly.

3. Release the Setup button.

4. Press and release the Mode button for the device you wish to control. The LED will blink once.

5. Press the Channel + button repeatedly until the device to be controlled changes channels.

6. If you go past the code, press the Channel – button.

7. Press and release the Enter button to complete the setup.

If those methods are not successful, the final step with this particular model is to "teach" the remote control.

10 MINUTES

Teaching the Remote

If the code for a particular device is not available for this remote, it is possible to teach the remote the correct code from the device's original remote.

1. Point your existing remote at the PUR09 with a distance of about 1 inch between the two.

2. Press and hold the Setup button until the LED indicator lights constantly.

3. Release the Setup button.

4. Press and release the Mode button for the device you wish to control. The LED will blink once.

5. Press and release the Learn button. The LED will blink once.

6. Press and release the button on the PUR09 that you want to teach (for instance, the Play button).

7. Press and release the corresponding button on the original remote control.

8. Repeat steps 5 and 6 for each button you wish to teach the remote control.

9. When you are finished, press the Setup button.

Setting Up for X10

The first step is to plug the receiver into an available AC receptacle and fully extend the antenna. It's a good idea to locate this as centrally in the house as possible, so you have the best range when trying to change your X10 devices. Set the House Code to the letter you will be using for your X10 devices. Since our devices will be using House Code "G," we will set the code accordingly.

HEADS UP!

Use the Receiver for Control of Another Appliance

The receiver has a port in the bottom to allow the connection of a device, like a lamp. This module will allow simple on and off functions, but will not allow a lamp to be brightened or dimmed.

⏱ **2 MINUTES**

By default, this particular remote has its House Code set to "A." However, since we've already explained why it's not a good idea to use the first few letters of the House Codes, let's first change the default House Code.

1. Press and release the X10 button.

2. Press and hold Setup until the LED lights steadily, then release the button.

3. Use the number buttons on the remote's keypad to select your chosen House Code. This number will be equivalent to the letter's position in the alphabet (1 = A, 2 = B, 3 = C, 4 = D, ...16 = P). Since the X10 devices we wish to control are using House Code "G," we enter "7."

4. Press the Enter button to confirm the new House Code. The LED will turn off.

Controlling an X10 device is straightforward, now. On the remote control, simply press the X10 button, then press the Unit Code of the device you wish to manage. Next, use the buttons in Table 16-1 to manage these devices.

Button	XI0 Function
On	Channel +
Off	Channel -
Bright	Volume +
Dim	Volume -
All On	Power
All Off	Mute

Table 16-1
X10 Functions and Their Corresponding Buttons on an X10 Remote Control

Advanced Control

In the preceding section, we talked about Smart Home remote controls. If you just shell out the money for the remote control and an X10 receiver, you'll be able to do some pretty cool things like turn on lights in the kitchen while you're in the bedroom, or maybe you want to turn on an electric blanket just before your late night movie wraps up. These individualized sorts of things are possible with an X10 remote, but if you want to do some really advanced stuff (like clicking a button on the remote and having all the lights in the family room dim, the television and DVD player come on, and the drapes shut, for instance), you need to couple the remote control with some other devices.

For instance, we've been big advocates of using a computer-based X10 control system. This allows you to set up very detailed and in-depth macros. For example, when an X10 command is issued from the remote control and it is "heard" by your computer's X10 interface, it can trigger a macro.

On the other hand, if you don't want to mess with a computer, you can still employ macros by using a two-way X10 controller. For example, you can use the Keypad Linc that we talked about earlier in this chapter to establish scene lighting schemes. However, the best and easiest control over your X10 gadgetry is to use a computer-based X10 control system, as it is easier to set up and much easier to manage.

To control your television set and other home entertainment components (automatically that is, not using an IR remote control), you need to connect an X10-to-IR Linc transmitter. We talked about this sort of configuration in Chapter 14. In essence, you position the X10-to-IR Linc transmitter near your A/V components, then attach an IR emitter to the component and plug it into the transmitter. When X10 signals come through the house's electrical wiring to the transmitter, it can be set up to turn on the television, DVD player, or other home entertainment components.

Once you've gathered and installed all your X10 devices, the fun part is making them do what you want. This section was about showing you different ways to get your X10 devices to do what you want, either by using a computer interface, a remote control, or an X10 controller, or possibly a combination of them.

❏ Do you have new batteries in your remote control?

❏ Are the House and Unit Codes for your X10 devices set correctly on your computer software?

❏ Are the House and Unit Codes for your X10 devices set correctly on your control panels or remote controls?

❏ Did you set aside an entire House Code for your X10 thermostat?

❏ When using an X10 remote, are you within range of your RF receiver?

Appendix

Smart Home Resources

You know what Smart Home gadgets are out there, but there aren't many corner Smart Home stores around. As such, your best bet is to find your gear through mail order or online resources. In this appendix, we'll give you a list of Smart Home retailers and their web addresses.

Also, if you decide you need a little help with one or more of your project designs or installation, there are a number of places to turn. This appendix lists ways to get in touch with qualified contractors, as well as some tips for separating the wheat from the chaff.

Smart Home Retailers

There are a number of online stores where you can find your Smart Home devices. Some are larger than others, some offer better deals than others. We've found the best deals, service, and support at Smarthome.com (www.smarthome.com). However, if you want to do some shopping around for your Smart Home devices and equipment, Table A-1 lists a number of online resources for your reference.

Finding a Contractor

If you decide to find a contractor to help design and install your project, your first stop might be turning to the Yellow Pages. However, once you get there, you're likely to be overwhelmed by the listings of contractors. They are sorted by specialty, like roofers, blacktoppers, and so forth. However, you're not likely to find a subcategory for home automation. As such, there are some good online tools that can help you find a contractor to serve your needs. This section talks about those

Name	URL	Notes
Baran-Harper Group, Inc.	www.baran-harper.com	Canadian distributor of X10 and DSC security panels
Bass Home Electronics	www.basshome.com	Alarm systems, security, and automation systems
Castle Control	www.castlecontrol.com	Customized home automation software
Domoselect	www.domoselect.qc.ca	Canadian resource for home automation products
Eon3	www.eon3.com	Australian resource for home automation products
Gadgitz	www.gadgitz.co.uk	UK resource for home automation products
H-Com International	www.hcom-intl.com	Home automation software, security, and video products
Habitek	www.habitek.co.uk	UK resource for home automation products
Home Controls, Inc.	www.homecontrols.com	Home automation, A/V equipment, telephone, and security systems
Home Control Systems, Inc.	www.homecontrolsystemsinc.com	Security and home automation systems
Home Tech Solutions	www.hometech.com	Home automation, security, and A/V systems
Home Technology Store	www.home-technology-store.com	Home automation, security, and A/V systems
HomeAutomationNet.com	www.homeautomationnet.com	Home automation, X10, and A/V systems
iAutomate.com	www.iautomate.com	Home automation, X10, IR, HVAC, and A/V systems
Laser Business Systems	www.laser.com	UK resource for home automation products
Let's Automate	www.letsautomate.com	UK resource for home automation products
People Technology	www.peopletechnology.com	Home automation and A/V systems

Table A-I
Online Smart Home Resources

Name	URL	Notes
Radio Shack	www.radioshack.com	Installation tools, cabling, and gadgets
Security and More	www.securityandmore.com	Security systems
Smarthome.com	www.smarthome.com	Complete line of home automation systems, including X10, security, A/V, and telephone systems
Smarthome Catalog	www.smarthomecatalog.com	Home automation, security, and A/V systems
Smarthome Systems	www.smarthomeusa.com	Home automation, security, and A/V systems

Table A-I
Online Smart Home Resources *(continued)*

online tools, then tells you how you can make sure the contractor is really well suited for the job.

Referral Networks

Because it is going to be difficult to track down contractors who are qualified to install home automation equipment, there are a few good online resources to help find a contractor in your area. This section examines some of the resources you can use to connect with a contractor.

Smarthome.com

Smarthome.com offers its referral program (www.smarthome.com/projref.asp) to connect Smart Home owners with qualified installers in their area. Following the aforementioned link brings you to a page asking you for specific information about your project, including personal information, how much you expect the project to cost, and the nature of the project. Project categories include the following:

❏ Home Theater-Remote Controls

❏ Home Theater-Screens and Projectors

❏ Home Theater-Speaker

❏ Home Theater-Whole house audio

❏ HVAC/Temperature Control

❏ Lighting

❏ Phone Systems

❏ Security-Hardwired

❏ Security-Wireless

❏ Surveillance

❏ Whole house automation/programming

Electronic House Magazine

Electronic House magazine offers a listing of custom electronics installers who provide customized wiring, lighting, security, home automation, and audio/video installation systems. *Electronic House*'s listing is found at www.electronichouse.com/Framesets/EHDealersFS.html.

When you visit the page, you are presented with a map of America (along with links for Canada and international installers). Simply click on your state and you'll be presented with a list of contractors in that state.

CEIDA

A very good resource for finding a qualified home automation contractor is through the Custom Electronic Design and Installation Association (CEIDA). This is an international trade organization of companies that specialize in planning and installing home electronic systems. According to CEIDA, their service is superior to flipping through the Yellow Pages because

❏ CEDIA companies subscribe to a strict code of professional conduct and ethics.

❏ CEDIA companies tend to participate in continuing education, keeping on top of technological advancements.

By accessing the finder tool (www.cedia.net/homeowners/finder.php), you are asked where you live and what type of project you're pursuing.

Questions to Ask

Once you've found a contractor (or you're trying to narrow the field a bit), there are several questions you should ask. These questions, courtesy of the folks at Smarthome.com, will help you determine if the contractor is what you're looking for, or if you should keep looking:

❑ *Are you licensed and bonded?* This should be the first question you ask a potential contractor. If they are not licensed and bonded and they cause damage to your home, you'll have a tough time collecting to get the damage repaired. Once they say they're licensed and bonded, check with your state to make sure they really are.

❑ *What is your main area of know-how?* It's a good idea to make sure that the contractor's area of expertise jibes with the project you want to complete. While a company may be good at installing home security systems, they might not be as proficient with home entertainment systems.

❑ *How long have you been in business?* You will be able to gauge how successful a company is by how long they've been in business. If the company is relatively new, find out about its installers' experience.

❑ *Can you provide a list of references?* Reputable contractors will have a list of previous clients who you can talk to about the company's performance. Be sure to tell them that once the job is finished satisfactorily, you'll be happy to be added to their reference list. This encourages them to give their full attention to your project.

❑ *How long will installation take?* This is important to find out, especially if you'll be without power, telephone, your security system, or even your home entertainment system. Ask for minimum and maximum amounts of time.

❑ *Who will perform the work?* Just because you signed a contract with this company doesn't mean they will perform the work. Find out if the company will be using trained installers, or if they farm the work out to subcontractors.

❑ *Are you familiar with my community's building codes?* Most home automation projects aren't going to require permits, but there might be some projects that require some in-depth work that will require permits and inspections (this is most likely to occur with electrical work.) However, it's best to find out if the contractor knows what he or she needs permits for and if inspections are needed.

❑ *Will you put that in writing?* Getting a written estimate lets you know how much the project is going to cost, but don't get married to that number. There are a number of factors that can cause a project to come in at a price over the estimate. It's also a good idea to ask what type of problems arose in similar, previous projects and what kind of impact that might have on the bottom line.

As we've mentioned throughout this book, planning and preparation will help you save time, money, and headache with your Smart Home project. The same is true when finding your Smart Home gear (check out different stores to find the best deals), and it is especially true if you decide to hire a contractor. A little time spent checking out some details will help greatly in the end.

Index

References to figures are in italics.

INTERNATIONAL CONTACT INFORMATION

AUSTRALIA
McGraw-Hill Book Company
Australia Pty. Ltd.
TEL +61-2-9900-1800
FAX +61-2-9878-8881
http://www.mcgraw-hill.com.au
books-it_sydney@mcgraw-hill.com

CANADA
McGraw-Hill Ryerson Ltd.
TEL +905-430-5000
FAX +905-430-5020
http://www.mcgraw-hill.ca

**GREECE, MIDDLE EAST, & AFRICA
(Excluding South Africa)**
McGraw-Hill Hellas
TEL +30-210-6560-990
TEL +30-210-6560-993
TEL +30-210-6560-994
FAX +30-210-6545-525

MEXICO (Also serving Latin America)
McGraw-Hill Interamericana Editores
S.A. de C.V.
TEL +525-1500-5108
FAX +525-117-1589
http://www.mcgraw-hill.com.mx
carlos_ruiz@mcgraw-hill.com

SINGAPORE (Serving Asia)
McGraw-Hill Book Company
TEL +65-6863-1580
FAX +65-6862-3354
http://www.mcgraw-hill.com.sg
mghasia@mcgraw-hill.com

SOUTH AFRICA
McGraw-Hill South Africa
TEL +27-11-622-7512
FAX +27-11-622-9045
robyn_swanepoel@mcgraw-hill.com

SPAIN
McGraw-Hill/
Interamericana de España, S.A.U.
TEL +34-91-180-3000
FAX +34-91-372-8513
http://www.mcgraw-hill.es
professional@mcgraw-hill.es

**UNITED KINGDOM, NORTHERN,
EASTERN, & CENTRAL EUROPE**
McGraw-Hill Education Europe
TEL +44-1-628-502500
FAX +44-1-628-770224
http://www.mcgraw-hill.co.uk
emea_queries@mcgraw-hill.com

ALL OTHER INQUIRIES Contact:
McGraw-Hill/Osborne
TEL +1-510-420-7700
FAX +1-510-420-7703
http://www.osborne.com
omg_international@mcgraw-hill.com

Sound Off!

Visit us at **www.osborne.com/bookregistration** and let us know what you thought of this book. While you're online you'll have the opportunity to register for newsletters and special offers from McGraw-Hill/Osborne.

We want to hear from you!

Sneak Peek

Visit us today at **www.betabooks.com** and see what's coming from McGraw-Hill/Osborne tomorrow!

Based on the successful software paradigm, Bet@Books™ allows computing professionals to view partial and sometimes complete text versions of selected titles online. Bet@Books™ viewing is free, invites comments and feedback, and allows you to "test drive" books in progress on the subjects that interest you the most.

Save money and do it yourself!

These highly visual, step-by-step, show-and-tell guides provide you with hands-on success!

Build Your Own PC Home Entertainment System
by Brian Underdahl

Build Your Own High Performance Gamers' Mod PC
by Joel Durham & Edward Chen

Build Your Own PC Recording Studio
by Jon Chappell

Build Your Own Server
by Tony Caputo

McGraw Hill
OSBORNE
www.osborne.com

Brilliance

Enlightened answers for your electronics, computers, and applications

How to Do Everything with Your Tablet PC
0-07-222771-0

Build Your Own PC Home Entertainment System
0-07-222769-9

Quicken 2003: The Official Guide
0-07-222618-8

Click! The No Nonsense Guide to Digital Cameras
0-07-222740-0

Available online or at booksellers everywhere.